Creating a New Public University and Reviving Democracy

Higher Education in Critical Perspective: Practices and Policies

Series editors:
Susan Wright, Aarhus University
Penny Welch, Wolverhampton University

Around the globe, universities are being reformed to supply two crucial ingredients of a purported 'global knowledge economy': research and graduates. Higher education's aims, concepts, structures and practices are all in process of change. This series provides in-depth analyses of these changes and how those involved – managers, academics and students - are experimenting with critical pedagogies, reflecting upon the best organization of their own institutions, and engaging with public policy debates about higher education in the 21st Century.

Volume 1
Learning Under Neoliberalism: Ethnographies of Governance in Higher Education
Edited by Susan Brin Hyatt, Boone W. Shear, and Susan Wright

Volume 2
Creating a New Public University and Reviving Democracy: Action Research in Higher Education
By Morten Levin and Davydd J. Greenwood

Creating a New Public University and Reviving Democracy
Action Research in Higher Education

◆ ◆ ◆

By Morten Levin and Davydd J. Greenwood

berghahn
NEW YORK • OXFORD
www.berghahnbooks.com

Published in 2017 by

Berghahn Books

www.berghahnbooks.com

Library of Congress Cataloging-in-Publication Data

A C.I.P. cataloging record is available from the Library of Congress
https://lccn.loc.gov/2016025395

British Library Cataloguing in Publication Data

A catalogue record for this book is available from the British Library

ISBN 978-1-78533-321-7 (hardback)
ISBN 978-1-78533-839-7 (paperback)
ISBN 978-1-78533-322-4 (ebook)

Contents

Dedication   vii

Acknowledgements   viii

List of Figures   ix

Introduction: Democracy and Public Universities   1

Part I: Public Goods, *Bildung*, Public Universities, and   19
    Democracy

Chapter 1. Public Goods, Democracy, and Public Universities   21

Chapter 2. Multiple Models and Meanings of Higher Education   37

Chapter 3. *Bildung*, Academic Freedom, Academic Integrity,   54
    and Democracy

Part II: Universities as Work Organizations: Stakeholders,   77
    Structures, Systems, Steering, Leadership and Anti-*Bildung*

Chapter 4. The Work Organization of Universities: Structures   79

Chapter 5. The Work Organization of Universities: Systemic   93
    Analysis

Chapter 6. Processes in the Work Organization of Universities: 111
    Socio-Technical Systems Design, Networking for Power,
    and Neo-Taylorism

Chapter 7. Leadership and Steering in Public Universities   135

Part III: The Road Forward: Action Research for *Neue-Bildung*   151
    in Higher Education

Chapter 8. Action Research as a Strategy for Organizational   153
    Change

Chapter 9. Practicing Action Research in Public Universities   168

Conclusion: What Difference Could Action Research in Public   194
   Universities Make?

Bibliography   199

Index   211

Dedication

Morten Levin dedicates this book to the grandchildren Oda Sæther Levin, Elise Skogvold Levin, Martin Sæther Levin, Sivert Sæther Levin, and Thea Skogvold Levin hoping that they will be critical and constructive citizens working for a democratic society.

Davydd Greenwood dedicates this book to Ella Luisa Greenwood in the earnest hope that the decline in higher education will be reversed in time for her to experience the joys and excitement of learning and teaching he experienced as a student and young faculty member.

Acknowledgements

This book is the result of nearly ten years of writing, revision, and re-thinking made increasingly urgent by the downward spiral of public universities. We wish to acknowledge the many fine colleagues and students whose intelligence, generosity, and sense of ethical purpose have enabled us to continue to believe in the future of public universities and of democratic societies despite the depredations of global neoliberalism seen everywhere. *Bildung*, academic freedom, academic integrity, social mobility through public education, and democracy go hand in hand. We especially want to thank, in alphabetical order: Rebecca Boden, Hirokazu Miyazaki, Christopher Newfield, Eli Thorkelson, and Susan Wright. They helped make this book possible. We also acknowledge the stimulus to urgent reform created by the many academic administrators, faculty, and students we have known whose radical individualism threatens civil society and democracy. They made this book necessary.

Figures

Figure 3.1: The Construction of University Democracy · · · · · 56

Figure 6.1: One of the Many Possible Variants of Matrix · · · · · 131
Organizational Structures

Introduction
Democracy and Public Universities

◆◆◆

Public universities have been significantly changed and undermined since the Thatcher–Reagan era, as have most of the public institutions of social democratic states. The link between the endangered state of public universities and the decline of social democratic institutions is direct. Both are victims of overwhelming neoliberal[1] policies that involve selling off key public goods and institutions built for the taxpayers and at taxpayer expense. Democratic societies are being undermined by processes and structures that remove key resources and issues from public control. Major social and economic decisions are increasingly controlled by global actors who benefit themselves and their supporters behind the scenes by privatizing and appropriating resources belonging to the public. These elites create decisions favorable to their own economic and political interests and work hard to maintain the charade that governments are enacting and protecting the public interest and thus to avoid social unrest.

We are not alone in linking public universities to democratic societies. Affirmations about democracy and economic development are invoked routinely to justify changes in public universities and other public goods on the presumed grounds of a need for reductions in expenditures. Given that even the neoliberals articulate a link between public universities and democracy, it is surprising how little systematic research and analytical discussion draws connections between economics, organizational dynamics, public universities, and democratic citizenship.[2] Instead, the literature is rife with right-wing and left-wing tracts about democracy and education. These do little to address the current decline in public universities in practical terms. In this book, we aim to get beyond these generalities and enter an arena of analysis and subsequent university reform.

Democracy has multiple meanings and so we must clarify our own positions for the reader. An in-depth discussion will be presented in detail in Chapter 2. The following presentation provides only a quick overview of our take on this important subject. For us, democracy, in its most general sense, is a mode of coming to agreements on shared action agendas through a combined process of stakeholder deliberation and action. The aim is to harmonize divergent interests and wishes of the legitimate stakeholders through democratic learning processes (Mansbridge 1983). The primary emphasis is on allowing the direct participation of stakeholders in making decisions that affect their lives. This is because they have both the relevant information about their own situations and the moral and political right to participate in deciding their own futures.

Representative democracy plays a strong role in society, but it necessarily coexists with other participatory democratic processes that can be found in families, neighborhoods, communities, businesses, churches, etc. Participatory democracy involves discussion, debate, collective learning and sharing knowledge and goals among the legitimate immediate stakeholders. This participation produces analyses and actions that, well handled, can harmonize the diverse interests of most of the relevant stakeholders. Participatory democracy can be a contentious, complex, and even frustrating process. However, it is built on honoring the rights, wishes, and knowledge of those involved. Participatory democracy also results in decisions that work because the stakeholders participate in making them and thus are responsible for them.

More specifically we advocate social democratic ideals. Social democracy is the intentional use of social and economic interventions and institutions to promote the redistribution of wealth to the degree necessary to protect vulnerable members of society and promote improvements in the lives of the majority of society's members. These redistributions and protections enable members of society to play an effective role in the social and political system and they protect the poor or marginalized from exploitation by the rich. Social democracy should not be confused with some of the self-identified social democratic parties in Europe, many of which do not actually support the development of social democratic societies. In any case the Labour Party in Great Britain and the various Scandinavian social democratic parties all differ in their platforms and practical politics. When we use the term social democracy, we are not referring to these parties but to the underlying values, norms and attitudes of social democracy.

We argue that democracy should be a vital part of the organization and the teaching, research and service activities at public universities. The alternative, hierarchical and authoritarian management of the many by the few, is what prevails now. Nevertheless, we recognize that very few key actors in the world of public universities agree that participatory democracy based on social democratic values is an essential feature of public universities. Rather policymakers and most higher education administrators articulate some kind of democratic and economic mission for public universities in their public relations campaigns and then rain down budget cuts and coercive assessment and ranking schemes on their institutions. Their actual behavior makes it clear that the democratic rhetoric is not tied to resource allocations or to the leaders' true goals.

The critical literature and policy statements about public universities are dominated by assertions about the evils of meritocracy, accountability, job preparation, the evils of corporatization and student debt (Lucas 1994; Soley 1995; Lucas 1996; Ehrenberg 1997; Shumar 1997; Slaughter and Leslie 1997; Strathern 2000; Kirp 2003; Slaughter and Rhoades 2004; Ehrenberg 2007; Greenberg 2007; Bousquet and Nelson 2008; Caanan and Shumar 2008; Ikenberry and MacLendon 2009; McMahon 2009; Schrecker 2010; Ginsberg 2011; Samuels 2013; Hyatt, Shear and Wright 2015). While these are all important topics and valuable analyses to read, it is remarkable how disconnected most of these arguments are from debates about the vital role of public goods like university education in democratic societies. It is a tribute to the power of neoliberal ideologies and authoritarian practices that debates about democracy in public universities have been marginalized in the current discussions of what was once seen as a key institution for social mobility and democratization. Thus, one of our agendas is to force the relationship between democracy and public universities back into the discussion arena.

Awareness of processes undermining social democracy is not new. It is a recurrent theme and has been analyzed before by thinkers like Mills (1956), Galtung (1989), Behn (2001), Gibson-Graham (2006), Klein (2007), and many others. Decades ago, Mills laid out an analysis of the political, administrative, industrial complex and its control over industrial production and innovations. In the years since, Galtung has talked and written about the economic blackmail of the Global South by international corporations, whether these are multinationals or colonizing regimes like the U.S. as Kjelstadli (2010) argues. Recently, well-known intellectuals like Habermas (2012) have pointed to the devastating consequences of a European Community that is being governed, including its universities, without democratic participation and social control. A fair society must be shaped by democratic ideals and practices. Democracy is about citizens having control over their own lifeworlds and, as a collectivity, being able to participate in the design and development of participatory, fair, and sustainable social processes.

Gaining participatory democratic control of the financial and political empires of the global elites is a daunting task, one beyond our ambitions in this book. Our focus is on the possible role of re-created public universities in helping to re-create participatory social democracy. To do this, public universities would have to be open to students and faculty from all social classes and races/ethnicities/genders. Students would be encouraged to develop their capacities as individuals and members of the social institutions that are the backbone of civil society. Public universities would have to educate these students in a way that enables them to enhance and advocate democratic praxis across the institutions of society. Along with this, they would gain a substantive education in fields they choose to work in after graduation. Within the university they would experience organizational processes that nurture and highlight social democracy. For this to be possible, public universities would have to treat the faculty, students, and staff as full partners in this citizen formation process.

The neoliberal public university reifies the teaching process as a commodity transfer having only instrumental training dimensions. For neoliberals, the new generation of professionals is simply a more skilled (and more indebted) version of the proletarian labor of their high-school-educated predecessors in previous generations. This reduction of the role of public education to a vocational training activity is a political economic strategy to create a new generation of well-trained but passive social actors, willing to meet the demands of global elites and not to disturb the neoliberal processes of elite wealth concentration.

In neoliberal universities, the faculty are treated as disposable fee-for-service labor and removed from governance functions, and occasionally blamed for indoctrinating students with anti-neoliberal ideologies. Faculty are subject to neoliberal competitions for merit through coercive systems of evaluation and their freedom of speech has been drastically curtailed. Thus neoliberalism supports a deeply political and authoritarian view of public higher education while claiming to banish "liberal" political indoctrination from universities.

The reduction of higher education to vocational training is as common as it is problematic and destructive. The message to public universities is this: "Stay in your own schoolyard and leave key societal questions alone." The leaders of public universities are required to offer training for the new "knowledge society" actors for their roles as a new proletariat. It is a new proletariat only because they now have a university degree rather than a secondary school diploma. In addition, they often have large debts caused by financing their own education after the neoliberal reforms.

In an op-ed published in a Norwegian newspaper, Levin, writing about the public Norwegian University of Science and Technology (NTNU), argued for democracy at departmental level (that the chair of the department should be elected by the faculty and not merely appointed by the dean of the college). The former director of The Norwegian Arctic University responded arrogantly that it was senseless to focus on democracy in universities, as democracy is irrelevant in any public institution of higher education. Universities, he argued, should prepare candidates for work life and nothing else.[3] It is particularly sobering that this acrimonious exchange took place in one of the few remaining European countries with a strong social democratic political tradition and free public higher education. Even in Norway, the prevalence of anti-democratic practices like the appointment of rectors or of department chairs at public universities is now expanding to a greater range of higher education institutions.

To counter this vocationalizing tide, we suggest that a renewed form of *Bildung* (education as human development) is essential to the future of public universities. This argument will be introduced in detail in Chapter 3. Here we simply point out that *Bildung* means that a university education is more than vocational training. It involves the development of an individual's sense of personal possibilities and potential purposes. This involves an understanding of the complex and multiple relationships among the many spheres of knowledge and an opportunity to learn about and critically rehearse the social, political and ethical values that help them become constructive and empathetic members of society, who behave with integrity in their families, communities and civil society at large.

Unfortunately, with few exceptions, university requirements for a *Bildung*-oriented educational experience have been debased into perfunctory "liberal arts" requirements or pre-university general education requirements. These liberal arts courses are usually taught in no particular relation to each other, without consultation among the faculty and departments teaching them, and without efforts at integration. Because this is what now passes for *Bildung* in most public institutions, we decided to call not for the restoration of *Bildung* but the creation of a *Neue-Bildung* suited to civic life in the twenty-first century. By *Neue-Bildung* we mean authentically integrated, system-based and interconnected courses put together in an educational process aimed at behavioral change and the promotion of civic values and practices.

We argue that the opposite of *Bildung* is neoliberalism. Neoliberalism feeds on socially repressive and regressive actions. Those neoliberals who are not merely cynical manipulators of ideas for their own benefit are free-market fundamentalists who believe that society is and should be a competitive free-for-all and that society is not a collectivity but an arena of competing individuals. They claim to believe that the world is a perfect "machine" that has been interfered with by foolish or even "sinful" people who have caused it to malfunction. For them, the ills of the world—governmental bureaucracy, waste, immorality, violence, drug abuse, pollution and global warming—are products of this improper interference. Their claimed goal is to stop people from interfering with the free market because free markets will automatically produce rational and fair allocations of all the goods and services on the planet. In their view, those who do well in the free market deserve their rewards and those who do poorly deserve their poverty and want.

The central contradiction in their behavior is that these supposedly free-market operators actually interfere constantly with the operations of the market through manipulations of the tax code, by changing laws, and trying to midwife their free market utopia into existence. They justify their actions by claiming to remove regulation, but their behaviors actually result in increased systems of control, assessment, surveillance, and managerialism. We have no sympathy for this ideology and the combination of concepts and cynical practices that this movement has spawned.

If we turn to the anthropological and historical evidence, unregulated markets do not now exist and never existed in the past. In addition to being subject to the law, contracts, the circulation of information, and the stability of currencies, all markets everywhere are inherently imperfect. No consumer has a completely ordered set of wants nor perfect information about available goods and services, nor perfect access to those goods and services, nor the interest or time to compare what is on offer. In addition, as Karl Polanyi pointed out (Polanyi 1944), neither land nor labor are commodities that can be moved around the globe at will. Trying to treat them as "fictitious commodities" has created a vast amount of human and natural wreckage. Thus, these free markets only exist as utopian ideologies: "stark utopias" as Polanyi called them.

This utopian belief in the perfection of the system and the imperfection of humans is a key part of neoliberal worldviews and it feeds elitist practices. Those who believe in the perfect free markets claim to be the enlightened ones, the rational actors, and are sure they should be in charge. Those who believe that markets must be regulated to protect society and it members against the depredations of the few are demonized as "liberals," communists, or fools who must be watched, corralled, and audited.

Trust is key. Neoliberals trust only themselves and their free-market ideology. Those who oppose them and believe in controlling the play of pseudo-free markets are treated as threats to the "good" and are subject to controls and constant assessment. They are systematically distrusted and treated as "enemies" of society. Thus the apparatus of neoliberalism is built on the distrust of the majority of human beings, of society, and of politicians who believe their job is to advocate on behalf of the less fortunate members of society. Neoliberalism is the repudiation of the notion of a civil society based on human solidarity, notions essential to the social democratic traditions and practices neoliberals detest. Consequently, neoliberalism is an implacable opponent to the role of public university education as a process of *Bildung* precisely because such an education promotes social democratic beliefs and behaviors.

We are now at a key juncture in history. The neoliberals have had their turn at remaking the world and the resulting path of destruction is clear. They have created a world more unequal and anti-democratic than it has been since the Industrial Revolution. This faces public universities with a choice. Public universities can either become an integral element in the recreation of social democracy or can continue to operate as an instrument of elite domination of the planet.

Public universities could provide both key social actors and research-based knowledge to make social democratic development possible. The character and education of these actors, the knowledge and skills they need to have, and the products and services they create would be vital ingredients in a transition to a social democratic future. But public universities as currently structured are also profoundly authoritarian and anti-democratic. Therefore, they must be remade if they are to play any role in reconstructing social democracy. In this book we chart a path toward their key role in recovering social democracy through the re-creation of public universities.

Accomplishing a social democratic re-creation of public universities is not a simple matter. It means that public universities would have to reshape their faculty and administrators as advocates and supporters of teaching, research, and community service to enhance social democracy. Policymakers would have to provide resources to promote democracy rather than to undermine it. This is the opposite of what is happening now.

At present, public universities have become important bulwarks in the consolidation of the hold of wealthy elites over the rest of the world, a role many public universities have willingly played since at least the 1980s. Elite private universities have played this role since their founding, since elitism is their promise and core function. Public universities once were a pro-democratic alternative to these elite institutions. They no longer are.

Thus we are as critical of current public universities as we are of neo-liberal higher education policy and administrators. We are not alone in taking these positions (Slaughter and Leslie 1997; Chomsky et al. 1997; Bok 2004; Newfield 2004, 2011; Giroux and Giroux 2004; Washburn 2005; McMahon 2009; Saltmarsh and Zlotowski 2011; Whelan, Walker, and Moore eds. 2013; Guinier 2015; Hyatt, Shear and Wright 2015, to name only a few). The difference is that we aim to move beyond general perspectives on these questions toward the development of specific views on the relationship between democracy and higher education as *Bildung* and as a set of organizational systems. Without these organizational specifics, the discussion of democracy in public universities leaves the subject on an abstract and polemical plane without concrete guidance and support useful to anyone who wants to engage in a democratizing change process.

The relationship between democracy and education in general and between democracy and public universities in particular is mainly rendered through tired statements about the way representative political democracy and a dynamic economy depend on an educated and socially responsible citizenry. Administrative and political "white papers" and nostrums abound. They are as prolific as they are disconnected from practice. Such pronouncements do not explain why profoundly undermined representative political systems and a vastly unequal world economy require educated citizens. What global elites want and what public universities mostly produce are obedient workers, fee-for-service researchers to serve business interests, and passive political subjects. Despite the inflated rhetoric to the contrary, this is their current function (Kirn 2009; Dereiciwizc 2014; Guinier 2015).

The contradictions between the behavior and rhetoric of the increasingly authoritarian and managerialist leaders of public universities, who advocate democracy in public statements while behaving in quite authoritarian ways, are clear. The democracy/economic dynamism argument is also empirically wrong, since dynamic economies can exist in non-democratic societies (e.g., China, see Brown, Lauder and Ashton 2011). In fact, the last thing many workplaces and stockholders want in most places is an activist democratic workforce trained in universities in the values and practices of democracy and willing to advocate for the social democratic rights of citizens.

One vexing issue in working through the literature on the crises in public universities is created by undisciplined use of the terms "marketization," "corporate," and "corporatization." Like other ideological terms, e.g., "traditional" or "modern," these terms evoke many different ideas in the minds of the readers. For example, when an academic colleague complains about a university administrative decision and calls it an example of "corporatization," there is no way to know what she means without further questioning. For many faculty, corporatization simply means a negative institutional decision forced on them by anti-academic administrators. By contrast, in many policy environments and among university administrators, corporatizing higher education is viewed as the road to its salvation. Together, politically and economically ignorant faculty and administrators have often made public universities into the costly and poorly functioning institutions they now have become. Later in the book (Chapter 5), we present some of the multiple meanings of marketization and corporatization. It is important to contrast the ideological use of these terms with their substantive organizational meanings so that a more responsible and realistic analysis of these processes becomes possible.

What is called neo-Taylorism in this book is also an important part of this story. Neo-Taylorism is a process of organizational mimicry, the implementation of an administrative fantasy that public universities are actually early twentieth-century nonunionized industrial mass production plants. Neo-Taylorism, like Taylorism before it, is built on strong hierarchies and hermetic structural units that are internally hierarchical and that report only upward toward the apex. These organizations purposely weaken cross-functional links to enable bosses in this fragmented system to exert control from above. The leaders at the pinnacle of the organizational structure are remote from the actual value-creation processes in the organization and yet reserve to themselves all decisional and disciplinary power. Importantly, without having any idea what their products are and how well these products work in society at large, these administrative leaders, remote from the actual value-production activities in the university, substitute phantasmagorical statements—about education for the knowledge society of the twenty-first century, community engagement, respect for diversity, or a decreasing environmental footprint—for meaningful organizational leadership.

Henry Ford would have loved this model, except for one crucial thing. Few of these bosses have a clue about what the public university's products are, what they are worth, how well they work, or how to get more good results and reduce poor results. Thus current public universities are modeled on a nineteenth-century manufacturing ideology of assembly lines but without cars or washing machines rolling off the line and onto trucks or trains and out for sale.

If, among the positive meanings of corporatization we mean being organized as current creative private sector companies are, then public universities are not corporate. They are increasingly hierarchical, inflating the numbers of administrators and the sizes of their salaries in relation to the number of faculty and students. The number of senior administrators and professional staff has skyrocketed, and with them the costs of running universities.[4] At some institutions, middle and senior administrative personnel outnumber permanent faculty and often are paid better than faculty are.

These are not successful contemporary corporate practices. In currently competitive manufacturing and service organizations, hierarchies are minimized, administrative structures are lightened and made flexible and adaptive, teamwork across functions (often around particular products or markets) is promoted, and leadership is a matter of helping coordinate and facilitate the work of the teams and supporting the organization in adapting to its larger environment.[5]

This kind of agile, flattened organizational structure, with room for diverse stakeholders to meet and cooperate around systems problems, bears no resemblance to public universities or private elite universities. To be sure, there are some multidisciplinary units, but these are often funded from outside the university with the money protecting the cross-structural space they occupy and fending off the structural anomalies they create. The core university organizational structures are authoritarian and hierarchical, with hierarchical professorial, staff, administrative and student statuses and roles, and departmental units competing with each other for the resources of deans, who compete against other deans for resources, all looking upward to a central administrative pinnacle. In this competition a vital strategic resource is the ability to shape networks supporting the interests of individual actors or small coalitions. These networks aggregate power to win decisions on resource allocation.

External systems of assessment and ranking of institutions strongly reinforce these neo-Taylorist behaviors. They rank universities, students, and faculties by using crude and often meaningless productivity measures. For faculty and students, they promote meritocratic competitions that discourage innovation and encourage short-term, quick-to-print academic work. They rank departments and colleges in ways that even beginning sociology students could see are methodologically flawed (Shin, Toutlkoushian, and Teichler 2011). Student outcomes also are ranked according to tests that show nothing about the ability of the students to do well in their jobs or to live meaningful lives.

Though nearly everyone understands that these systems of ranking and evaluation are methodologically invalid, neo-Taylorist senior administrators and their governing boards make or ruin their careers by moving their institutions up or down in the rankings. In the United States, faculty make or break their careers by accumulating ranked chits on their CVs, and students get jobs on the basis of the rank of their institution, even if the rankings are meaningless in any educational sense. This is what we mean by neo-Taylorism. It is Fordism without Ford cars, a vast neoliberal simulacrum. Perhaps the one business parallel is to be found in "casino capitalist" investment banks and hedge funds where huge hierarchies exist and where performance, salary and bonuses are diffusely and even inversely related to performance (Cohan 2010; Brown and Hodgson 2012). The current organizational structures and dynamics of public universities are inimical to *Bildung* in any form and promotion of *Bildung* would be opposed by many of the inhabitants of these institutions, now including most administrators and many faculty and students. *Neue-Bildung* requires the kind of coordination and organizational integration that can only be achieved through participatory democracy in the universities themselves.

Public universities graduate people and train researchers, some of whom, even under current dismal conditions, manage to become the future leaders of society in both the private and public sector. Let's be clear, though, that these are the winners. Many graduates, however, do not end up being high-level leaders. The majority end up as salaried workers in low- or middle-level management positions (Abel, Deitz, and Su 2014). After the latest world economic crisis, such graduates are lucky now if they have a career that includes stable employment. A generation or two ago, a vital role for public universities was to make it possible for students from the working and lower middle class with adequate talent to obtain the academic degrees needed for social mobility. This is no longer the case. Under current conditions in the U.S., without a university degree young people have few meaningful economic options other than in the military or in wage labor under increasingly precarious conditions. Even now, economic security depends greatly on access to higher education. Public universities remain important gatekeepers in the process of social mobility and increasingly function as life preservers for the declining middle class.

Our position is that university education must be much more than technical training. It should be understood to include knowledge and skill acquisition, civic socialization and the potential for social mobility after graduation. In all universities, students and neophyte researchers are taught how to operate within structured organizational systems. This is an important life skill. Importantly, this means that the structure of public universities and how they teach students matters in their subsequent working and civic lives. If they are treated as neoliberal market customers, universities act to augment the corrosion of social democracy. If, however, these same students and young researchers are treated organizationally and educationally as future citizens of social democratic systems, then public universities can exercise pressure toward the redevelopment of democracy in civil society at large.

For all these reasons, we argue that public university organizational structures and dynamics matter in preparing students and faculty for organizational and civic life. At the core of this is treating students and faculty in such a way that their social roles involve more than individualistic, competitive economic actions (Guinier 2015). When they participate in organizational processes or take on leadership positions beyond the university, it matters to the welfare of society at large if they have democratic values and know how to enact them in their behavior toward others and toward society generally. If their mentors and university administrators do not behave in a democratic and pedagogically respectful way toward them, any talk about civic socialization becomes a fraud. It is not enough to write position papers and give speeches about these issues, which is what most university administrators do.

The focus of this book is public universities both in Europe and in the United States. Their expansion in the national higher education systems after the Second World War was exceptional, greatly increasing the number of students getting a university degree and broadening the social origins of the students to include the lower middle class and the working class. By contrast, except for token policies of inclusion based on systems of scholarships, elite universities (the Ivy League, Oxbridge, etc.) have remained relatively and purposely immune to the massification of higher education. They lived and still live by their privileged position and vast wealth. Despite the occasional working- or middle-class student who makes it in and is used to manage the public image of these institutions as something more than finishing schools for elites, they do not play an important role in national social mobility. This is why public universities matter.

From the 1950s through the 1970s, increased access to higher education had the obvious effect of enhancing class mobility by creating access to middle-class status and beyond. In this process of social democratization, the upwardly mobile entrants brought diverse values and interests with them, shaped by their social and material backgrounds (Bourdieu and Passeron 1979). This in turn caused new voices to be heard in the public domain, and issues emanating from university campuses pressing for democratic revitalization in the late 1960s and early 1970s. They created a great deal of productive social turmoil including a significant expansion of civil rights, environmental justice, gender equality, etc. During this period, the goals to create a fairer and more sustainable world were real, shared and acted on.

Elites recognized this threat and mounted the counter-offensive that gave us Thatcher and Reagan's neoliberalism in the form of an all-out attack on public higher education, among other public goods. That neoliberal counter-revolution has engulfed our societies up to the present. Their reforms have produced major increases in inequality and the global financial crises that quickly pushed the working and middle classes back down into precarious work and poverty. We argue that without educationally based social mobility, there can be no social democracy. The public universities both in Europe and the U.S. hold the key to mobility based on talent and effort rather than on inherited wealth and nepotism. This grounds our arguments for the importance of public universities.

There is a potential downside to increasing the social availability of higher education. University education poorly done, and without fundamental changes in the curriculum, teaching methods, and institutional organizational structures and processes, can pull new generations away from their social origins in a personally and socially unproductive way (Guinier 2015). Inclusion and homiletic statements about diversity not accompanied by a critique of the debased liberal arts curriculum and of authoritarian university organizational structures and practices are a sham. Without fundamental changes in the structure and management of public universities, inclusion means only the assimilation of more students into the structures controlled by and for existing elites.

Our own commitment to diversity is not based on political correctness. For us, democracy, politically and socially, is not about inclusion only for its own sake. We do believe that respect for diversity is vital to the health of democratic institutions for moral reasons. Democracy is premised on granting equal rights to all members of society to have a say in decisions affecting them. However, we also argue that democracy is practically important. Power sharing is pragmatically essential because it permits the inclusion of knowledge, experiences, and unique capacities of all kinds of people in the deliberative process and the development of new social actions. This inclusion permits us to come up with better (fairer, more sustainable) courses of future action (Guinier 2015). Such inclusion requires having a meaningful say in all the institutions people operate in, including public universities, a say not based on a vote only but centered on translating personal experiences and insights into collective, socially beneficial actions.

Our views grow directly out of our long experience in universities in the United States and Europe and in the private and public sectors on both sides of the Atlantic. They also emanate from our efforts over the past twenty years, during which we both have engaged critically with the transformations taking place in higher education. We have analyzed, taught about, and published on the ongoing degradation of public universities in the United States and Europe and on the search for remedies.[6] In this book, we intend to tie all our efforts together in a single overall analysis accompanied by an action research strategy for change.

Much of our collaborative research and writing to date has been in the doomsday mode. At this point in our trajectories, we want to go beyond engaging in analytical laments and to trace a path toward the better future we hope for. We are aware of the collapse of social democracy but we are persuaded that critical reflection, truly public universities, and social democracy can and must be re-created and expanded. A key element in this process is the creation of a public university system to replace the one that has been wrecked.

The Plan of the Book

This book contains four interdependent lines of argument that together lead to a different way of thinking about re-creating public universities. In Part I, we discuss the substance and the connectedness between public goods, *Bildung*, public universities, and democracy. Chapter 1 presents neoclassical economics in order to engage in a critique of the pseudo-economics of neoliberalism and pseudo-corporatization. We begin with a review of the logic and premises of neoclassical economic analysis. We do this because neoclassical economic analysis, while not being our preferred economic approach, reveals the falsity of the pseudo-economic arguments used to justify neoliberalism and neo-Taylorism in structuring and managing universities. We simultaneously issue a challenge to those who decry "marketization" and "corporatization" to demonstrate that they know what they are talking about, that is, that they actually know how successful corporations currently work.

Chapter 2 presents the multiplicity of models and ideologies of higher education and situates our specific focus on public universities in the context of debates about higher education generally. Chapter 3 takes up the multiple meanings of democracy and links public higher education to social democracy. Revitalizing concepts like *Bildung* and the related ideas and practices of academic freedom, academic integrity, and shared governance requires a significant effort. These have long been treated as separate concepts, rendered as abstract principles, and often given quite restricted or common sense meanings.

Part II analyzes universities as work organizations, reviews the positions of all the relevant stakeholders in universities, and analyzes some of the most common organizational structures. In addition, we portray some of what passes for leadership in public universities and show how unfavorably this kind of leadership compares with leadership in well-run corporate organizations.

In Chapter 4 we place *Bildung*, and neoliberal anti-*Bildung* in an organizational context. Chapter 5 details our ideas about universities as work organizations. We show that much of what has been written about universities as organizations fails to capture the organizational complexity and power dynamics that characterize them. In Chapter 6, we lay out the kinds of work and value-creation processes typical of public universities. These chapters argue that without sound organizational structures and practices, democratic change initiatives in public universities are impossible. In Chapter 7, we devote attention to the use of ideas like "steering" used by neoliberal policymakers and university administrators unilateral control while they appear to be freeing local actors to act in accord with the principles of the free market.

Part III lays out the road forward. In Chapter 8, we provide a primer on action research and its major characteristics, because participatory institutions cannot be built by authoritarian imposition. We also present socio-technical systems design as a proven alternative to neoliberal authoritarianism. Chapter 9 links the practice of action research to public university re-creation by showing how it is possible to reorganize public universities to produce a *Neue-Bildung* that would bring public universities back to the center of social democratic development.

In this final section, we intend to be practical. It is one thing to advocate participation and democracy. It is quite another to trace a path and lay out a set of practices that could actually bring this about. Separating research from practice already has created socially disconnected social science and humanities disciplines in higher education. We do not intend to reproduce that split here. We believe that the only way forward is through participatory organizational development and fundamental changes in teaching, research, organizational dynamics, and community engagement. In other words, the democratization of higher education is the only path we can see toward a redevelopment of social democracy itself.

Why Does This Matter?

We do not have to look far to see the devastating effects of the decline of social democracy in most parts of the West. We can point to the overwhelming problems created by the current economic crisis. Millions are out of work. There is massive youth unemployment, including university-age and even university-educated youth, while the global elites continue to monopolize wealth and power, suppressing voices and institutions that would challenge them. The earth itself is being devastated by predatory capitalism and its systematic destruction of the universal commons. Given this, striking out in a new, pro-social democratic direction is amply justified.

Notes

1. By neoliberal we mean an emphasis on privatization of public resources and function, fiscal austerity, deregulation of industry, removal of trade barriers, and shrinking the role of government in the economy. We will define it in more detail later in the book.
2. Walter McMahon is a rather lonely exception (McMahon 2009).
3. See http://www.adressa.no/meninger/article7160667.ece (accessed 30 September 2016), and http://www.adressa.no/meninger/annenside/article7210631.ece (accessed 30 September 2016).
4. The increase in academic administration can be seen in many reports. An example is http://www.huffingtonpost.com/2014/02/06/higher-ed-administrators-growth_n_4738584.html (accessed 30 September 2016).
5. Key texts in this field supporting our views are Thorsrud and Emery (1964, 1970), Davis and Taylor (1972), Herbst (1976), Trist (1981), Lawler (1986), van Eijnatten (1993), and Levin et al. (2012).

6. Our major works in this field include the following publications: Greenwood (2007, 2008, 2009, 2012), Greenwood and Levin (1998b, 2000a, 2000b, 2001, 2005, 2008), Levin and Greenwood (2001a, 2001b, 2007, 2011), Levin and Martin (2007).

Part I

◆◆◆

Public Goods, *Bildung*, Public Universities, and Democracy

Part I addresses the broad social, moral, and political arguments for the key role of public universities in democratic societies. There exist individual studies of the meaning and importance of public goods, of the concepts and practices associated with *Bildung*, the social importance of public universities, and the diverse meanings of democracy. In this opening part of our argument, we explore each element and argue they form a mutually necessary set of factors for sustaining and developing public universities and democratic societies. After discussing the concept of public goods and the variety of meanings of democracy, we argue for the key importance of public universities in democracies. We then present the multiple models of the purposes and structures of higher education institutions and review some of the ideological positions now attached higher education generally. This section closes by bringing *Bildung*, academic freedom, and academic integrity together and arguing that there is a mutually necessary relationship among these elements as well as between strengthening them and revitalizing the practice of democracy both in public universities and in society at large.

CHAPTER 1

Public Goods, Democracy, and Public Universities

◆◆◆

In this section of the book our focus is the uneven and often incoherent approaches to universities in the (supposed) light of market economics. This topic is difficult because economic concepts are invoked and distorted by people on all sides. A key function of this section is to clear away some of this underbrush so it is possible to think more systematically about what economics has to do with universities. Economic analysis is relevant but methodologically and theoretically meaningful economic analysis, not invocations of pseudo-markets and pseudo-corporatization as ideological weapons.[1] There are serious economic problems with the way universities operate. They are not addressed by careless or intentionally distorted manipulation of economic concepts and evidence.

A key element in our analysis is understanding public universities as a public good. We show how the concept of public goods is actually argued from a neoclassical economic perspective. We emphasize the neoclassical economic perspective here, not because it matches our preferences for analyzing the political economy of universities but because contemporary discussions of the "business model" and "corporatization" of universities have converted simulacra of neoclassical economic analysis into revealed truths. We show that the actual deployment of neoclassical economic perspectives contradicts neoliberal ideologies and practices in higher education. This matters because neoliberals masquerade as economic analysts to support an authoritarian, hierarchical view of society. They use models that serve the interests of global elites and their local representatives. These obfuscations also prevent public universities from addressing the real economic challenges they face. Substituting pseudo-accountability and ranking for reflection on the serious allocation decisions they must make and that a genuine economic analysis would require permits authoritarian administrators and policymakers to do as they please and cover their tracks (or even confuse themselves) with false economic arguments.

The Neoliberal Construction of Higher Education

The first problem in analyzing the economics of higher education is figuring out which institutions we are actually talking about. Current debates on the future of public higher education tend to refer to higher education in abstract, generic terms without always distinguishing among the multiple types of higher education institutions existing everywhere. Doing this is already an ideological move as well as an analytical non-starter. There are community colleges, for-profit colleges and universities, vocational schools, liberal arts colleges, regional colleges, private universities, flagship public universities, land-grant universities, state university and college systems, and national public university systems in Europe. Failing to distinguish among them is an analytical and strategic error because homogenizing them produces analyses and reform proposals that confuse the part with the whole and that ignore the key differences among these types of institutions. It also overshadows their analytically relevant commonalities.

Currently, dominant policy models homogenize public institutions, including public education. These policy models ideologically reconstruct the public sector as a set of market-driven service organizations that are supposed to deal with clients (i.e., the public that pays the taxes and fees to support them) by means of putatively market rational allocation of resources and by administrative efficiency and transparency.

This ideological fantasy looks nothing like observable reality. The neoliberals use the failure of reality to match their market fantasies as a justification to lay waste to public sector institutions. Among other things, this neoliberal construction of higher education denies the unique functions and institutional logics of not-for-profit and public organizations in general and undermines the public goods creation essential to public higher education in any democratic society.

The obliteration of public goods is evident in all sectors subject to the "new public management" (Behn 2001) and has deeply compromised the institutions of public higher education along with most other institutions that provide public goods (e.g., utilities, healthcare). Public resources are stripped from these institutions and used to enrich global financial elites. The goal is nothing less than the destruction of all the social democratic gains made since the Second World War.

This "marketizing" and homogenization is accomplished by invoking but not applying neoclassical economic theory and methods to public higher education. It trades on the, to us dubious, scientific legitimacy of neoclassical economic theory and analysis. Rather than being about economic choice and rationality as they claim, these policy efforts focus on undermining both the social and educational functions and the institutional autonomy of public higher education to further consolidate the political and financial hegemony of global elites.

These are bold claims, and to support the contention that neoliberalism is a purely ideological distortion of neoclassical economic theory, it is necessary to make a brief foray into the fundamentals of neoclassical economic theory and generations of research in economic anthropology.

Neoclassical economics is an elegant theory of allocation driven by a small set of operating assumptions. The first assumption is that human beings universally have wants that exceed the resources they have to meet them, an assumption generations of anthropological research have called into question (Polanyi 1944; Sahlins 1972).

These supposedly endless wants are not all equally important and thus they are hierarchically ranked so that some receive a higher priority than others. Humans then must allocate their resources to satisfy their wants, resources gathered either by directly creating them with their own labor, through exchange, or through other means of accumulation. In satisfying our wants, we supposedly wish to expend the smallest possible amount of our resources to acquire the largest amount of goods and services that satisfy our most highly ranked wants. That is, we must engage in allocating scarce means among alternative, hierarchically ranked ends. Since suppliers also are attempting to maximize their incomes, they want to sell their goods and services at the highest price possible and spend the resulting income to acquire those things that they value most. Thus the whole system is built on chains of interrelated decisions among putatively rational, perfectly informed actors. Each of the actors is maximizing their gains in competition with each other to get the best personal outcomes (Marshall [1890] 1920; Robbins [1932] 1937).

Valid critiques of the realism and details of this theoretical model abound. They have been available for decades and are ignored by the neoliberals and their policy operators. Still, even neoclassical economists agree that, no matter how it is framed, there is nothing in this theory of allocation that determines which ends will be ranked highest. Thus different actors will not necessarily rank their ends in the same ways. In addition, the marginal utilities that various actors realize from these transactions are not easily commensurable.[2]

A genuine application of neoclassical economic theory to public higher education necessarily would have to start with the way purchasers and sellers of public higher education define and rank the ends they associate with higher education. Whether or not it is acceptable to call consumers of higher education "students" or "customers" (an important issue that we will come back to later) does not matter as much as recognizing that the first step in doing an economic analysis of public higher education is to figure out what those who pay for it value about it. What other things they are willing to forego to access public higher education, what those who fund it through taxes value about it, what components the faculty and students in these institutions value, and how those elements are ranked and transacted in relation to each other are necessary data for using such a model. We would need similar information about the providers of higher education as well.

The complexity of the interactions among the supply and demand crowds, each with their hierarchies of wants, their different interests, their different resource endowments, and the different marginal utilities for the things they can "buy" with their goods, is obvious. Further, we know how imperfect the information all the actors use actually is and how heavily decisions are affected by non-rational elements. Trying to reduce this complexity to a simple calculus is a fool's errand. But clearly there is a sufficient supply of people willing to keep this fiction going.

For the neoliberal construction to be reasonable, the following conditions have to be met: all students are only seeking high paying jobs through education; all non-student university customers are seeking high value research and development work at the lowest price; all faculty want the highest salaries for the least amount of work; and the sellers of higher education are also rationally motivated. Further, it must be assumed that transparency and accountability will be complete, so that perfect information can inform economic maximizing decisions by all actors; that the rationalities of the supply and demand crowds will match up; and that public higher education institutions will be forced by consumer demand to provide precisely what the consumers want at the lowest possible cost and in the most efficient way and nothing else. If this scenario is persuasive to you, this book will not make sense to you. Versions of this tale guide a great many higher education policy prescriptions and administrative strategies. Competent neoclassical economic analytical thinking is in short supply at many universities and in most branches of government.

Among the many missing elements in the neoliberal construction is whether or not what the student "customers" will want and get will turn out to be an "education" in any meaningful sense of the word. Nor is it clear what kind of research and development non-student consumers are trying to purchase and whether or not universities are positioned to provide this at the lowest possible price. No clarity is presented about faculty motivations in teaching and conducting research. Instead, the empirical gaps are filled in with negative and positive stereotypes to make this construction work.

Another manipulation common to this neoliberal scheme conflates minimizing costs with achieving efficiency. It is easy to show that what is low cost and what is efficient are rarely identical, particularly when the time perspective is added and the sustainability of particular strategies is taken into account. Such a conflation is simply wrong. Yet arguments abound claiming that what is "efficient" according to neoliberal political and social ideas is market rational.

There is a deeper theoretical and mathematical problem that goes beyond the foregoing problems. There is no theoretical justification for combining students and non-student consumers into groups with a homogeneous set of preference scales. There is no reason to assume the preferences of the university demand and supply crowds are homogeneous, just as it would make little sense for any other categories of actors. The first step in speaking about "students" in the neoliberal scheme is to improperly homogenize the stakeholder groups by asserting that stakeholder groups each have a collective preference scale (Elster and Roemer 1993). Vaulting over this analytical mistake, neoliberals then proceed to examine how institutional behavior responds, rationally or not, to their fictitious homogenized preference scales. Put more baldly, they fabricate the preference scales and then pretend that institutional behavior either satisfies them or fails to satisfy them. Where institutions fail to meet these imagined preference scales, public universities are then subjected to neoliberal reforms.

Economic theorists have long known that combining interpersonal utilities is mathematically and conceptually dubious and thus scientifically uncertain (Elster and Roemer 1993). While there is a great deal of work on this subject, the mathematical difficulties of comparing individually created preference scales responsive to different resource endowments, values, and contexts was demonstrated clearly years ago but is ignored in the bulk of economic analyses in higher education, regardless of the analysts' ideological commitments.

To hide this problem, both neoclassical and neoliberal exponents of reform export their own preferences scales to fill in the blanks in the combined utilities of the actors. This means that, prior to the analysis, the analysts have already imposed their own preferences (including their politics and ethics) on what is presented, but portray it as if it were a simple objective calculation. In the case of higher education, the ideological preferences of the analysts are converted into the goals that universities have to meet or, more commonly, that they fail to meet. Since universities fail to meet these imposed goals, the analysts and policymakers feel justified in imposing their preferred political control systems and organizational models on universities to force compliance with their ideological vision. All of this is carried out under the veil of supposedly objective quantitative analysis.

Typically, this ideological strategy emphasizes the preferences of one group (usually students or the private sector). It ignores the preferences of the faculty, staff, community members, taxpayers, and other stakeholders. We searched in vain for books that balance the interests and wants of all the stakeholders in universities. Analyzing universities this way actually discourages serious empirical study of what diverse and complex student constituencies actually want and what diverse faculties do and do not want. Also ignored are the diverse and often divergent goals of administrations and policymakers, the wants and interests of community members, and the complex and dynamic structures of the research and development and employment markets. The neoliberal operators and their administrative enablers already "know" what people should want and punish them when they don't conform.

These points could be considered elementary in neoclassical economics and yet they rarely are taken into account in policy actions or policy critiques regarding public higher education. In place of a solid theoretical and empirical grounding, ideological notions of transparency, efficiency, and consumer choice are recommended as the solvent to banish irrationality from the system, protect the public from the selfishness of faculty and administrators and from the fecklessness of students, and to stop the waste of public funds on the middle and working classes. All the while, these operations hide the ideological agendas of the analysts.

Operating this way ignores the key requirement of any economic analysis to define the ends to be met, their relative priorities, and the complex mix of supply and demand crowds with their dynamic, diverse, and perhaps inconsistent or incompatible preferences. When economic analyses are done seriously and these fundamental violations of economic theory and method are avoided, the resulting conclusions are much more complex and differentiated (see Ehrenberg 1997, 2007; McMahon 2009; McGettigan 2013). Not surprisingly, the neoliberal solutions turn out not to be solutions at all but a significant part of the problem. The neoliberals are the ones who must be held to account.

To return to our point of departure, when these neoliberal operations dominate the scene, democratic debate about the multiple missions of public higher education is shut down. The unexamined and ill-defined ends are taken for granted and institutions are simply held accountable for meeting them by the "authorities." Such operations reinforce current behavior and organizational structures, are inherently backward looking, oversimplify institutional missions, and consolidate administrative power at the expense of everything else. The results are predictably negative and fundamentally anti-democratic both in terms of university operations and in terms of a key institution's contribution to the promotion of a democratic civil society.

In this context, many institutional leaders support the neoliberal accountability scheme by trying to spin their numbers to look good or using external accountability demands as a way of consolidating their own authority over internal constituencies. Others turn themselves and their institutions upside down trying to meet these externally imposed demands and act in ways that nullify or entirely shut down discussion about the potentially unique missions and situations of their institutions. Still others count on their institutional reputations and wealth to overcome any problems with their numbers. The overall scene involves pseudo-compliance or naïve compliance to imposed, irrational objectives. These circumstances often bring out the worst in institutions and have been central to the radical decline of public universities.

For these reasons, we highlight the resulting absence of substantive discussion of the meaning and ends of public higher education on campuses, in state governments, and in national and international arenas on the right, in the center, or on the left. Taking for granted that everyone knows and accepts the missions of public higher education kills democratic debate in its tracks. Engaging in the complex and demanding multi-party dialogues between students, faculty, staff, administrations, legislators, policymakers, and other funders about the missions and evolving contemporary meanings of public higher education is long overdue and is an essential, if disappearing, feature of healthy democratic societies.

Rather than confronting this challenge, the majority of critical authors produce denunciations from all positions on the political spectrum (see Soley 1995; Shumar 1997; Kirp 2003; Giroux and Giroux 2004; Washburn 2005; Schrecker 2010; Arum and Roska 2011; and Ginsberg 2011 for a sample of these works). Few arenas for meaningful discussion of these issues exist. Their absence on campuses, in state and national governments, in philanthropic organizations, in national organizations like the American Council on Education, or in international agencies shows how far neoliberalism has managed to undermine the operations of civil society.

This does not mean that such arenas are unnecessary. In case anyone is confused by our broadside against neoliberalism, we strongly favor holding all stakeholders in democratic societies to account regarding important social decisions, but we argue it is not possible to establish democratic accountability processes without first holding democratic deliberations about what institutions should be accountable for. When accountability is measured unilaterally by the power holders and not by collaboratively generated community standards, then accountability it is an exercise in coercion and cooptation.

Diverse student bodies and their families have a significant part of the information about what they want, need, and can afford. Graduates who have been out of the system for a while have their work lives and personal experiences to share about the value, relevance, and failures of their prior education. Faculty members, old and young, male and fe-male, minority and majority have relevant information about the quality of their working lives, the organizational pluses and minuses they deal with, the pressures they struggle with, the goals and hopes they have, etc. Staff members who execute administrative plans have an ample supply of information about the organizational failures and successes of systems imposed on them that do or do not work as planned and make them more or less productive. Administrators are rarely asked to go beyond meeting short-term management objectives to think and talk seriously about what they value, what they hope for, what they are frus-trated by, and what changes they feel are necessary. And so it goes, up-ward to state and national governments, foundations, and international agencies. The absence of substantive, democratic, non-adversarial dia-logues about these matters leaves the definition of the missions of pub-lic universities in the hands of the neoliberals and their accountants.[3]

Modeling the Goals of Public Higher Education

In the light of the above discussion, it is clear that all institutions of higher education have to engage in a selection among the many dimen-sions of their activities, weighing and programming them into action-able future plans that include budgets, recruitment, retention, physical plant improvements, etc. How social mobility, access, job preparation, technical training, research training, civic formation, public service and to whom, the conservation of knowledge, and the rest fit together is an institutional decision, not a universal formula-driven plan. These allocation decisions involve balancing multiple ends. They include the development of organizational structures and management systems to support these choices, the evaluation of success and failure at meeting them, and summing the activities into an overall understanding of the direction of the institutions. These choices must be intelligible to those who work there, study there, support the institution, and regulate its operations. Attempting to rank such institutions on a national or world-wide scale, given these different mixes, is meaningless. Obviously, this does not prevent such ranking from being widely practiced. University administrators and political authorities (and some faculty and students) are constantly concerned with the position of their institutions in the national and international rankings.

Product Mix, Factor Proportions, and Distribution of Product

One way to conceptualize these choices in neoclassical economic terms is by analyzing them in terms of the basic questions addressed in economic analyses: product mix, factor proportions, and distribution of product. Deciding the product mix institutionally is essential to any kind of economic planning and academic policy. What should we do and how much of each thing we should do are key decisions. Once those decisions are made, how the production is to be done requires another kind of allocation choice. Given what we produce, what is our best way to do it? More labor intensive, less labor intensive, with permanent staff, with contract staff, with what kind of facilities, etc.? Finally, we must allocate our efforts among the possible users, in this case the students, the various parts of the academic community, the private sector, and the public sector. What mix, how it is created, and for whom it is created are questions now often answered by unilateral administrative action without significant consultation with the affected internal and external stakeholders who have a legitimate interest in these choices.

The near absence of thoughtful and inclusive discussions of these basic economic matters on campuses and in policy environments is striking. Instead, much of the literature and the policy prescriptions implicitly claim that the key allocation decisions in public higher education have already been made. The assumption then is that institutions can be neatly organized to meet these known goals and that the only problem is how to be more "rational" in allocating resources to these known ends. In the absence of complex and yet potentially fruitful discussions, the result of closing down such discussions has been the vocationalization (the conversion of a broad concept of educating persons into job training) of public university education and the commercialization of public university research.

The lack of attention to these larger matters is not neutral nor is it an oversight because many interests are arrayed to keep these discussions from taking place. Still it should now be obvious that in each type of higher education institution, these fundamental economic choices will differ because the missions of these institutions also differ. We will return to this discussion in Chapter 2.

Public Goods and Private Goods

For the moment, leaving aside the pseudo-economics of neoliberalism and the real complexities of allocation decisions universities must make, there are inherent difficulties in the economic analysis of institutions like universities. Among the key difficulties in approaching this subject are the inherent ambiguities surrounding of the economic concepts of public and private goods. The scope of these dilemmas is masterfully laid out in Raymond Geuss' philosophical treatise *Public Goods, Private Goods* (Geuss 2001).

Geuss argues that the current distinctions between public and private goods are both confused and ideologically inflected. Though there now is now a broad literature on public choice and public accountability, the technical history of neoclassical economics' development of the concept of public goods is not very long. What is generally accepted to be the key formulation was made by Paul Samuelson in 1954 in an article "The Pure Theory of Public Expenditure" where he coined the term a "collective consumption good" (Samuelson 1954). For him, the defining features of public goods were "non-excludability" and "non-rivalrous consumption." Basically this means that public goods are those that no one can be prevented from consuming and whose consumption does not reduce the supply available.

Before we move to the history of deployment of the notions of public and private goods in higher education, we want to pause briefly over what is perhaps the most comprehensive and impressive book linked to this subject, Walter McMahon's *Higher Learning, Greater Good: The Private and Social Benefits of Higher Education* (2009). McMahon, a senior economist of education, takes a neoclassical line of argument in his book. He shows clear admiration for the market fundamentalism of Gary Becker and for social capital theory in general. In other words, he is a devotee of the rational choice model of economic behavior and believes that this model can apply very broadly. Given this background, one might think McMahon would not be a good traveling companion for the present authors. That is not the case.

What makes McMahon's book uniquely interesting to us is that his rational choice position, generally associated with a conservative conceptualization of social systems, does not take him to the neoliberal position. Rather he argues that to take the numbers seriously means to count all the private benefits accruing to individuals who get a higher education (something that few analysts in educational economics have done) as well as the public benefits emanating from their subsequent behavior in society. He also insists on a methodologically and empirically demanding analysis of the "public" benefits of higher education, including better health, more participation in the operations of democratic society, more volunteerism, and others. When he makes these calculations, he finds that the public benefits of higher education have been drastically underestimated and understated. In other words, the justifications for decreasing public expenditures on higher education are both wrong and economically irrational, leading to a general undermining of the economic competitiveness of our society. McMahon's argument does not center on an ideological preference for public goods but on an economic calculation of the value of the private and public goods created by higher education and what he believes ought to be the rational policy consequences of these calculations. His views are not good news for those trying to further undercut public investment in higher education on the false grounds of neoclassical economic rationality.

Thus far, we have presented a discussion about public and private goods, about the ambiguity of the concepts and the controversial economic consequences of some public goods, because arguments about higher education as a public good are an ideological centerpiece of both the neoliberal attack on higher education and the left and liberal defenses of the value of such an education. Since at least the Thatcher era of the 1980s in the U.K., public higher education has been under an all-out neoliberal attack as inefficient, opaque, and unaccountable. The constant repetition of this litany of faults has, as often is the case, gradually created a public understanding that higher education is deeply flawed and highly suspect.

For neoliberals, a public good is simply a good that has yet to be properly privatized. A public good is also a good that is inefficiently allocated, since they claim without justification that the market for public goods does not discipline their distribution and consumption. Private goods, by contrast, are supposedly always disciplined by the market and, therefore (a false syllogism) rationally allocated. Finally, what is private is regulated by the market and any form of regulation that is not driven by the market is dismissed as a form of "socialism."

These fallacious positions have enormous traction in Europe and the U.S. where they have gradually garnered bipartisan support at the EU level, the national level, and (in the United States) at the state government level. This explains why we spent effort on a theoretical discussion of public goods. Nothing in the neoliberal position bears an analytical relationship to the complex meanings of public and private goods and their value in higher education. Nothing in that position acknowledges the difficulty of making a hard distinction between the public and the private. Nothing they do shows an understanding of the institutional missions and organizational structures that make it absurd to affirm that every single actor and unit should be a "tub on its own bottom" facing its internal and external market demands directly.

This is a serious problem because universities, public or private, both produce and rely on public goods for their very survival. Not all faculty, departments, or activities pay for themselves nor could they. Innovative basic research is rarely funded externally. Having a great research library used only by a fraction of the faculty and students is a public good that is hardly fully utilized in a neoliberal sense. Yet basic research facilities, libraries, and a host of faculty experts in fields for which there is currently low demand and not necessarily an immediate use is essential to university survival and knowledge development. Having this kind of supposedly excess capacity is key to innovation, research and development, thinking outside of the box, and ultimately to university sustainability. It generates inefficiency from the neoliberal point of view but is essential to the trans-generational survival of research, universities, and of democracy itself. Trying to solve the puzzle of paying for and supporting the creation of public goods with simpleminded rational choice models is not only hopeless, it has destroyed public universities as institutions.

Here are some of the kinds of dilemmas that emerge. If a university requires a heating system and a security force to operate, are these legitimately public goods? If so, how are the costs of having them to be allocated? Should the creative writing program pay the same cost per faculty, staff, or student for these services as the nanofabrication laboratory with significant grants and patent income? If some of the professional schools within a university collect their own tuitions and therefore pay the university rents and utilities for the use of university facilities, how should these payments be set? On a per capita consumption basis? On the basis of the amount of profits shared with the central university budget after costs are deducted? If the department of economics has four times as many students per faculty member as the department of religion, but both of their tuitions go directly into the coffers of their college administration, should economics pay four times as much for the public goods or one fourth of the amount the department of religion pays? Who should pay for the departmental, college, and university administrative staff and how much?

These questions can be multiplied easily. The answers can be calculated, but only after decisions about the kind of institution and the systems of internal distribution that should characterize it have been made. In the real world, heterogeneous, historically conditioned, and politically charged patterns of allocations generally exist. They persist from year to year in which some things that don't pay for themselves receive subsidies from other activities that generate supposed surpluses. These redistributions are based affirming that these subsidized activities are necessary to the existence of the institution as a "university" that must have a requisite complement of departments and disciplines represented. Certainly saying that those who receive the redistribution are "public goods" welfare beneficiaries and those who lose in the redistribution are "private goods" losers is a non-starter. Taking the same argument down to the levels of popular and less popular subdisciplines within departments falls prey to the same problems of analysis and institutional solidarity.

Whatever else the public and private goods distinction might be useful for, it is not useful for day-to-day operational decisions about allocations within a university economy according to rational choice logics. This directly undercuts the neoliberal logic of a perfect higher education system in which every individual in every unit of every institution is disciplined by the "market" to produce whatever it is they produce in the most efficient manner possible. The overall system's structure is the direct result of the full play of market forces driven by the demands of student, private sector, and governmental "customers" who pay for the services.

Why Focus on Public Universities?

We have chosen to focus attention on public universities because, after the Second World War, they became a dominant arena for social mobility in the U.S. and Europe, fueled by the expansion of higher education to include a much broader social spectrum. These universities once were major creators of knowledge through research and scholarship as well and were the envy of the world for a number of generations. Now there is a consensus among liberals, conservatives, and radicals that the public university system in North America is collapsing and that the public systems in Europe may indeed be in the vanguard in leading the downward spiral (Soley 1995; Lucas 1996; Ehrenberg 1997, 2007; Caanan and Shumar 2008; Garland 2009; Hill 2009; Cole 2010; Newfield 2011; McGettigan 2013; Guinier 2015).

These universities are public because they bring new generations of working- and middle-class people into productive and pivotal roles in our societies, and because they used to engage, at least to some degree, in research and service of benefit to the public in their states and nations. Because of this, their decline has considerable social, economic and political importance. It directly impacts democracy through limiting the possibility for social mobility and thereby the opportunity for students not born with a backpack filled with money to aspire to an improved social position. Instead, the decline of public universities re-concentrates social control and resources in the hand of global political and financial elites.

The ongoing conversion of public universities into vocational training schools deepens the divide between the powerful and their subjects and aims to convert public university students into an indebted, university-educated new proletariat and the faculty into fee-for-service trainers rather than educators. Put another way, we see in the decline of public universities the educational expression of the growing global gap between rich and the rest, aided by the neoliberal economists and policy analysts who work for governments, the financial industry, the International Monetary Fund, the World Bank, and other global players (Graeber 2011). These self-interested operators claim all these changes are the rational outcome of the workings of the "free market."

Democratic Institutions Create Democratic Actors

Some graduates from universities take on important positions in the public or private sector, and how they have been educated matters to society at large. Those who end up in middle-management positions in organizations are in positions where their ability to work in teams, to show initiative, to write synthetically, etc., is understood to count for a great deal. However, with the international consolidation of global economic elites, such employment is now no longer guaranteed to public university graduates and they cannot count on achieving senior leadership positions. There is a clear correlation between this and the new higher education ideologies that frame the majority of public university graduates as workers in the "knowledge society of the twenty-first century." They are, in effect, a new proletariat. Yet even if leadership positions are now nearly foreclosed for many graduates, employment in organizations where teams work on projects and where collaborative skills and initiative are required is increasingly common. The disconnection between the student as an individualistic consumer of higher education and the employed graduate as a practiced collaborator in organizations is becoming evident.

Team-based organizations are now commonplace in the private and public sectors. To prepare students for successful participation in team-based organizations that are dynamic and to meet changing demands on employees, public universities cannot limit themselves to individualistic technical training. They have to provide training in leadership, team membership, group processing of complex problems, knowledge acquisition in new areas, and so on, for their graduates to operate successfully in most organizations. Of course, such training could also prepare them to play a constructive role in a democratic society.

A great deal stands in the way of doing this. The most serious problem is that this kind of education cannot be carried out in an institution whose internal structures and processes are a daily denial of democracy, collaboration, and teamwork. If students are expected to be democratically competent organizational actors and citizens, then they must be active participants in their own academic institutions. These institutions would have to operate through democratic structures and processes. Authoritarian universities cannot produce collaborative organizational members or democratic citizens.

This matters a great deal now in view of what is happening globally with democratic societies. The emergence of trends toward fascism once again (for example in Hungary, Poland), and proto-fascist elements appearing on the political scene in many other countries including the United States, it appears that humanely oriented democracies are under increasing threat. One counterweight to this is democratically-inspired and organized public higher education that reaffirms the values and practices that underpin democracy. Public universities treated as training camps for a new generation of corporate workers do nothing to counter this trend.

The challenges here are serious. For universities to be democratic in the above way requires a serious revaluation of academic freedom, free speech, and integrity in research and teaching. Universities ultimately can only teach democracy by exhibiting it in their own institutional structures and behavior. Doing this would be key to preserving and developing democracy in an ever more hostile global environment. The deteriorating state of democratic governments around the world correlates neatly with their neoliberal policies of higher education, citizen disaffection, increasing political corruption scandals, and the sale of a country's assets to the highest bidder. As Piketty (2014) argues, in the face of this, one of the most important investments a country can make is in public education. The virtues and value of free speech, academic freedom and integrity are never safe, as we will show in Chapter 4. They always have to fought for, and now fighting for them is the only way to recreate democratically relevant public universities.

Notes

1. By this we mean to refer to the kinds of analyses that have been canonical in academic economics since Alfred Marshall's *Principles of Economics* ([1890] 1920) became the dominant text to be followed by Paul Samuelson's *Economics* (1948, and at least fifteen subsequent editions). Perhaps the most elegant and succinct statement of the neoclassical argument is Lionel Robbins, *Essay on the Nature and Significance of Economic Science* (Robbins [1932] 1937). Whatever one thinks of these works and their arguments, they have been the core of non-Marxist economic thought and analysis.
2. See Elster and Roemer (1993) for a portrait of the whole debate.
3. This is compatible with the argument of Ronald Barnett (2003) who argues that universities are not and should not aspire to be ideology-free. Rather, to use his term, they are "saturated" with ideology and the issue is to promote virtuous ideologies and suppress vicious ones.

CHAPTER 2

Multiple Models and Meanings of Higher Education

◆◆◆

While denunciations of the degradation or destruction of public higher education abound (see Chapter 1), proposals for reform based on nostalgia for a supposedly golden past are doomed to fail. Equally unacceptable is a forced march toward a neoliberal "stark utopia." While a return to the past is not feasible or desirable, no discussion of the future of higher education makes sense without a review of this history of the various institutional designs that have been tried and modified so far. The road forward has to be built on awareness of the best features of historical academic institutions, now reformulated to promote both democratic ideals and their own economic sustainability.

Though in this book we focus on public universities, they are only one component of a broad array of institutional forms of higher education. To situate them properly, we briefly contrast them with the many other higher education institutional types in existence. This is particularly important for European audiences since it can be argued that there is less diversity within European higher education. Higher education worldwide is composed of multiple kinds of institutions. It is particularly important to distinguish public universities from the other institutions in both their mission and organization.

We are aware that the following pages contain abstract idealizations of models of higher education. They suffer from all the limitations of such abstractions. To become actionable, they would need to be incarnated in real contexts. What follows, then, is just a sketch map of the territory we will traverse later in this book.

This discussion moves from the medieval university to the "for profit university" passing through a variety of institutional types with different histories and missions. Building on this, we then focus on different teaching models or meanings of education, e.g., technical training, professional training and civic education. This flows into a discussion of the role of research in different kinds of higher education institutions. Proceeding this way enables us to include an examination of the relationship between teaching and research in higher education, an issue often treated as an afterthought in tracts about reforming universities. We keep these linked because so many of the current reforms and critiques reduce universities to their undergraduate teaching functions (e.g., Arum and Roska 2011).

Models and Meanings of Higher Education

If an economic analysis of higher education must be specific to the particular institutional type as we argued in Chapter 2, it also has to be mission-specific. Homogenized analyses are not helpful to anyone. Thus, in addition to distinguishing types of higher education institutions, we attend to different teaching models, teaching purposes, research models, and research and teaching linkages. These are interacting dimensions of complex organizational processes, not separate variables.

Types of University

The Medieval University

There were many types of medieval universities, mostly growing out of monastic models and gradually changing by the thirteenth century into the early urban European universities like Bologna and Salamanca. We will be brief here since this is not our central focus. These institutions were created by contractual agreements among a group of professors and an association of students who paid the professors' salaries in return for the instruction the students demanded. Most of the professors necessarily had an ecclesiastical education. The *trivium* (grammar, logic, and rhetoric) and *quadrivium* (arithmetic, geometry, music, and astronomy) dominated most of the teaching. The students generally came from families with enough money to allow them to study and included only a small fraction of the total population in their age group. These elite students presumably were being prepared for life in the court, the clergy, law, and the family businesses. Philology, philosophical disputation, calculation, and the ability to write well were for the privileged few.

Humboldt's University

Because of the multiplicity of ways the legacy of the Humboldt reforms in Germany has been conceptualized, this is a hard model to characterize fairly. Still, there are a few basic principles common to most discussions. One is that the goal of education was *Bildung*, the formation of students and enhancement of their capacity to play constructive roles in public and private life. Reading and interpreting canonical works was an important element in the formation process. A parallel element in *Bildung* was the ongoing development of the faculty as teachers and researchers. A concept with strong roots in Romanticism, *Bildung* has protean meanings ranging from liberal to reactionary. What it means in any particular context always needs to be specified.

Humboldt's model, though never fully implemented (Bruford 1975), had certain core elements. It was based on a contract between students and professors that assured the students the "freedom to learn" and professors the "freedom to teach." These two freedoms obligated the parties to participate in a developmental dialogue about reconciling their freedoms and choices in any given place at any given time. The link between learning and teaching in the Humboldt model eventually gave rise to the German research university. The students and faculty negotiated their relationships to achieve a satisfactory balance. Insofar as one can tell, there were no "administrators" and the Prussian police state did not begin regulating these universities until later (Clark 2007). The two threads, teaching and research, went hand in hand, albeit for a small elite of wealthy students.

The Newman model

Cardinal Newman's lectures, *The Idea of a University* (Newman [1852] 1907) were enormously influential in both British and U.S. educational circles. Newman saw education as driven by a set of transcendental moral values oriented around spiritual and ethical development. However, that development required substantive education to be effective. As a result, the curricula Newman recommended were a complex amalgam of classical educational sources and the sciences. Many elements were consolidated in this model, including the notion of a community of scholars and learners and the collegiate residential system, a concept that had an enormous impact on university life in the U.K. and the U.S., particularly in the form of the residential collegiate model.

The "American" Model

In Europe, there is a surprising amount of talk about the "American model" of universities. The term, when used by most Europeans, conflates the American model with what are mainly the elite private U.S. universities whose basic features are great wealth, prestige, and social exclusion. These institutions are fundamentally unlike the European universities, other than Oxford and Cambridge, that currently want to emulate them but lack the money and residential systems yet to make the model work.

It should be noted that there is no such thing as an "American model." Rather, there are a wide variety of American models. The current invocation of the American model in Europe now is very much like the invocation of the German research university model in the U.S. at the end of the nineteenth century. They are ideological and manipulative operations by self-interested power holders who want to reform higher education to suit their purposes.

The Liberal Arts College Model

In many ways, the United States liberal arts colleges—smallish, four-year institutions built on a residential campus—were a direct heir to the Newman model. Most liberal arts colleges began as schools to train Protestant pastors but quickly evolved into the myriad liberal arts colleges that dot the landscape. Their liberal arts curricula include the physical sciences, biological sciences, social sciences, and humanities. They stress two years of coursework in general areas of history, language, mathematics, the sciences, literature, and philosophy after which the students select a field in which to "major," and take the equivalent of about a year of coursework in that particular field. There is an emphasis on the dynamic tension between a broad general education and residential collegiate community life that aims to produce thoughtful and ethically aware citizens. The vitality of these institutions is as great as is their diversity. They range from confessional schools to fully secular schools. The faculty's activity is dominated by teaching, with only modest (though now increasing) pressure to do research. The faculty play a significant role in the governance of the institution.

The Private University

Private universities come in many varieties, since they were founded and financed mainly with private capital and thus can be chartered to have quite specific missions and foci. In the U.S., the elite universities in the country are private—Harvard, Yale, Princeton, Columbia, Stanford, Pennsylvania, Dartmouth, Chicago, etc. In structure, they generally combine a collegiate system for the first four years of university study with specialized graduate education in an enormous variety of masters and doctoral fields. Their budgets are composed of very high tuition and fees charges, the income from multi-billion dollar endowments, research grants, and patent income.

More modest private universities exist in various forms. One model is a strong liberal arts college with a few attached postgraduate programs, such as law, medicine, or business. Another is a kind of special purpose private university dedicated to particular lines of research and training in certain fields. Examples would be MIT, Rockefeller University in New York City or the New School for Social Research.

In Europe, private universities are just beginning to make their influence felt. A few, with significant financial backing, are becoming successful at attracting some faculty and students away from the public system but they still have a distance to travel to become the elite institutions in most countries. An interesting example is the Central European University founded by George Soros, which he framed as an alternative to massified, impoverished, and bureaucratic state universities. Also a number of business schools that, though private, receive a good deal of public funding are relevant cases. Such private universities are attempting to create a niche for themselves as a counterweight to the public systems. In some countries, they do so with the active support of national governments deeply frustrated in their attempts to reform their public higher education systems.

Vocational Colleges

Vocational colleges have long been part of the higher educational systems of both the United States and Europe. In the United States, what were once called junior colleges and vocational schools now are called community colleges. These are supported by the local or county tax base, charge modest tuition fees, and offer certificate programs in specific vocational fields, such as information technology, nursing, criminology, and accounting. Tuned closely into the employment needs of the local area and structured to deal with adults, many of whom are employed or have families, these colleges enroll over 50 per cent of all higher education students in the United States and are a core part of the higher educational system. In Norway, the "university colleges" play a similar role though they mostly wish to become full liberal arts colleges now.

The U.S. community colleges tend to have few permanent faculty and they change programs and curricula quickly in response to local needs. The original model included both vocational training and two years of preparation after which students who wished could continue on to the liberal arts colleges or the universities in the system. While this did happen and still does, the shorter-term vocational training and retraining of local workforces tends to dominate their activities.

In Europe the polytechnics, regional colleges, and other vocational schools have long formed a key part of higher education, preparing local people with modest incomes for more skilled work or retraining them to meet the needs of the shifting economic environment. In recent decades, many of these vocational schools have aspired to become full colleges and even universities, blurring the line between them and the rest of the system. Nevertheless, they do not easily compete for national research funding with the older public and private universities and end up usually finding some kind of particular regional or local socioeconomic niche where they and their students fit. Certainly this is the case in Norway.

Public Universities

There are two different types of public universities in the United States, those funded by the individual states and those publicly funded and also designated as the land-grant universities of their states. The state universities are public institutions founded and chartered by the states. In Europe, they are set up and regulated nationally. In both cases, they used to receive significant allocations of public funds drawn from the tax base. They are organized as not-for-profit entities that do not pay taxes on their core activities.

In return, their mission is to provide higher education for the residents of their state or nation. They once were open to people from all social classes regardless of their financial situations. These systems vary in size, scope, and quality a great deal. Some state systems in the United States are huge. The University of California system has ten campuses and 238,000 students and the California State University system has twenty-three campuses and 447,000 students. The State University of New York has sixty-four campuses and about 460,000 students. These campuses range from large public universities to specialized small and technical colleges. Typically, in the United States, attending these universities used to cost students very little because the major part of the budget came from state tax revenues. They coexist side by side with private universities, liberal arts colleges, and community colleges as part of an array of nearly 4,000 higher education institutions.

European public university systems typically did not charge tuition or charged very little. This has now changed in most countries. While the percentage of the population getting a university education has increased greatly in Europe, none of the European public university systems approximate the numbers of campuses found in the United States. The European systems, until the imposition of the Bologna reforms and subsequent European Union regulations, were quite idiosyncratic in structure and operations. The English, French, and German systems were radically different in conception and operations and the status of the professors as civil servants, contract employees, etc., varied greatly.

Another feature of public universities in Central and Western Europe was the system of shared governance that involved the election of the rector (or vice chancellor) and other officials by the combined bodies of student representative, staff representatives, and faculty. This system of comanagement is being eradicated in country after country.

Another difference in the United States system is the set of public "land grant" universities. The land grant system was created by the Morrill Act of 1862 and was based on the idea that each state in the union had some state land that could be sold to create a fund to support the creation of a land grant university, one per state, with a special public mission. The land grant university was to engage in teaching and research for the benefit of the people in its state but also to engage in direct service to the people of the state. This service came to be called the "extension" system. Problems that needed research support in each state were brought to the university for research and the results were "extended" to the people though an organized extension service with trained professionals. The initial land grant focus was agrarian but extension moved into urban and industrial settings as the structure of the economy changed.

The prestige of the land grant universities was considerable, and many of them evolved to become some of the major teaching and research universities, such as Cornell University, Ohio State University, the University of Wisconsin, the University of Minnesota, Michigan State University, and University of California at Davis. For a long time, the public service mission combined with relatively open access to any high school graduate in the state made them key avenues for social mobility and community and economic development. These functions are in radical decline under neoliberalism.

For-Profit Colleges and Universities

Though they have existed for generations, for-profit colleges and universities have grown explosively in recent decades. These differ from the institutions we have discussed so far because they are not tax exempt and explicitly intend to make a profit for the owners or shareholders. Operating on tuition income along with federal student loans to students to pay tuition, they have grown in number to include over 800 institutions. The largest university in the world, the University of Phoenix, is a for-profit university run by the Apollo Group and its stocks are traded on world financial markets.

These institutions concentrate heavily on job training, use contract faculty, and make heavy investments in online teaching. They often contract with not-for-profit university faculty to create syllabuses for them and then have the courses taught by temporary lecturers. The jury is out on their educational quality. Some are quite good and some are frauds. Their topical focus and emphasis on satisfying their student customers are key to their business model. They are accredited to offer university credits by the same agencies that accredit not-for-profit universities (Ruch 2001).

Models and Meanings of Teaching

In addition to distinguishing types of higher education institutions, it is important to attend to the different modalities of teaching that take place in them. While some institutions specialize in a particular teaching model, more than one variety of teaching is found in most. These teaching models operate differently in the classroom, laboratory, and studio, and the teaching purposes, research foci, and the relation between them differs in institutions where both take place.

In the broadest sense, teaching is a form of communication across and within generations aimed at imparting valuable information and skills, capacity building, competence, and standards. Students are not blank slates and an important part of teaching is articulating what they know and think with new ideas, skills, and possibilities. A key element in most teaching is helping students learn what they themselves can aspire to accomplish, so that their motivation to learn and perform competently continues beyond their formal enrollment in higher education.

Teaching varies, from the "banking model" (Freire 1970) that construes students as passive recipients of the teacher's expertise and knowledge to active learning models in which teachers and students collaborate in inquiry and problem solving to enable students to learn how to formulate and solve problems on their own (Dewey 1990). Settings vary from amphitheaters to seminar rooms to studios to laboratories, each with their associated modes of teaching. Except in the worst cases of overcrowded public universities and predominantly online systems, most of these teaching approaches are employed at most institutions. Increasingly, though, with the systematic impoverishment of public higher education, public institutions are moving to the amphitheater, passive learning approach. This combined with contract instructors and a reliance on graduate teaching assistants has caused an important decline in the quality of public higher education overall.

Surprisingly, what has been done to public universities is now appearing in elite universities. Large classes with a single professor are a great temptation to administrators for whom serving more "customers" with the same money is a goal regardless of the educational consequences.

Types of Education

Many types of education are commonly found across the spectrum of institutions as well as within the confines of individual institutions. Since we are making an argument about higher education, we need to be clear about the multi-dimensional character of education to be able to focus our analysis and critique properly.

Vocational Education

Vocational teaching treats job training as a central goal. The teacher is presumed to know what the students need to know on the basis of the teacher's ample experience in the relevant work settings. The teacher is the practiced expert and the students are novices with clear vocational goals. Vocational education is not restricted to vocational schools and community colleges. A great deal more of what is taught in public and private research universities involves this kind of vocational training than is ordinarily recognized. Nor is vocational education restricted to amphitheaters. Many vocational programs have laboratories and workshops where students engage in active learning under professorial and peer supervision.

Technical Training

A clear distinction between vocational training and technical training is not to be had, but we maintain the terminological difference to point to forms of more advanced work training. Here we are referring to the sort that is given in engineering, computer science, and similar fields at universities. In addition to the mastery of the conceptual and methodological dimensions of particular fields, students are trained in the use of apparatuses, technical problem solving, etc., under the direct supervision of professors. Technical training is a key part of any kind of higher education because knowledge without and understanding of methods for applying it, education is a dead end.

Liberal Education

The "liberal" meaning of education extends well beyond the satisfaction of the aims of the students. A liberal education seeks to have students reconsider their initial aims and goals by broadening their familiarity with ideas, methods, and fields unknown to them from their prior schooling and experiences. An aim is for them to learn the consequences of taking different positions and different methodological approaches to issues of importance, and to learn about the meaning and consequences of different behaviors when they become practicing professionals and members of society after graduation. The liberal education approach involves the formation of tastes and preferences rather than the satisfaction of wants and is a centerpiece of both the Humboldt and Newman models. It is incompatible with a conceptualization of students as customers.

Professional Training

Professional training is a key part of vocational and technical training and of liberal education. It involves preparing students to enter particular professions such as anthropology, public policy, planning, literary studies, medicine, law, engineering, etc. This involves the transmission of knowledge and practical expertise but also the modeling of professional experience and norms. Students are situated to some degree in the historical trajectory of their fields, the current mores and life ways of professionals, and the major controversies that divide and unite groups. They are given an initial sense of professional belonging, practice with the current tools (theories, methods, mindsets) that dominate their professions, and they learn about the major funding sources, the main publication venues respected by each professional group, and the job market. How to conduct professionally acceptable research and teaching, how to write up publishable results, how to select journals, how to write grant proposals, how to administer grants, etc., all form part of this professional training. In this model, the professors are expected to be exemplars of their professions (Abbott 1988; Schmidt 2001).

While vocational and technical education are a focus of vocational and technical schools, liberal arts institutions with graduate and professional schools engage in a significant amount of vocational and technical education. The liberal education approach and extensive professional socialization is more restricted to liberal arts colleges and the wealthier private and public universities.

One of the most important consequences of neoliberalism has been the impoverishment of the concept of higher education to reconfigure it as solely a matter of job preparation. Consequently, liberal education is under constant threat, including the preparation for active citizenship that is a part of the liberal arts. Professional education is increasingly narrow, practical, and limited to fields where universities can make money by training professionals for jobs. Within the professional fields, neoliberalism has also skewed the selection of areas of practice toward the most remunerative specialties both by promoting an ideology of self-aggrandizing greed and imposing such high educational debts on students that they seek high-paying careers to get out from under the educational debts they have incurred.

Teaching Purposes

There is no neat distinction between teaching purposes and teaching models, but it is useful to add a categorization of the different kinds of knowledge aims emerging from teaching in higher education. Below we lay out the diverse aims of teaching processes.

The Creation of Competence

One aim of education is to teach students how to do particular things well.

The Transmission of Prior Knowledge

A significant emphasis in education always involves transmission of knowledge gained in the past. This knowledge presumably has been weighed and sifted and is transmitted to the next generation. This necessarily involves the conservation of knowledge from the past in the form of broad training of the teachers, libraries, curricula, and activities that have proved to be worthwhile over generations of teaching.

The Application of Prior Knowledge

Part of education is to take knowledge (theories, methods, techniques) already extensively used and transmit this knowledge to the next generation in a way that the students can make this knowledge part of their own repertoire of possible resources and behaviors.

The Critique of Prior Knowledge

Prior knowledge is not inert but only exists as the subject of constant examination, interpretation, and reinterpretation. A large amount of the activity of teaching involves the critique of prior knowledge as a way of moving the current fields and potential future practitioners into new emphases, new areas of development, along with the avoidance of activities that proved not to be as fruitful as they once seemed.

The Generation of New Knowledge

Part of teaching is to provide students with the tools to generate new knowledge on their own while at school and in the future. Students are taught how to do research and how to manage discovery processes in the hopes that they will become innovators and inventors for the next generation.

The Application of New Knowledge

Another part of teaching is to show students how new discoveries can be converted into useful innovations. Advanced undergraduates often engage in research projects, sometimes independently and sometimes with existing faculty teams, and learn how to critically generate and apply new knowledge as preparation for a creative professional life.

In most teaching situations, these elements are mixed but in different kinds of institutions and settings, one or another is emphasized more heavily. We note that the transmission and application of knowledge is heavily emphasized in neoliberal schemes at the expense of critique, the generation of new knowledge, and the application of new knowledge to create innovative processes. There is no support in this framework for the student as an innovator or as a critical and reflective adult in the making. This reflects the proletarianization of higher education that lies at the center of neoliberalism's agenda.

Research Models

Research in higher education involves a multiplicity of streams and each leads in different directions. There are also various classifications of research universities according to the diversity, amount, and funding of research. Our aim only is to distinguish some of the main categories of research.

Ongoing Disciplinary Research

Many disciplines make their way through time by the ongoing development of existing, funded research projects in areas where the local professors are well known and have a track record. These "research shops" have usually accumulated the personnel, equipment, library resources, and organizational structures needed to keep relatively long-term projects going with constant infusions of external funding from governments, foundations, and the private sector. This kind of research generates multiple products including research publications, technical innovations, patents and patent income, etc. In the social sciences, ongoing research groups exist but rarely produce patents and patent income. Teamwork in law schools might produce significant and actionable outcomes. In the humanities, ongoing research groups are quite infrequent, the research practices tending to be highly individualistic.

Individual Research Projects

In many public universities and most private universities, there is an expectation that faculty will maintain a personal research profile. This is less emphasized in liberal arts colleges where teaching is the first priority but it still is an important part of many liberal arts faculty members' work life and the process of evaluation they go through as they rise through the ranks. At public and private universities, research is emphasized as a key part of appointment, renewal, and promotion procedures. Annual reports detailing research activities, grants, and publications are required of all faculty members. Individual research projects are created autonomously by faculty who select their own topics, theories, and methods and who engage in their research at a self-defined pace. There is relatively little collaboration in this kind of work and often very little guidance or oversight of what is being done. Rather it is seen more as a qualification for being a university professor to have and demonstrate research competence, no matter what the research is about.

The neoliberal impact on social science research has been documented in *Great Expectations* (Commission on the Social Sciences 2003) and many other studies. The emphasis on neoliberal accountability has increased pressure for short time horizons for projects, multiple deliverables, more individualistic publication and research styles (because coauthoring counts less), and projects more narrowly defined to fit disciplinary boundaries that are reinforced by the accountability system. The sacrifice to multidisciplinary research, collaborative research, and long-term research projects on large-scale phenomena (e.g., global warming, sustainability, arms control, racism, terrorism, etc.) has been documented. It is resulting in a massive dumbing down of the research apparatus in higher education generally. The long-term consequences of this strategy for the polity and economy of the United States and Europe are likely to be negative.

Research and Teaching Linkages

The relationship between teaching and research takes multiple forms in different institutions and in different units within the same institutions.

Research without Teaching

In some units, the faculty engage in their research without communicating much about it to their students. Those faculty are fully engaged in communicating about their research with their professional peers in their national and international professional organizations. If they get major grants, they are relieved of teaching duties partly or completely and basically become full-time researchers.

Research and Teaching

In some areas, students are directly engaged in the faculty research projects as research team members or assistants. It is relatively common for the best students to be engaged in faculty research and in ongoing training to enter working life in that profession. In the social sciences, funded research projects often involve student assistants. Generally the assistants are postgraduate students but there are also projects where undergraduate students participate actively.

Teaching and Research as Directly Linked

An underlying element in the *Bildung* view of education once involved the necessity of linking teaching and research so that students and faculty together would engage in inquiry processes. Students would learn how to do research and become autonomous researchers in the future. In the process, they would also learn to work in teams of people with different statuses and capabilities and thus also learn skills in group work and leadership.

Linking teaching and research, based strongly on pragmatist knowledge generation, is not dominant in contemporary higher education. The increasing separation of teaching and research at universities is the hallmark of the period from 1960 onward. While teaching and research are evaluated in hiring and promotion decisions, research trumps teaching dramatically at most universities. A good researcher with a bad teaching record is rarely denied a promotion but a great teacher with a poor research record is unlikely to survive a promotion review.

At universities, teaching and research faculty are increasingly separated, with teaching faculty occupying inferior positions with lower salaries, less generous benefits, and less job security. Of course, the implication is that the students, even at research universities, are increasingly taught by people distant from the research process and so socialization into the research world is unlikely to be a significant part of their experience.

Models of the Public University

Because images, ideologies, public relations, and actual practices vary widely and often contradict one another, it is worthwhile approaching the public university in terms of an analytical dichotomy articulated by Chris Argyris and Donald Schön (Argyris and Schön 1996). They distinguished "espoused theory" and "theory-in-use" as a way of contrasting what people claim or think they are doing (espoused theory) and what their behavior reveals (theory-in-use). This division is fruitful in creating a deeper understanding of the public university.

Espoused Theories of Public Universities

It is commonplace to see in the literature a relatively timeless idea of the public university and then to view the present as a deviation from that ideal. There are both positive and negative historical views that provide a charter for critique and reform proposals. The positive view is that there has long been a stable model of the public university in which these institutions provide broad social access, high quality education at a low price, conduct important research, and disseminate that research to the research community and the public effectively. This public university was integrated through a shared understanding among students, faculty, administrators, policymakers, and the public about its mission. While elements of this view could find some confirmation in examples, it is an attempt to capture the essence of the institution outside of a context of constant socioeconomic and political change and without consideration of the internal organizational changes visible over its history.

The negative view is that the public university is a mediocre hotbed of leftwing thinking with lots of lazy and irresponsible faculty. Supposedly these faculty members substitute ideological indoctrination for teaching and conduct research on trivial subjects of no interest to society at large. These universities are administered incompetently by people with no business sense and are a drag on the public purse.

The positive view justifies the critique of corporatization and the politics of accountability and the negative view justifies corporatization and the imposition of accountability and efficiency measures on public higher education. Both are stereotypic, ahistorical, and fundamentally useless in charting a meaningful path toward organizational change.

Theories-in-Use of Public Universities

Against these views, we pose the actual behavior of public universities. This is not a simple matter because the literature suffers from a conflation of espoused theories in the absence of careful ethnographic work on how universities operate. Still we can say that all public universities are now Tayloristic institutions with sharp hierarchies. At the apex are university administrators, increasingly hired from the outside with the help of executive search services and handsomely paid; in the middle are faculty (increasingly on contracts and part-time) and staff; and students are at the bottom. Increasingly authoritarian, non-consultative decision making at the apex is common.

When we survey what public universities now prioritize in their behavior, we see a consistent public relations emphasis on accessibility, diversity, public engagement, and job preparation; teaching functions separated from research; an emphasis on profitable research; and a primary concern with institutional ranking. Along with these go a litany of explanations for the constant cutting of teaching budgets, the substitution of permanent faculty positions by contract faculty, and the need to increase tuition costs and administrative numbers and salaries. The theories-in-use basically configure public universities as administratively top-heavy service industries wrapped in the patina of education for participation in the "knowledge society of the twenty-first century" while they are actually moving towards vocational approach to knowledge transmission.

It is notable that these models provide no principled prioritization of the diverse elements that make up a public university. Rather, efficiency, diversity, engagement, internationalization, teaching, research, fancy buildings, salaries, and so on all compete with each other in a political free-for-all refereed by senior administrators who use their positions at the apex to support some groups and functions at the expense of others. Rather than adding up to a coherent model of a public university, most institutions are a ragtag conjugation of these elements. Stated another way, instead of finding a broad theory-in-use, we constantly come across partial theories-in-use or unidimensional views that do little to assist the participants in the more demanding task of reconciling the wide variety of goals universities necessarily have and organizing them into intelligible and actionable plans.

These partial and competing theories-in-use and the positioning of senior administrators as referees actually stand directly in the way of principled campus-wide debates about the proper balances of activities and budgets for the institution. In the absence of such principled debates, policies and models drift on the global processes and fads in higher education reform and are subject to local political bossism. Together these factors provide ample support to authoritarian, hierarchical management, increasingly Fordist, segmentary, discipline-dominated academic structures, the deterioration or disappearance of shared governance, increasing use of contingent faculty, and the use of accountability schemes as the central method of institutional policing.

Modeling the Goals of Public Higher Education

In the previous chapter, we discussed the kinds of economic decisions all institutions of higher education have to make. In this chapter, we have diversified the many types of higher education institutions, their multiple missions and activities, the diverse meanings of research and teaching, and the multiple ways research and teaching can be linked. From our perspective, this means that every institution of higher education has to engage in a selection among, weighting of, and programming of these multiple dimensions into actionable plans. These plans include budgets, recruitment, retention, physical plant improvements, and the like. How to weight social mobility, access, job preparation, technical training, research training, civic formation, public service and to whom, the conservation of knowledge, and the rest, and how they fit together, is an institutional decision, not a simple, formula-driven plan. Doing this involves allocational decisions, the development of organizational structures and management systems to support these choices, the evaluation of success and failure to meet these multiple ends, and summing up the activities into an overall understanding of the direction of the institution. This direction must be intelligible to those who work there, study there, support the institution, and regulate its operations. One-size-fits-all ideological prescriptions about what public universities should be or do reflect either ignorance or a wish to undermine the institutions and their role in democratic societies.

CHAPTER 3

Bildung, Academic Freedom, Academic Integrity, and Democracy

◆◆◆

In current discussions on the future of higher education, four concepts have circulated freely: *Bildung,* academic freedom, academic integrity, and the role of democracy in the future of higher education. Few discussions pursue the important links among these concepts. We see them as highly interdependent. The substance of and relationships among these concepts form the centerpiece of this chapter.

We claim that a democratic university is grounded in formation processes (*Bildung*) that include all stakeholders. We assert these can only be effectively built and maintained through democratic principles of education broadly understood as a developmental process involving free speech, academic integrity, and collaborative institutional management through democratic deliberation. In such an environment, students would graduate imbued with the values and practices of *Bildung* and with a concrete, practical, and, substantial understanding of democracy in education, organizations, the public sector, the family, and in government. Faculty, staff, and administrators would behave according to democratic and participatory norms of conduct in teaching, research, and administration. Together these institutions and their graduates would be capable of making essential contributions to revitalizing the democratic societies so undermined by neoliberalism and elitism.

Of these concepts, *Bildung* is less known in the current educational environment. *Bildung*'s link to higher education can be traced back to the work of Wilhem von Humboldt. His concept of *Bildung* located it in the interaction between students and faculty engaging in joint teaching, learning, and research activities. For him, *Bildung* was a formation process that created skillful students and faculty who could critically approach problems while being intellectually creative and coming up with constructive ideas about how to solve them.

Understanding the relation between *Bildung* and democracy requires rescuing the concept of democracy from its current limitation to a narrowly political representational process. For us, a democratic society includes the whole lifeworld of the individual. Democracy is just as central in education, family life, community dynamics, and working life as it is in the exercise of political liberty. This broad view of democracy was the centerpiece of the design of the Norwegian Industrial Democracy Program (Emery and Thorsrud 1976), perhaps the boldest of all the social democratic developments in Europe after the Second World War. In that case, workplace democracy was viewed as the beachhead for the development of a truly democratic society via the expansion of participative and democratic processes from work to the whole lifeworld.

Academic freedom is the academic equivalent of the free "public" speech essential to any democratic process. In academic contexts, this freedom implies that the teachers have the freedom to teach what they see as important and to do so in ways they believe will best clarify their ideas and benefit the students. For their part, the students must be free to choose to study subjects they find of interest and potential value to them and to do so in ways that work for them, unimpeded by the differential costs of instruction in different fields.

Often overlooked is that, in a properly functioning academic institution, these freedoms require a collaborative dialogue between faculty and students who together must arrive at the curricula, teaching systems, and research subjects that satisfy the needs and wishes of both groups. In a context of genuine academic freedom, the administrator's role is to facilitate and champion these dialogues and negotiations, not to control or suppress them. The suppression of these freedoms are now common administrative practices in higher education through the imposition of speech codes, disciplinary procedures, the use of term contracts, and the imposition of promotion and salary decisions on faculty and staff.

Academic integrity, beyond the common meaning of not cheating on examinations, not plagiarizing the work of others, and not misrepresenting the results of research, has broader meanings. Academic integrity depends on creating knowledge through systematic and verifiable procedures open to inspection to other scholars, to students, and to other users of the knowledge. Such integrity can only be maintained through transparent, democratic structures in universities that make research processes open. They encourage the development of scientific insights regardless of their immediate economic, political, or ideological consequences. When this openness exists, academic knowledge can be trusted and is worthy of dissemination to society at large. When it does not, integrity is compromised.

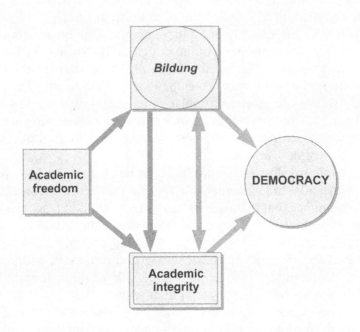

Figure 3.1 The Construction of University Democracy

The interrelationship among these concepts is shown in Figure 3.1. The relationship between the elements in this figure can be understood to flow from academic freedom. It is the basis for academic integrity because it is fundamental to the formation process of students and faculty (*Bildung*). Without the freedom to speak up and to research issues salient to faculty and students, *Bildung* is not possible and the foundations for academic integrity cannot be built. Democracy in higher education rests on the presence and integration of *Bildung* and academic integrity. This, however, is not possible in an authoritarian organizational structure. Participative democracy including all the stakeholders—students, faculty, staff, and administrators—is a sine qua non for academic freedom to exist.

In recent times, academic freedom has been reduced to a different and rather diluted meaning. It is largely limited to free speech for some of the faculty and to permitting some of them to engage in research on topics they see as important (usually meaning whatever they can get funding for). Student and staff free speech is barely mentioned. In the United States now, most universities have restrictive speech codes that they impose on students, staff, and faculty. Transgressions can result in significant punishments or expulsion (Kors and Silverglate 1999; Lukianoff 2014).

Academic Freedom

Current faculty-focused views of academic freedom are a great deal less ambitious than the original concept of the freedom to teach and to learn. While we recognize that academic freedom has an individual dimension, ultimately it is the product of a set of organizational relations and processes that produce conditions making freedom of speech for all stakeholders possible, championed, and protected. Academic freedom is a product of the whole institution, not merely an individual right. It is a public good in the institution and for society at large (Kahn and Pavlich, eds. 2000).

Despite this, even the narrower concept of academic freedom also plays an important role in *Bildung*. It legitimizes the faculty's right to engage in critical examination of topics and to forward critical discourses in research and in the classroom. This kind of critical reflection is essential to the production of reliable knowledge and to modeling democratic speech behavior for the students.

A partial cause of distortion in these discussions is that the debate on academic freedom currently is centered in the United States. This causes distortion because the protection of free speech for employees of any organization in the United States is very weak compared with most countries in Europe. This is true despite the existence of the American Association of University Professors founded by John Dewey and Arthur Lovejoy, among others, to protect faculty free speech, despite the experience of the destruction of academic freedom in the McCarthy era (Price 2004), and despite the ongoing examples of control of academic speech in contemporary United States universities (Lukianoff 2014). Precisely because nationally such protections of free speech are so limited in the United States, academic freedom is more hotly debated there.

Louis Menand edited a major book on academic freedom in 1996, *The Future of Academic Freedom* (Menand 1996). Menand and his collaborators expanded the concept of academic freedom from freedom of expression to include the ethics of free inquiry, a view we see as vital. They also point out that the focus on controlling hate speech is now one of the central forces limiting free speech in higher education. As we have already mentioned, United States universities all now have speech codes, many suppressing free expression on the grounds of hate and now even upsetting speech. More than a few universities impose the requirement on speakers and faculty that they issue "trigger warnings" if they are going to say anything that might upset anyone from any group (Lukianoff 2014).

These codes are part of the more general move in the U.S. to limit freedom of expression. It is a historical paradox that in U.S., the right to free speech is clearly stated in the first amendment to the Constitution. This alone should grant unlimited support for open and free civil discourse in all contexts. But campus speech codes abridge this constitutional right as part of administrative politics, power relations, and political correctness. One impact of these codes has been to "domesticate" universities into being supporters of the social and political status quo. This is not just about speech. These speech codes are accompanied by many instances of attempts by university administrators, private sector actors, and politicians to suppress faculty research results when they offend the interests of businesses and government officials (Kirp 2003; Washburn 2005).

Contemporary versions of McCarthyism are very much with us. For example, though not true across the board, arguments critical of the behavior of the Israeli state and of Zionism are barely tolerated on many campuses in the U.S. or Europe. The case of Steven Salaita and the University of Illinois at Urbana-Champaign is an example.[1] In Norway, professors' critical perspectives on Israel have been targeted by pro-Zionist Israeli groups. An associate professor at the Norwegian Business School in Oslo wrote a newspaper editorial that did not please the Israeli Embassy in Norway. The Israeli ambassador publically demanded that the rector fire the professor, an outrage in the Norwegian environment, a demand that was rejected. Historically, there have been many parallel cases in the United States where the "speaker" has lost a job or had to withdraw and application after having exercised free academic speech (Ross 1992; Finkelstein and Birn 1998; Finkelstein 2000; Price 2004; Pappe 2010).

These incidents show that the power of university governing boards is very extensive and that, for them, the maintenance of an anodyne, apolitical, or even actively pro-conservative institutional image is a high priority. On campuses, many groups—racial, gender, religious, disabled, and others—can and often do attempt to control campus free speech to match their own wishes and political agendas, right or left. Tenured professors have had a privileged position, being somewhat difficult to fire for exercising free speech. Now an increasing number are being fired or disciplined for exercising their free speech rights. Staff, administrators, adjunct faculty, and students have few such speech protections. The increasing number of contract and part-time faculty and staff has also increased the percentage of employees with no institutionally supported free speech rights.

The attack on free speech also comes from another angle. Authoritarian university administrators, concerned with their span of control and with managing the "brand" image of their institution, regularly usurp the rights of free speech and civil discourse on campus. By publicly stating their positions on major issues without consulting the faculty, students, or staff, they purposely misrepresent their views as expressing the "institutional" position. This behavior makes a sham of campus-based civil discourse. In the Salaita case referred to above at the University of Illinois at Urbana-Champaign, the university administration unilaterally broke the contract for a job, already awarded to Salaita, on the basis of the substance of his declarations about Israel and its supposed incompatibility with the university's position, a position only created and articulated by the senior administrators and the board of trustees.

These problems are not new in United States academia. The nineteenth century saw many suppressions of academic freedom and the firing of faculty for socialist and other nonconformist views (Ross 1992). Activist researchers, feminists, socialists, and others came in for abuse and subjugation between the founding of the social science disciplines and the end of the Second World War (Furner [1975] 2010; Madoo-Lengerman and Niebrugge-Brantley 1998).

More recently, Hollingsworth (2000) draws the genealogy of this issue back to the Cold War era (1950–1989) and how the "House Un-American Activities Committee" (HUAC) hunted down academics who sympathized with the "enemy" (Socialists, Communists, Stalinists). Being accused of holding Marxist or communist sympathies destroyed the basis for many academic careers in United States universities. This "red scare" environment created a lot suspicion and animosity among professionals, staff, administration, and governing boards. Far from being a dead issue, this Cold War mindset regularly erupts whenever academic free speech is abridged (Price 2004).

Equally important to academic freedom is the freedom to choose what subjects to research, how and for whom to conduct that research, and how to disseminate the results. This dimension of academic freedom gets less attention, with the exception of egregious episodes like the Novartis coup at Stanford University and its aftermath. (Washburn 2005). Though it holds a marginal place in the current debates on academic freedom, it may well be academic freedom's most problematic side. Freedom to research whatever problem a professor deems important is relatively unproblematic as long as the research can be done without external funding and without publishing results that might not be to the liking of corporations, politicians, and governments.

In Scandinavia, about half the faculty members' work time is allocated to doing research of their own choosing based on their own interests and expertise. U.S. faculty at research universities are also expected to conduct research and usually some conditions are created to make this possible. In principle, this means that there is research freedom. However, if this research does not result in publications in major professional venues, then this freedom becomes an invitation to become academically marginal or to be dismissed. This scheme makes prestigious academic journals and publishing houses and their reviewers (usually senior academics and their circle of editors) arbiters of what constitutes valued academic speech. Thus practical academics conceptualize their research so it will be publishable in the ranking professional journals and many journals steer away from any issues that are politically or socially controversial.

This problem is reinforced by the current generation of "accountant" administrators who count grants and publications in "A" journals as their metric for promotions, salaries, and other resource allocations. Complicity in this process effectively determines the topics of research by restricting people to the most conservative and discipline-centered academic journals and book publishers.

Added restrictions are created by university research policy priorities. At most major universities, research is an entrepreneurial activity as well as a scientific one. Universities compete for research funds from the government, foundations, and private sector sources. Many universities want the income from patentable research discoveries as well. Most university administrations have created statements (strategic plans) about their research profile and priorities and they support or discourage research in different areas, often with little or no faculty or student consultation. These administrative choices are bolstered by the neoliberal point and ranking systems used to enforce compliance with administrative objectives.

Funding agencies also exercise a key influence on research topics. Governments, foundations, and private sector funders have their own research priorities and send out requests for proposals in those areas and do not accept proposals in other areas. Sometimes they consult with panels of faculty experts in developing these priorities. More often they do not. Governmental research funders may have strategic and economic priorities to meet with the research they support. They now generally discourage basic research of any kind in the United States. Corporate foundations have mission-driven priorities of their own and generally only support research in their areas of business development.

Even after requests for proposals are sent out and applications made, funders often discuss the proposals with faculty researchers to press them to fit the agency's vision or interests. Such discussions can be problematic, because the funding agency may well express interests and methodological or theoretical preferences that were not in the minds of the researchers when they wrote the proposals. Sometimes these discussions can improve projects but they become problematic when there is an obvious conflict between the original intent of the proposal and the funding agency's de facto perspective. The researchers can either decide to adjust to meet the agency's demands or withdraw the proposal. In either case, the result is an abridgment of academic freedom.

Academic Integrity

Most people would agree that it is admirable for a person to be characterized as demonstrating integrity in her or his conduct. In everyday language, the concept of integrity identifies a wide range of behaviors. It can refer to a person that has a harmonic personality or it can refer to integrity in political processes where the individual stands up and speaks the same language in any situation, hostile or supportive. Intellectual integrity describes a person who expresses a consistent conceptual understanding of what they have learned and yet is open to learning. Finally, it can refer to the general moral and ethical coherence seen in a person's behavior. Here it refers to "character."

Academic integrity is rarely central to debates on the future of higher education, except where the issues are students cheating on examinations, professors falsifying research results, students and professors engaging in plagiarism, and administrators misrepresenting their careers in their job applications. These are important issues but we focus on a broader concept of academic integrity, one that refers simultaneously both to the individuals and to the institution.

As we have argued, at a personal level academic integrity refers to intellectual integrity in which the individual is seen as capable of expressing her or his perspectives independently and honestly without regard for the potential political and social pressures being exerted on them. However, we believe that what is appropriate behavior is not universal and singular. It is partly determined by the organizational context. If we expect people to act with integrity in a certain professional context, then our judgment of them should be based on understanding of this context: special duties, obligations, rights, competencies, and so on.

Seen this way, an institution of higher education has institutional integrity when it is capable of supporting research and teaching on issues that the local faculty and students deem relevant and important regardless of who is supported or offended by the results. It also makes sense to view academic freedom as a precondition to creating this kind of personal and institutional academic integrity.

Democracy

We have invoked democracy repeatedly throughout this book and will have more to say about democratic practices in the final chapters. Now a detailed presentation of what we understand democracy to mean is necessary. This is a complex topic and requires an extended treatment. We have made the case that understanding the transformations of public higher education requires a general reflection on democracy. In the current situation, democracy is a trivialized and denatured concept that is rarely clarified and discussed. In daily use, it has accumulated many different meanings that depend on social position, values, and interests and so we need to bring the various meanings of democracy back into analytical awareness.

The concept of democracy is usually traced back to the governance of the Greek city-states. The word combines *demos* (people) and *cratos* (steering). It identified a governance structure in which people had the power and the structures granting them the right to participate in political decision making. Understood this way, the contrast made is between democracies and kingdoms and religious despotisms.

The philosophical development of concepts of democracy owes a great deal the Greek philosophers Aristotle and Plato. As we know from these texts, in the Greek city-states, key elements in democratic praxis unfolded in a common meeting space (the *agora*) where the citizens met, debated, and decided political issues. This particular kind of democracy was restricted to a minimal group of men. Women and slaves had no right to participate. Even now, with general suffrage in many countries, we can still see similar problems of inclusion in current debates over voting rights. Beyond offering the equal right to vote, democracy depends on who decides which issues get on the political agenda, on who has the resources to develop knowledge about issues of public interest, and on which societal institutions influence the political agenda.

Leaping forward in time, current debates on democracy often take their point of departure from the United Nations' Declaration of Human Rights adopted by the General Assembly on 10 December 1948. Two articles (21 and 26) of this declaration relate to democratic institutions and practices and also to educational rights.

Article 21

(1) Everyone has the right to take part in the government of his country, directly or through freely chosen representatives.

(2) Everyone has the right of equal access to public service in his country.

(3) The will of the people shall be the basis of the authority of government; this shall be expressed in periodic and genuine elections which shall be by universal and equal suffrage and shall be held by secret vote or by equivalent free voting procedures.[2]

Article 26

(1) Everyone has the right to education. Education shall be free, at least in the elementary and fundamental stages. Elementary education shall be compulsory. Technical and professional education shall be made generally available and higher education shall be equally accessible to all on the basis of merit.

(2) Education shall be directed to the full development of the human personality and to the strengthening of respect for human rights and fundamental freedoms. It shall promote understanding, tolerance and friendship among all nations, racial or religious groups, and shall further the activities of the United Nations for the maintenance of peace.[3]

Article 21 identifies the core of democracy as the right to participate directly or indirectly in governance. In the broadest sense, democracy is a system that grants the participants meaningful social authority through participation in deciding on the rules (laws and regulations) of the society they live in. In addition, democracy deals with the distribution of power because, in principle, democracy should derive from all citizens. This remains a challenging position because many institutional arrangements are purposely created to reduce the peoples' ability to decide their fate collectively, including many of the arrangements at work in the United Nations itself.

Article 26 focuses on education as a human right. Unfortunately the discussion is weakly developed because it focuses only on access to education as a democratic right and does not include education's role in the daily work of democracy. Because of this, it ignores the vital impact of knowledge and knowledge construction processes on the effective and fair functioning of democracies. If people do not have the knowledge and the ability to participate in knowledge construction, democracy cannot function. For a democratic system to work as the people's "tool" for creating and improving society together, citizens both need to be well informed and to be able to generate relevant information and proposals for change on their own. Among the implications are that both general education and access to research capacity and research results must be available to stakeholders to employ in articulating and defending their interests.

Competing Meanings of Democracy

Democracy has given rise to multiple interpretations. Before making the intellectual linkage between democracy and higher education, we need to clarify some of the competing meanings. Democracy is "essentially a contested concept" (Gallie 1956) and so we also need to clarify our own position in relation to others. We follow Gallie's argument that some concepts like democracy have different meaning depending on who uses the concepts and what interests these actors have. Being "essentially contested" means that many different interpretations, including ours, compete for hegemony.

The genealogy of democracy relevant to higher education begins, as we already have mentioned, with the work of Wilhelm von Humboldt (1767–1835), Prussian Minister of Education in the first quarter of the nineteenth century. The university he founded, now called the Humboldt-Universität zu Berlin, became a model for research universities worldwide. Humboldt linked *Bildung* and certain democratic practices, such as the faculty's freedom to teach and the students' freedom to learn. As we have pointed out earlier, this meant there had to be some kind of deliberation between students and professors to find a middle ground that could satisfy both parties. Despite Humboldt's importance, there is no documentation showing that any institution ever fully implemented the Humboldt idea of a university.

John Dewey (1859–1952) was the preeminent American pragmatist philosopher and educator. His work is of particular interest because it integrated educational philosophy with theories of democracy. He made a direct link between the practices of public education, good pedagogy, and the strength of a democratic society. Dewey insisted that knowledge development and acquisition are best practiced in democratic learning communities and that decisions made through democratic deliberation are superior in quality to decisions made by other means. This position is developed in his book *Democracy and Education* published in 1916 (Dewey [1916] 2009). Westbrook, in his book *John Dewey and American Democracy* (1991), credits Dewey for his work on participative democracy: "Dewey was the most important advocate of participatory democracy, that is, of the belief that democracy as an ethical ideal calls upon men and women to build communities ... to realize fully his or her particular capacities and powers through participation in political, social, and cultural life" (Westbrook 1991: xv).

A common argument built on Dewey's pragmatism is that democracy should be valued only because it produces the best quality decisions. While we believe this instrumental value is significant, we reject arguing for democracy solely in instrumental terms. We argue that democracy is a fundamental right that can and does produce good for society. But we also want to emphasize the scientific and intellectual value of democratic processes in academic discovery and analysis.

Another central voice on democracy in political science was Robert A. Dahl (1915–2014). His work centered on representative democracies and he did extensive research on who exactly the power holders in Western democracies were. Dahl argued in his most famous book *Who governs?* (1961) that a key characteristic of Western democracies is that more than one elite fights for power. Dahl's view contradicted C. Wright Mills' (1956) position that only one specific elite controlled power in society.

Finally, Jürgen Habermas (1929-) is one of the most famous social philosophers in Europe. Over a long and productive career he has covered a broad array of issues in research and publications. His *magnum opus* and major contribution to democratic theory and practice is found in his volumes on social communication (1984,1989) where he develops the theory of communicative action.

Habermas argues that ideal speech communication implies a situation in which a person delivers an argument to support a specific position. The other persons present reflect on and then judge the content of these utterances before making their responses. The ethics of this pattern of communication require the listener to decide if the received utterances represent the best possible understanding of what was said or not. If not, the listener must put forward a new suggestion and so on.

In these ideal speech situations, differences are sustained and explored rationally though debate and dialogue.

In his later years, Habermas has felt it necessary to return to the more general problems related to democracy in the European Union. He advocates democratic decision making in the current financial crises in the Mediterranean countries of the Union, democratic decisions that he rightly argues have been absent (Habermas 2012).

With this brief genealogy in mind, we now take a closer look at how democratic systems operate in contexts relevant to this book.

Elements in Democracy as a Social Institution

We again turn to Robert Dahl, but this time to his book, *Democracy and Its Critics*. In this work, he presents five elements as core features of any democracy (Dahl 1989: 39):

Effective participation
Equality in voting
Gaining enlightened understanding
Exercising final control over the agenda
Inclusion of adults

These features overlap with or expand the conceptualization of democracy conveyed in the United Nations Declaration of Human Rights, but still follow the same general principle of granting rights to every citizen to participate in deciding on matters that concern them in everyday life and in larger political arenas. Democracy amounts to a right to have a say in social decision making.

Dahl provides an exhaustive list of the social goods that democracy creates (1989: 44– 61). The difficulty is that his list of ten items includes almost everything that in the West is seen as desirable, including factors such as prosperity, avoiding tyranny, supporting human development, creating political equality, and seeking peace. This utopian thinking can dissuade readers from taking democracy seriously since it's obvious so far that democracy has yet to produce all or even many of these outcomes.

Democracy is a process in which citizens have the right and the obligation to participate in decisions regulating daily life as well as broader political matters. However, this does not mean there is one proper form of democratic praxis. Dahl is not sufficiently clear in recognizing that democracy can be embodied in a variety of practices. Schumpeter took a broader view (1943: 242): "Democracy is a political method, that is to say, a certain type of institutional arrangement for arriving at political—legislative and administrative decisions." For him, these practices covered a wide range, from voting on candidates for a parliament through electing municipal administration to participative decision making in public administration or business life. These practices might overlap, be aligned, or be in conflict with each other.

Democracy, from this perspective, does not per se focus on the quality, relevance, or consequences of the decisions taken. It deals fundamentally with the nuts and bolts of the processes by which people are able to take part in social decision making. Democracy requires us to clarify who is eligible to "cast their vote" and how the participation in the process is organized.

For the purposes of this book, we focus on three key different democratic forms: representative democracy, deliberative democracy, and participative democracy. All three depend on participation, but the kind of participation ranges from just voting for a representative to a participative process wherein each member has the right and responsibility to decide on issues important to them in private as well as working life. Thus the practice of democracy spans a fairly wide range of social arrangements, all enabling the individual to impact issues related to their own interests and perspectives.

Practicing Democracy in Universities

There is no single system for governing today's universities. The political economies and histories of different countries shape different opportunities and constraints on the organization and role of institutions of higher education. We expanded on these differences in Chapter 2. Here our focus is how democratic governance structures could be or have been implemented in universities.

For many thinkers, the answer rests with designing a system where students, staff, administrators, and faculty are elected to boards, councils, and committees all around the campus. This parallels the system we know in many democratic societies, where citizens elect their representatives for a limited period of time. The representatives generally are supposed to act on behalf of those who elected them. In most societies, this kind of representative democracy is the only democracy there is.

Aside from the fact that this is a narrow perspective on democratic processes as periodic moments of citizen input, merely electing representatives does not guarantee democratic institutional operations, integrity, high quality research, or excellence in teaching. Furthermore, this kind of representative system that typified West European public universities from the period beginning after the Second World War has been almost completely dismantled by the neoliberal wave that has overtaken public education generally. Thus even this limited idea of representative governance is all but gone in most universities.

There are many other dimensions to democratic processes in such institutions. For example, having a say in the guidance and operation of a small research group poses different challenges when compared with the problem of how to influence the university's governing boards' decisions. In a research group, democratic processes can be very much linked to the individuals' ability to impact their daily working conditions. Shaping real influence in such a research group has little to do with electing representatives who meet with the university board every three or six months.

One dimension of democracy does not exclude the other. Direct participation by means of grand plenaries is probably not a fruitful democratic process for influencing a board's decisions, just as electing representatives to manage a small research group would be foolish. Thus we need to expand our perspective to include perspectives on democracy that link the participative and representative systems but that go beyond them.

Representative Democracy

We have already discussed the particulars in representative democracies, but we find it worthwhile to recapitulate the argument contrasting representative democracy with forms of direct democracy. The essence of the representative model is the election of representatives to decision-making boards and committees. There is a competition between possible contenders to get elected. The candidates are supposed to represent different perspectives and preferences. In this regard, the representative system actually produces adversarial relationships. The strength of the representative system is that it grants access to forums where decisions are taken. Strategic and long-term decisions are for example sometimes possible in a representative system.

Direct Democracy

The vital side of direct democracy is the access to control immediate factors in the lifeworld. Pateman (1970) in her book, *Participation and*

Democratic Theory, contributes to the discussion of democracy by arguing for a model where everyone has the right and the obligation to participate in processes that shape that person's working and living conditions. Participation in everyday decision making is the pivotal point. Accordingly, the organization of work and community life needs to be designed in such a way that it creates opportunities for direct participation.

Direct democracy through participation is not productively developed as a "free-for-all" where everyone states and advocates a position. Years of organizational research have shown us that new organizational forms have to be developed to make participation effective. A good example from early experimental work on participation is the work on semi-autonomous groups (Emery and Thorsrud 1976). These groups had the internal freedom to decide on how they wanted to do the work, the only requirement being that their contribution to the total production process was maintained. Along with the emphasis on these organizational practices came the hope that people working in semi-autonomous groups would be able to spread these ideas and practices to the rest of the society. While the semi-autonomous group turned out to be quite effective in work organizations (Gulowsen 1971), the hoped-for automatic diffusion of participative democracy from the workplace to society at large did not take place (Gustavsen 1992; Gustavsen, Finne, and Oscarsson 2001; Levin 2002). This is one of the reasons we argue for the importance of engaging higher education in promoting democracy internally and in society at large. Students are not yet full participants in society and can be taught and can practice the skills of participatory democracy in preparation for private, professional, and public life, thereby creating more momentum for democracy in general.

There are models for direct democracy that emphasize other dimensions of participation. Mansbridge (1983) argues for a democratic model that builds on consensus decision making instead of the competition and the adversarial relationships inherent in the representative model. She calls her model "unitary democracy." The fundamental idea is the aim to reach a common platform for understanding issues and for finding solutions. Listening and learning are central to this. It is interesting that Mansbridge builds her model on research on small town meetings in the northeastern United States, meetings that somewhat parallel democratic processes in the Greek city-states.

Another participative model of democracy is based on deliberation (Forester 1999). This approach structures the interaction between professionals and ordinary citizens to promote both knowledge development and fairness. This concept of participation is particularly important to us. Given our perspective on graduates from public higher education institutions and their role in a democratic society, their ability to participate in and manage deliberative processes is an important dimension of their formation.

A core idea in deliberation is to create effective communication between lay people and professionals so that everyone can have a voice and will be understood. Ideas from ordinary citizens have an equal opportunity to influence decisions as those of the professionals do. Various kinds of knowledge and experience are shared: professional knowledge and experience and stakeholder knowledge and experience. The influence of Habermas' perspectives is clear here.

A democratic classroom at a public university faces some of the same challenges. The professor has, by definition and training, a broader perspective on the themes relevant to the teaching than most of the students. But the ostensible goal of the teaching is to train students to be able to deploy their knowledge effectively in their professional careers when they are dealing with non-professionals and with other professionals as well. Accordingly, the professor must be open and willing to adjust the teaching processes so the students can learn by actively participating in the deliberative processes in the class. This implies that the professor has to cede control to the group, just as Forester's deliberative practitioners cede control to the stakeholders. The professor negotiates the teaching, including the subject matter and the teaching processes, to benefit the students, while still meeting professional standards of knowledge and competence.

Democracy and Bildung

There is a tension between an educated citizenry and the formation of social elites through restricted educational opportunities and social networks based on existing wealth and power. This plays out in the tension between public and private higher education, but even in the public systems some of the students come from existing elites and are being supported to maintain elite status through a university education.

The multiple meanings of education or *Bildung* unfortunately obfuscate this point. Nearly everyone claims that higher education prepares the next generation of social leaders but carefully avoids pointing out that this process is fundamentally different from the processes in higher education that involve achieving social mobility and those processes using higher education to consolidate elite status (Bourdieu and Passeron

1979; Armstrong and Hamilton 2013). Instead, the discussion of higher education carried out on this general level is an exercise in vague and homiletic talk about the "educated" person and the value of such people to society as a whole. This vagueness is evident in the level of analysis of the meaning of "education" in the current neoliberal and liberal attacks and defenses regarding public higher education (Kronman 2007; Arum and Roska 2011; Ginsburg 2011).

It is easy show that higher education is no guarantee of democratic or pro-social behavior. For example, research on the recruitment to the German Nazi security police in the 1930s is a case in point. Wildt shows in *The Uncompromising Generation* (2003), how graduates from universities (most with excellent academic transcripts) became the perpetrators and the central destroyers of democracy under the Nazi regime. Many of the architects of the wars in Vietnam, Iraq, and Afganistan, and of the policies of the World Bank and International Monetary Fund, actions and institutions that are highly authoritarian, were graduates of or even faculty at elite universities. Higher education alone is no guarantee of the promotion of democratic ideals and practices. Other authors agree. For example, Dereciewicz, in *Excellent Sheep* (2014), rehearses a similar view.

For higher education and democracy to link, specific higher education institutional structures and processes are necessary. Public universities cannot prepare citizens for a role in democratic processes if these institutions are authoritarian, meritocratic systems that promote cutthroat competition and exclude students, faculty, and staff from key institutional processes and decision-making structures. Merely taking a set of courses and getting a degree in higher education does not necessarily make a meaningful contribution to the development of an increased understanding of and training in how to behave in a democracy. It often seems to have the opposite result. Thus, we insist on calling attention to the substantive link between the institutional structures of public universities, their educational research and service missions, and the daily life and work experiences of all the university stakeholders, a subject hardly discussed in the current literature in the field of higher education, political science, or political philosophy, or in the literature on higher education reform.

There are at least four different ways public higher education can contribute to democracy. First, it supplies society with candidates that may come to play key roles in private sector or public sector organizations. These candidates must be acquainted with both the theory and praxis of democracy. Second, it supplies society with research-based knowledge to be used in making key societal decisions. This knowledge must be available to all segments in the society and it must be possible for all groups in society to commission university research to assist them in examining and resolving their problems. Third, universities can critically examine the class and ideological bases of existing knowledge to make it clear whose interests particular knowledge claims serve and what consequences these claims will produce. And fourth, in universities, the knowledge generation process must be transparent so it is possible to understand the premises upon which new insights are built and old ideas are discarded.

To summarize, we argue that democracy in society depends on (among other things) having democratic institutions of higher education, and that democracy in higher education depends on processes and structures that promote democratic knowledge production, acquisition, and examination. There is a symbiotic relationship between a democratic society and democratic institutions of higher education, making it clear why higher education has to play an important role in a democratic society. Training in the ability to make arguments and to conduct scientific research to support them is a key citizen skill. Public higher education thus impacts democratic processes in society though citizen education, research on issues of social importance, and also by educating some citizens who will play prominent roles in key social decisions and creating a democratically capable and active citizenry.

What is the Current State of Democracy in Higher Education?

Representative Democracy in Higher Education

Among the many meanings of democracy found in higher education, representative democracy is the most common one. Representative systems used to be fairly common in higher education in Europe. It is increasingly difficult to find more than token representative systems in North American universities. In the U.S., the presidents, provosts, or chancellors now are only responsible to their board of trustees and superordinate political authorities, except in the rare cases of a vote of no confidence from below. These boards of trustees are composed through closed procedures in which members already on the board control who will be appointed to or stay on the board and who will be the chair. In these systems, members strategize to form supportive coalitions for their projects, all without much if any linkage to the faculty, students, or staff.

In Europe there are two common university democracy models. One involves electing the rector or the vice chancellor though a vote that includes every member of the institution—faculty, students, administration, or staff. Different candidates compete for these positions through electoral campaigns. Then the rector usually becomes the chair of the governing board. In some cases, other members of the board can be elected from the university faculty, staff, and student groups. In addition, the state can appoint members to the board.

The second and now increasingly common model has the rector appointed by the ministry of education (or any other ministry responsible for higher education). This rector serves on the board, together with other external persons and some internally elected representatives. Despite some similarities, these two systems are very different. In the first model the authority of the rector is granted to that person electorally by the faculty, students, and staff while in the second model the authority is granted by the ministry that makes the appointment (Wright and Ørberg 2009a).

Deliberative Democracy in Higher Education

As we discussed earlier, deliberative democracy builds on participation by all involved in a communicative learning process, where the aim is to jointly reason about and act on the issues at stake (Habermas 1984, 1989). This kind of democracy involves those who actually do the daily work at the institution and who are able to contribute competent information about the issues they face and the facts they are dealing with daily. Despite images of deliberative faculty meetings and considered and reflective conversations between faculty and students, deliberative democracy is extremely rare in higher education. The conditions for it seem to be present but they do not produce it on their own.

Cooke identifies five elements that support the development of deliberative democracy: "(1) the educative power of the process of public deliberation (2) the community-generating power of the procedure of public deliberation (3) the fairness of the procedure of public deliberation (4) the epistemic quality of the outcomes of public deliberation, and (5) the congruence of the ideal of politics articulated by deliberative democracy with 'whom we are'" (2000: 947).

Deliberation builds on reason and sense-making through communication processes where all relevant stakeholders in the public are involved. In this regard, it requires a participative process in which the problem owners engage fairly and openly. The reasoning process is intended to shape agreements on desirable solutions and mutually acceptable plans of action to arrive at those solutions. Basically the idea is to create a workable agreement (not a consensus requiring unanimous decisions) in favor of a specific solution.

From the perspective of higher education, deliberative democracy can be promoted as a universal teaching and learning principle. This includes reducing passive lecture learning to a minimum and employing deliberative democracy in all university decision-making venues from departmental meetings to university-wide meetings. Doing so is consistent with both Dewey and Freire's view of education as a participatory, deliberative process in which all the stakeholders play a role. In the case of university classes and seminars, the professors operating this way present substantive themes and issues in an introductory way to provide an opening for a collaborative reasoning process with the students. Teaching this way builds on the practice of communicative reasoning and democratic dialogue. After graduation, these students are in a position not just to participate in such processes but to take the lead in promoting them in their workplaces and communities. This is a robust expression of the concept of *Bildung*. It is drastically different from the kind of vocational training that now passes for education in many universities. Deliberative democracy is almost never found in higher education where authoritarian management dominates.

Participative Democracy

This is a third operational model of democracy and it moves beyond deliberative democracy. The term was coined by Carol Pateman in her book, *Participation and Democratic Theory* (1970). The book has become a canonical work with major impact both in the theoretical debates on democracy and in the democratic practice in organizations. Its publication coincided with the drive for democracy in workplaces in North America and Western Europe at the time. Much of the inspiration for the Norwegian experiments on democracy at work (Emery and Thorsrud 1976) came from Pateman's initial work.

Recently, in 2012, she published the paper "Participatory Democracy Revisited" (Pateman 2012) in which she reflects on the merits of participatory democracy after some forty years. She notes that: "By the 1980s the attention of most political theorists turned in other directions, interest in democratic theory waned and, in particular, participatory democratic theory became unfashionable." She thinks it is now enjoying a revival, a view for which we see no evidence at all.

The *modus operandi* of participative democracy centers on the idea that the stakeholders have the right to control and change the immediate lifeworld variables in their surrounding environment. It treats this as a fundamental democratic right. The individual should be involved in a knowledge creation process related to making sense of her/his own lifeworld and also have the opportunity to and the necessary remedies available to change his/her immediate lifeworld in a desired direction. This view includes elements from deliberative democracy: making sense through reasoning processes and potentially having voting power based on the insights generated. What it adds is an explicit and necessary focus on organizational development: that is, on how to change the lifeworld of the stakeholders in a desired direction.

We advocate participative democracy in university life. We believe that participative processes are essential parts in all activity related to governing, developing, and reforming the actual operations of higher education institutions. Democratizing university life would create change processes built on real involvement by the respective faculty, staff, and students rather than on administrative fiat, tokenism, and "input" as generally happens now. Participative democracy, unlike neo-Tayloristic authoritarianism, also represents the necessary alignment between teaching, research, and engagement that is supportive of *Bildung*, academic freedom, and academic integrity. These key dimensions of university life can only fit together in a participative democracy.

Despite this, participative democracy is practiced almost nowhere in higher education. The only true exceptions we know is the Mondragón University (Wright, Greenwood and Boden 2012) and a few liberal arts colleges whose small size and commitment to humane values incline them toward *Bildung* and participative democracy.

Conclusion

The extended discussion in this chapter leaves us with the key question: how would it be possible to democratize higher education? Since history tells us it is impossible to mandate democracy, it means democracy can only emerge though processes that nourish democratic engagement. Accordingly, the transformation process must be under the control of the stakeholders and not of external actors. All categories of stakeholders must be involved. Students, staff, administration, and faculty all occupy different positions in a university and the change process must involve them all in shaping a participative democracy.

Given that those who gain most from the current authoritarian system would oppose any such effort, it is reasonable to ask if reforming universities as participative democracies is a fool's errand. We hope not. The two most promising approaches seems to be either models based on liberation pedagogy (Freire 1970) or action research (Whyte 1991; Greenwood and Levin 2007). Both approaches have their possibilities and pitfalls but we see no other course of action.

Despite the dreary realities of contemporary higher education, we believe such change is possible. No one thought the authoritarianism and union-busting of the robber barons in the Tayloristic world of nineteenth- and twentieth-century manufacturing could be overturned. Change came partly through activism and partly because these regimes collapsed under their own weight and incompetence. We believe neoliberal higher education is reaching a similar turning point because the organizational life in such universities is unsustainable for the majority of the stakeholders. The administrative bloat, inefficiency, and failure to satisfy the needs and desires of most of the stakeholders creates a ready environment for change. Change is not achieved by marching in the street and shouting through a bullhorn. The kinds of change we are writing about and our sense that we are reaching an endpoint for neoliberal higher education needs an extensive justification and analysis. We turn to this in the next section of this book.

Notes

1. See http://mondoweiss.net/2014/09/untangling-salaita-case/ (accessed 19 May 2016).
2. http://www.un.org/en/documents/udhr/index.shtml (accessed 30 September 2016).
3. Ibid.

Part II

◆ ◆ ◆

Universities as Work Organizations: Stakeholders, Structures, Systems, Steering, Leadership, and Anti-*Bildung*

Beyond the substantive meanings of *Bildung* we have discussed extensively in Part I, there are a set of organizational requirements that must be met for this concept to become a real part of everyday life in higher education. We now focus now on these organizational dimensions of higher education in detail.

The extensive literature on the social and cultural construction of the person (Berger and Luckmann 1966; Strathern 2000; Messer-Davidow 2002; Wright 2003; Bousquet and Nelson 2008; Hill 2009; Kirn 2009; Caanan and Shumar 2008; Deresiewizc 2014; Guinier 2015) makes it abundantly clear that different kinds of ideologies require different kinds of organizational designs and processes to be sustainable. Particular kinds of organizational settings and dynamics call forth particular kinds of human behavior and suppress others. In this section of the book, we examine which kinds of organizational structures and processes favor *Bildung* and which do not.

CHAPTER 4

The Work Organization of Universities
Structures

◆◆◆

Within the broad array of published work critiquing contemporary universities and proposing reforms, analyses of these institutions as work organizations are rare. Despite their potential value to understanding the higher education scene, the significant and extensive literatures on the organization of work, organizational behavior, leadership, steering, and the impact of changing work structures on institutional functioning are seldom applied to analyzing universities. One possible cause is that a portion of this literature is written by people who do not live and work in academic settings themselves, but also we see another cause. Most of the academic authors of these organizational literatures do not engage in critical examination of their own organizational behavior and work practices.

This lack of organizational self-analysis is a trait academics share with many other professional groups like doctors and lawyers (Schmidt 2000). This contrasts with non-academic business life. There many actors operate with some basic organizational self-understanding. They are aware that their contributions involve helping (or obstructing) the organization's operations and its leadership. Issues of efficiency, occupational health, benefits, and quality of working life are regular subjects of most actor's reflections. They recognize that organizational factors impact the daily operation of their own organization and ultimately their own fates. By contrast, the available literature suggests that this sort of organizational self-awareness is rare among many stakeholders in the world of universities.

A long-time leader in research on universities as institutions, Burton Clark, barely touches these issues in his 1995 book *Places of Inquiry* (Clark 1995). A few key works now do highlight the organizational dimensions of university life, such as Newfield's, *Ivy and Industry* (2004), Tuchman's *Wannabe U* (2009), and Ginsberg's *The Fall of the Faculty* (2011) but these important works do not engage the extensive and relevant literatures on work organization in developing their analyses. Exceptions are the excellent work of Susan Wright and her collaborators

(Wright 2003; Wright, Brenneis, and Shore 2005; Wright and Ørberg 2009a, 2009b and 2011). Despite their importance, these works are not widely read as yet. More popular are the models of Weick (1976) and Cohen, March, and Olsen (1972). Universities as "loosely-coupled systems" and as "organized anarchies" are often referred to, despite the weaknesses of both models. We will comment on these models later in this chapter.

Framing Universities as Work Organizations

Institutions of higher education, whatever else they may be, are organizations in which work is done. Accordingly, they can be appropriately analyzed and understood as work organizations (See, for example, Taylor 1911; Mayo 1933; Weber 1947; March and Simon 1958; Weick 1976; Whyte 1948; Pfeffer 1981; Mintzberg 1983; Barley and Kunda 2001; Bolman and Deal 2013). Key operational choices about what the purposes are, what kinds of structures and processes are appropriate to them, how to overcome particular problems or obstacles, how to change the kinds of behaviors the organization promotes, and about the kind of leadership that is appropriate, all are documentable and can be analyzed. These organizational dimensions are relevant to the study of universities because no one in universities is a solo actor. Threads of mutual expectation and accommodation bind the institution together (Nelson and Winter 1982). Participants on all levels—students, faculty, staff and administration—depend on or contend with each other to make the institution work for themselves (Barley and Kunda 2001).

Work Organization and Bildung

Our own organizational analysis is driven by our commitment to the idea that a core goal of public universities is to produce *Bildung* for students, faculty, staff, administrators, and society at large. This is our central position based on our combined total of about seventy years working in academic and non-academic institutions. We have concluded that without *Bildung*, public universities are not truly "public" and cannot survive. Achieving the rededication to *Bildung* involves integrating learning and teaching, becoming more skillful in diverse fields, knowing the basic elements of research, effectively communicating research results, and coming to value and being able to practice ethical participation in social change. The virtues and skills associated with

Bildung can only be generated through direct and sustained interaction and participation among the students, faculty, staff, and administrators.

If the interaction of these elements is structured as a competitive power arena, laced with hierarchies, it does not produce *Bildung*. It creates a competitive meritocracy. If it is structured to promote collaboration, mutual understanding, and participation by all categories of stakeholders, then *Bildung* is possible. Thus, for a public university to produce *Bildung*, its own organizational structure must be participatory and democratic. Every stakeholder must have the freedom to act to improve and manage their own working conditions and their longer-term life choices.

Structures and Groups

Even in the best-functioning organizations not everyone interacts with everyone else at all moments. Tasks must be accomplished, energy and resources are finite, and some issues are more salient than others. Surveying universities, we do see a great variety of collaborative structures and processes, many of which are task dependent. Researchers form teams (Emery and Thorsrud 1976; Herbst 1976) that make deep and long-term collaboration possible. Students can study by creating peer groups where substantive academic and professional issues are dealt with. Such interactions can also occur in seminars, lectures, or laboratories. There are university interest groups that promote certain political positions; some of these are composed of students only, some of faculty only, and some have mixed participation. Administrators and staff create taskforces and commissions to handle specific issues either needing immediate attention or that engage in long-term strategic planning.

This small sample of activities could be multiplied because the work organization of a university is quite diverse and complex. A work organization is set up to "produce" desired outcomes, but members need not necessarily agree on every goal or strategy. An organization may function successfully even if some members advocate different purposes for the organization or for their own role in it.

Together the aggregation of these working systems and the way they connect constitute the work organization of a university. No one in these subsystems refers to the "organizational chart" to guide their conduct because such schematic diagrams reflect little about the real organization of work processes. Confusing the organizational chart with the organization itself confuses a map with the territory it refers to.

These diverse nodes can be created by many different members or subgroups in the work organization. Many subsets of organization members, within one category or across organizational categories and levels, work more closely with each other than with other organization members even within their own organizational box. These networks may form relatively permanent structures or sub-systems (von Bertalanffy 1969). They may be convened temporarily to solve a particular problem. These sub-systems may interact with others to build new, larger, or more adaptive networks, or they may create conflict and instability in larger organizational structures.

These larger systems may be hierarchical, depending on the task being handled (Luhmann 1982), the institution's mission, internal power relations, and the type of leadership exerted. Except in small face-to-face organizations, the subsystems can be articulated in various ways. They can be organized to operate independently according to a strategic plan arrived at through joint engagement. This is the case of cooperatives and trusts. They can be matrix organizations with cross-functional teams specializing in particular products or services. Or they can be bounded as separate units only integrated by a small leadership group at the apex of the organization, as in the case of Taylorist and neo-Taylorist organizations.

Leadership

To survive, all organizations require an overall direction to orient and coordinate the work processes. The coordination that keeps the parts in some kind of sustainable relationship to each other is what organizational theory means by leadership (Jackall [1988] 2010; Kotter 1996; Northouse 2004), a topic we take up in detail in detail in Chapter 7. While leadership is an essential organizational function, it is not necessarily the most important organizational function. Leadership must fit into the work organization alongside other functions such as communication, coordination, and control. Contrary to the thinking of many in the new generation of academic administrators, good leadership is not achieved by personalizing this function in the figure of the boss. Leadership is a function and not an individual trait. Different persons and subsets of the organization take on leadership roles in particular areas and, under some conditions, leadership emerges from collective efforts by members of a team or subsystem (Emery and Thorsrud 1976; Trist 1981) and can be productive for the overall organization.

Conflict

Conflicts are endemic and even useful in organizations and they may emerge in almost any area (Coser 1956). For example, developing operational strategies is an area where conflicts often arise because choices about the allocation of resources are involved. These conflicts may be a positive contribution to the *Bildung* of the organization because, treated properly, they can create the conditions for knowledge sharing and organizational development through dialogue and the mediation of diverse positions. We see conflicts as an integral, even essential part of everyday organizational life and a source of potential energy for improvement if they are handled properly. Unresolved fundamental conflicts, of course, are not good for any organization. Neo-Taylorist leaders often forget that authoritarian leadership often provokes and intensifies unproductive conflicts.

Power Relations

Like leadership, power relations are a core feature of all organizational life. They involve the ways members or subsets of members work to gain leverage to support their own interests through their actions, ideas, and subsystem activities. While it was long unfashionable to talk of power and fundamental conflicts of interest in United States universities, it is impossible to understand universities without making sense of the many power positions and their accompanying interests and actions (Pfeffer 1981; Lukes 2005). There are no real universities without internal conflicts, debates, and a multiplicity of exercises of power.

Adaptation and Change

Organizations do not exist forever. The overall dynamics of organizations, changing environments and new structures are a central element in organizational analysis (Lewin 1948; Klev and Levin 2012a, 2012b). Precisely because universities should be *Bildung*-producing organizations, they are inherently unstable. They are often disturbed by the emergence of new ideas and practices and the discrediting or surpassing of old ones, without which universities cannot not be "learning organizations" or knowledge creators. (Argyris and Schön 1996).

No organization operates in a vacuum. Material constraints in the form of technology, resources, the larger political economy, and the plethora of ideologies that surround organizational structures and practices play an important role in daily operations. Analyzing organizational dynamics without understanding these contexts and the ways they are handled is a dead end.

These basic organizational dimensions are ignored by many faculty, students, staff, and administrators in their everyday practices and thinking. Because so many contemporary university actors understand themselves as solo meritocratic operators and individualist entrepreneurs, the lack of organizational self-understanding itself has become a central part of the problem we address. In the current situation, many organization members refuse to see themselves as forming part of a work organization (Schmid 2000).

We believe this to be one of the central consequences of neo-Taylorism and neoliberalism. The social production of meritocratic persons blinds these persons to the system they are a part of. Running a competitive race while wondering who set the course, whether the timers and referees are fair, if they are counting the right things, and whether the prizes for the winners are worth having is unlikely. The neo-Tayloristic model has penetrated university organizational structures and practices and sets the conditions for working life even though its hegemony is not entirely clear to the runners in the meritocratic races. We affirm, with Christopher Newfield (Newfield 2004) that Taylorism has been and remains almost unchallenged as the core organizational design for universities, so much so that many of the actors in the system cannot imagine an alternative way of organizing university life.

We explore these issues in more detail later. Here we initiate the organizational analysis by presenting a picture of the four main organizational sub-systems in universities: teaching, research, students, and administration. We then contrast our understanding of the ways these fit together with the most often-cited views of universities as organizations, Karl Weick's metaphor of "loosely coupled systems" and Cohen, March, and Olsen's "organized anarchies" or "garbage can" model. We show why we find such models quite misleading.

Meritocratic Individualism and the Denial of Work Organization

We have already pointed to the disconnect between the literature in organizational theory and the study of universities. A general failure to deal analytically with organizational structures and dynamics in academia is evident. In place of organizational analysis, there are many works blaming particular groups—students, faculty, administrators, or policymakers—for whatever ills there are in higher education. In the organizational models developed by Chris Argyris and Donald Schön, this blaming behavior is called "Model O-I" behavior. It is an organizational behavior routine in which problems are blamed on others while the person or group allocating the blame does not understand or accept their own role in creating the problems (Argyris and Schön 1996). This blame game generally trumps the challenge of analyzing universities as organizations and results in repeated cycles of unproductive behavior.

A great deal of the writing on universities focuses on the intellectual (individualistically analyzed) tasks of teaching and research. Many works encourage us to envision university life as a set of activities executed by individual professors and students, operating in their classrooms, offices, and laboratories by themselves. These actors may be altruistic, malevolent, lazy, brilliant, or stupid but they are treated mainly as voluntaristic individuals (see Weick 1976; Tuchman 2009; Arum and Roska 2011). Often these individuals are blamed for not desiring or doing the right things. This individualistic emphasis is not surprising since it is compatible with meritocratic competitive systems.

Despite its dominance, this individualistic, meritocratic view is empirically and intellectually indefensible. Academic life involves complex interrelationships among individual reflection and interest, the desire for and need to engage in broader professional discourses, and the need to operate in a variety of interconnected organizational venues both on campus and beyond. Academic life is not possible without this combination of individual effort and reflection and communication, critique, and synthesis in the presence of knowledgeable colleagues, students, and administrators. Students are not students by themselves, faculty do not control their own destinies alone, and administrators, whatever their power, are directly dependent on the organizational and policy structures of which they are a part.

The coerced reconceptualization of universities as competitive meritocratic arenas directed by neoliberal management is a sea change. For about a century and a half before this, for all of their defects, universities operated with a certain kind of solidarity among the parts. Most administrators were drawn from the faculty of the institution and had experience as faculty members (Ginsberg 2011). Most university faculty taught, conducted research, supervised students, and engaged in institutional service by leading departments and programs as administrators and by serving on a number of committees and taskforces. Most of the student body expected to have an organized curriculum presented to them and to be guided to some degree in making academic choices and in developing a personal trajectory through and beyond the university. The majority of administrators, even if they had given up on returning to the faculty, conceived of administration as facilitating and protecting the activities of the faculty and the students. They conceived of administration more as service than as a high-paying career track. Underlying all of this was a general notion of solidarity and mutual obligation, a solidarity necessary for all parties to perform their tasks. This sense of interdependence was based on all parties understanding that their own well-being depended in part on supporting the well-being of the others, on at least understanding themselves as parts of the larger university system. When any actor or group overstepped, they usually received a rebuff.

Linking research and teaching was understood to be valuable both to the students and to the faculty, permitting students to learn how knowledge was created and transmitted. This also caused the faculty to take what they were learning through their research and figure out how to communicate it to publics not aware of their findings and their importance. Teaching, writing, lecturing, and learning interacted and were central to the creative life of the university. Put another way, participation in this kind of university work organization provided the conditions under which academic work used to be possible.[1]

It is necessary to emphasize these obvious points because few current faculty, students, and administrators understand sufficiently the consequences of their participation in and dependence on a work organization that links their fates together in particular ways. Instead, each of these categories of actors is encouraged to see themselves as solo, perhaps even heroic actors, and collectively deny their mutual interdependence. Many professors, ironically including social scientists, prefer to see themselves as free-floating intellectuals whose achievements are the result of their own abilities and capacities only, institutional organization being irrelevant. Students are encouraged to see themselves as individualist consumers of educational services in competition with their classmates and later with other graduates in the job market.

This same radical individualist dreamwork has given rise to the "audit culture" (Strathern 2000). This accountability model for academic and administrative work is imposed by neoliberal administrators and policymakers everywhere. Many of these organizational actors deny their own role in reinforcing the neoliberal agenda while they enforce the process of rewarding and punishing only individual efforts by faculty, students, and administrators. This neo-Taylorist model of organization has become "naturalized" to the point that it is taken for granted by many participants. The imagination of most participants does not include the possibility of alternative organizational structures (Gibson-Graham 2006).

Alienated Labor

In approaching this subject, we frame the issues in terms of what is called the "social construction of the person" (Berger and Luckmann 1966; Levinson, Weis, Holland and Foley 1996; Holland and Lave 2009). This perspective connects to our arguments for the crucial importance of work organization in understanding universities.

Our understanding of the social construction of the person starts with a Marxist historical framing. Labor is seen as creating and sustaining human beings by satisfying our requirements for survival. The subsequent exchanges of this labor created society itself. So long as humans controlled the use of their own labor personally or in close kinship and domestic group arrangements, the person was not strongly subordinated socially by work. When labor was alienated from the person and bought and sold on a market as a condition of physical survival, work still created the person and society but it created a very different kind of person and society. The alienated laborer person was individualized into a striving competitor. Ownership of the means of production was concentrated in the hands of controllers of land and financial capital and laborers had to sell their labor in order to eat, clothe themselves, and have a place to live.

From that point on, the way work was organized and the kinds of market conditions imposed on labor created new kinds of "society" and new social actors. The organization of alienated labor not only created the structures of production and distribution, but dictated the social person appropriate to playing the necessary roles: individualistic, competitive, unorganized and often unskilled, clerks and other functionaries, foremen, senior managers, owners, and stockholders. All of these categories of actors now are encouraged to conceive of themselves as persons principally in relation to the work organization they are in.

The "social construction of the person" can be applied as a framework for studying work life in universities as well. Despite the "exception"[2] from the constraints of work structures that some privileged academics claim, universities are organizations whose participants (faculty, students, administrators, staff, external boards, and policymakers) operate in a structured system to produce teaching, research, and service. Leadership is executed and collective coordination and integration is present.

The challenge in understanding universities is not that the work organization of universities is under-specified or spontaneous. Nearly everyone knows how to behave. Rather universities are under-studied and under-analyzed as organizations and the virtues and consequences of alternative ways of organizing universities are treated as vague abstractions that provide no basis for changing the current systems. Since present modes of university work organization are inimical to the creation of *Bildung*, we assert that they must be changed in a participatory and democratic direction. This is a practical matter requiring informed attention to organizational designs and processes.

How Taylorism Structures Universities

All forms of work organization require certain key processes to link the parts together in a system. The academic production process can be differentiated into knowledge generation and transmission in teaching, research, and service. Both research and teaching rely on the dynamics of diverse learning processes. Unlike the neo-Taylorists,[1] we conceptualize universities as centering on these learning and teaching processes. These processes are organizationally situated and involve multiple nonlinear social and psychological processes. They center on teachers and learners consolidating and moving beyond the prior boundaries of their knowledge and altering their projections and plans for the future courses of their lives.

Teaching, Research, and Learning

While this view of learning is hardly controversial, it is incompatible with a linear authoritarian neo-Taylorist model that views teaching and learning as a commodity transfer. For neo-Taylorists, knowledge is what fills the passive brains of researchers through reading journal articles and books, conducting research, and attending professional meetings. Teaching fills the passive minds of students through one-way communication of these professional "contents." Freire's critique of the impossibility of this "banking model" of education is certainly correct (Freire 1970).

The commodity model of research is misleading. Research processes are not linear sequences of hypotheses and deductions, starting with a formulation of a research question and ending with new theory. Rather, research processes are a complex spiral of activities moving cyclically between data, analysis, contestation, and conclusions. The communication of research has similar qualities to oral and written presentations. It is reviewed and critiqued and then revised to take account of the knowledge generated from these interactions. It is a dynamic process and not simply market-driven commodity creation and transfer.

For researchers to discover the limits of their understanding and for students to learn, to get things right and to be mentored, requires active and often conflicting processes that push the prior boundaries of their knowledge. Strong emotions and high personal stakes abound. These have to be dealt with in work systems that permit the actors to be collaborative, operate in a solidary and relatively conflict-free environment, and yet be able to confront one another intellectually. These processes require a sense of personal safety to be effective. They also require these organizational actors to be comprehensible to one another as people and respectful of each other's interests. As abstract as these knowledge creation processes may sound, they must be enacted in very concrete and practical ways. How they are organized matters a great deal to how well they work. This is why organizational analysis is central to understanding what is happening at universities now.

Commoditization of Teaching and Research

Over the past century, neo-Tayloristic forms of university work organization have been developed and have conventionalized these processes in counterproductive ways. These conventionalizations became internationally hegemonic as an extension of the general hegemony of Western industrial capitalism in the global system (Newfield 2004). That this has happened historically does not mean that neo-Tayloristic work organizations are optimal for the central tasks of university life. To believe this would require believing that "this is the best of all possible worlds" and that history is a story of linear progress to the present state. These organizations, like the once hegemonic forms of work organization that developed in industrial capitalism (e.g., Taylorism or Fordism) turned out to be anything but optimal for the successful and sustainable functioning of firms, for human health, and for the environment. They also are radically dysfunctional for universities, as the current crisis in public higher education shows.

Christopher Newfield's important insight that universities adopted the Tayloristic models dominant in industry in the early 1900s is key. Universities, as they grew into the large institutions we recognize today, were wrenched away from the guild organization and "community of scholars and students" model of the prior centuries and converted into neo-Tayloristic organizations mimicking industrial manufacturing, with one important exception. Universities had and have no clarity about what exactly they produce.

We differ from Newfield in one way. While he states that this mimicry was fundamentally inappropriate to a service activity with few clearly definable products, he does not engage in the explanation of the specific ways this organizational model has been dysfunctional. We accept his fundamental and important insight and we add an analysis of the organizational inappropriateness of Taylorism based on our experience working in contemporary industrial organizations and our familiarity with the organizational literature.

In universities, the expansion of the Taylorist model gave rise to the current pattern of disciplines, departments, divisions, colleges, and central administrations laid out in a bureaucratic or hierarchical manner and disciplined from above. Indeed, this disciplinary specialization is a key feature of what the non-German world "borrowed" from the German research university. Claims about *Bildung* had nothing to do with importing this disciplinary design.

The emergence of the disciplines themselves is a complex story that we will only allude to briefly here. In an excellent new book, *Organizing Enlightenment*, Chad Wellmon chronicles the emergence of the disciplines. From the 1750s onward, scholars became ever more concerned as the massive expansion of the print media made the project of integrating and verifying knowledge at first difficult and then impossible. Faced with the impossibility of any one person or a group of general scholars to manage this expanding intellectual resource, they eventually hit on the idea of dividing knowledge into fields and attempting to guarantee comprehensive understanding of each field by having each discipline manage and verify the knowledge within it. This taxonomy was intended to organize all knowledge and gave both a new structure and meaning to the "university". This taxonomy resulted in the Tayloristic system we now find to be so counter-productive (Wellmon 2015).

Despite the ongoing dreamwork of many academics who try to view themselves as part of a self-regulating guild of colleagues in the same discipline and academic field, organizationally they are individualized meritocratic subjects managed from above when it comes to working conditions, salary, contracts, promotions and dismissal, benefits, and job expectations. Rather than analyzing themselves in this organizational context, they often blame the stupidity and authoritarianism of "administrators" for the many experiences they have that do not conform to their guild and craftwork idealization. They do not spend effort learning how things came to be as they currently are.

Students too live in a hierarchically organized world in which bureaucratically imposed standards, rules, and learning conditions prevail. Students are encouraged see themselves as voluntaristic individual actors who select institutions to study and work in, choose courses of study, and choose courses and make life plans individually. They too are subjects of a neo-Tayloristic system. They compete against each other to get into universities. While at the university, they are boxed in by requirements and rules, allowed in or excluded from particular courses and curricula, have little influence over the content of the courses, and, except for unusual crises, have little impact on the management of universities. Now many of them are debtors in the world system of finance.

The non-academic staff and administrators most closely fit and take for granted the neo-Tayloristic system. They work according to hierarchically organized job classifications and definitions, within a multiplicity of organizational units that report upward, and they generally must obey chains of command. Senior university administrators sit atop these multiple hierarchies. It might seem that they are therefore in control but those familiar with organizational analysis also know that these administrators are themselves subject to the system. They compete with and discipline each other and they report upward to boards of trustees, state educational authorities, higher education associations, and markets of various sorts. They also compete with similar administrators at other institutions for better jobs, reputations, and salaries (Tuchman 2009). They enforce national and state higher education policies while they are also driven by them.

In the next chapter, the organization of universities is treated as a set of subsystems and the ways these are integrated into an overall neo-Taylorist organizational framework inimical to the development of *Bildung* is examined.

Notes

1. Taylorism comes from early generations of industrial goods manufacturing. Its application to universities, medicine, law and other areas where the product is not a material good began as an analogy and was infused with bureaucratic logic. Current neo-Taylorism is a radical break with Taylorism that converts services like teaching, medicine, and social services into fictitious commodities

      subject to "casino capitalist" control by apical authorities via accountability, and extraction of surplus for administrative salaries for the benefit of external businesses and governments.

2. It will immediately be countered that research institutes and think tanks are exceptions to this view. We do not say that academic reflection is impossible in other venues. Rather we call attention to the success of universities as productive work organizations over a couple of centuries because their work organization balanced research, teaching, and service.

3. This reference to exceptionalism evokes an old argument common to U.S. historiography. Basically, in the United States, the dominant historical interpretive tradition was that the United States was an exception to the European structuring of society into conflicting social classes. Some writers went so far as to claim that class was irrelevant in interpreting society in the United States and most neoliberals still hold this belief. Not a few people in universities appear to subscribe to a version of this exceptionalist argument. That is, they want to see universities as a place outside of the constraints of their surrounding societies, a place of reflection and learning, uncontaminated by power relations, class conflict, and other undesirable social traits.

CHAPTER 5

The Work Organization of Universities
Systemic Analysis

◆◆◆

Building on the structural analysis presented in the previous chapter, the focus here is on the multiple modes of interaction of the parts. These collaborative routines operate between the key subsystems that compose the organization of a university and these subsystems set the basic parameters for the overall organization of work (Nelson and Winter 1982). Understanding their structure and dynamics is key to understanding universities as a whole. Other than literature pointing to the deployment of neo-Tayloristic models, there is little analysis of how the whole system of any university works. To encourage such an analysis, this chapter applies systems thinking to the structure of university work. The first step is to identify the larger system by examining the relevant subsystems that compose it, because they and their interactions create the backbone for the whole organization.

Systems Thinking

Systems thinking rests on a distinction between closed systems and open systems. In closed systems, the capacity to adapt is entirely internal to the system. Open systems, by contrast, have permeable boundaries and can rearrange those boundaries and internal structures to achieve the necessary internal balance and transactions with the environment that allow them to persist. Universities are clearly open systems. However, many of the stakeholders operate as if they were in closed systems, an error that leads to destructive choices in strategy and poor judgments in all the stakeholder groups. In what follows, we will present the teaching, research, student, and administrative subsystems of universities and then examine their integration.[1]

The Teaching Subsystem

The university teaching system has a long trajectory. While research organizations have existed for millennia in non-university contexts, teaching has been, historically, a foundational aspect of university life (Clark 2007). Teaching began in seminaries and then in secular classrooms where the faculty were paid or hired directly by the students attending the classes (Clark 2007). Since then teaching has developed into an activity hedged around with hierarchical bureaucratic structures and control systems, tying up the professors rather like Gulliver in Lilliput. Course scheduling, curricular requirements, credit hours, enrollments, tuition payments, classroom structures, textbook ordering, copyright clearances for reprints used in teaching, teaching evaluations, grading, delivery of grades, privacy of student records, codes of integrity, etc. are all now subject to regulation and control in disciplinary departments, colleges, universities, and through external accreditation agencies.

Most universities have created standardized teaching segments in the form of courses composed of a certain number of "classes" per week for a certain number of credits over the academic term. These classes each have a determined duration such as the 45-minute class in Norway, the 50-minute academic hour in the United States, conventionalized 2–3 hour advanced seminars, etc. Each class carries an a priori approved number of credits toward the students' graduations and the results of the students' performances are inscribed on their permanent academic records. Each semester of work is also hedged with limitations on the number of courses students may and must take, and these differ widely within and across institutions. Departments and colleges compose specialty and degree requirements and force choices among the variety of courses and demand a specified number of courses be completed successfully.

None of these structures is put forward with detailed academic rationales. They are treated as if they were "natural" laws of university life. They structure the teaching lives of faculty and the learning lives of students. One could ask why 45 minutes has become the teaching mantra in Norway and 50 minutes in the U.S., but such questions rarely arise. The same lack of rational explanations goes for the number of course credits required for graduation and the host of other requirements students have to meet.

The hidden assumption is that these requirements are the necessary conditions for a "learning" process, a claim that is never empirically justified. Rather, it is clear that the whole teaching structure is a top-down, hierarchical one built on Tayloristic conventions that have little educational justification. The board, president, rector, dean, or other unit head resides at the apex of teaching decisions and has the authority to decide whether a course can be accepted for the course catalogue.

Once published in the catalogue, the course is scheduled using complex timetables, now computerized, making it possible for the students to fulfill the necessary course requirements for their particular degree program and also trying to optimize the use of the academic physical plant throughout the day and week.

The length, number of credits, timing, and sequence of courses are determined without much thought about their pedagogical implications. Hedged between conventions, accreditation standards based on unjustified conventions ("we have always done it this way"), the structure of the teaching system is determined without reference to what makes sense in organizing learning experiences. Bureaucratic control trumps pedagogy. Any learning that takes place has to be accomplished within and by overcoming these constraints.

The overall composition of a degree program is decided through a complex combination of external accrediting standards, often imposed by people who know little about education. Then the availability of teaching staff, power plays by different disciplinary departments, ideologies about higher education, and the demands of administrative professionals of the university are taken into account. Then the execution of teaching is handed over to the professorial workers (the faculty). This is a neo-Tayloristic model based on fragmented teaching structure separated from a controlling administrative staff (Greenwood and Levin 2000b).

This may sound simple but the authority relations here are unexpectedly complex. When a course first enters the catalogue, the individual professor has great autonomy and control in teaching. It is only in highly unusual situations or in particular scientific and engineering fields, where curricular standards are set by national and international professional governing bodies or in sectarian institutions that any high-ranking university person or accrediting agency would interfere. Generally, the professor has the freedom to be good or to fail as a teacher, to engage with the students or to be disconnected.

The tension between this autonomy in the classroom and the neo-Tayloristic system is endemic. For some faculty, this freedom in the classroom, once the course has been approved, is experienced as "academic freedom" because, at that point, the professor has the choice to teach what he or she sees as important within the framework of the actual course[2]. The downside of this classroom "freedom" is that it also means that personal professorial preferences dominate teaching. The same course taught by two different faculty members is often substantively not the same course despite having the same number, credits, name, and fulfilling the same requirement. This creates the illusion of a consistent set of offerings while hiding, for better or for worse, a much greater diversity (if not chaos) of teaching activities.

A key part of the teaching subsystem, then, is neo-Tayloristic as regards creating the course structures, approved courses, curricula, hours, rooms, schedules, etc., but the actual specification of tasks within the parameters for the courses themselves is minimal. This lack of specification offends the sensibilities of neo-Taylorists. Getting control over course content through arguments about relevance and accountability is a key current agenda of neoliberal administrators. Even now they do not find their existing authority to be sufficient.

The structural ambiguity between neo-Taylorism and classroom autonomy actually allows the persistence of an idealized version of the "craftworker" view of academic faculty as members of a guild. Within this system, faculty are encouraged to view their teaching as craftwork while simultaneously they conform to a neo-Tayloristic system of work organization. This neo-Taylorist system encourages non-university actors to try to regulate what actually occurs at a key point of academic production: the classroom. Faculty salaries and other job conditions are determined by criteria having little to do with craftwork.

In practice, senior administrators have little idea of what goes on in most classrooms, tutorials, and laboratories unless a particular professor gets in trouble by saying or doing something that outrages a student or a political, ethnic, gender, or religious group. Sitting at the top of the hierarchy, the administrators look as if they are leading the organization in producing teaching and research. The faculty and students look as if they are following instructions while they also generally believe they are making autonomous choices.

Autonomy inside the classroom does not therefore imply that contemporary best practices in pedagogy are deployed often. While the situation in advanced seminars may be somewhat interactive, the default pedagogy increasingly treats teaching as a one-way process where the professors transfer knowledge to students and, if possible, to the maximum number of students at a time or online. Accordingly, students are expected to be passive recipients of the knowledge decided on and presented by the professor. In this context, the professor is the boss and the students are the workers. Professors who lecture to larger numbers of students receive financial and political rewards for Taylorizing the teaching process.

Breaking with this one-way knowledge transfer is complicated but it is possible. It already happens in some seminars, in tutorials, art and music studios, architectural design courses, theater arts, and in some scientific research groups where collaborative group processes and shared learning take place. There are emerging pedagogical practices that build on project-based teaching where students actively decide on the curriculum and move forward through working on actual projects. These practices directly confront the neo-Taylorist structures that administrators prefer and reward, and faculty take these approaches at their own risk. Under present conditions, good teaching is done against the grain or incentive structures of universities and usually without proper financial and logistical support.

Under these circumstances the dominant form of teaching remains close to the medieval cathedra form of teaching from the pulpit (Clark 2007). As it was then, it mainly relies on one-way communication staged as the teacher's monologue aimed at the student receiver of knowledge, followed by examinations or other exercises to see how well the students are listening. When faculty complain about the current hierarchical behavior of administrators, few stop to consider the neo-Tayloristic ways many manage their own courses and student supervisions.

These teaching sessions are a key structural element in many professors' workday. They have to spend time in advance of a lecture to prepare, show up in the auditorium at the correct time, and possibly remain afterwards for a while to answer the questions from interested students. This sequence of teaching events is, for many professors, the only mandatory campus presence required, other than some required office hours to answer further student questions. The rest of the time, excluding faculty and university meetings, is mainly up to the professors to manage.

While most full-time professors cannot avoid teaching, they do have a great deal of freedom in managing their work choices, a freedom not paralleled in many other professions. Their teaching performance may be evaluated, but these evaluations, until recently, have depended on local conditions and policies. More important, it is rare for the quality of teaching in general to have a major impact on the hiring, promotion, and compensation a professor receives. At most public universities, research and research-based publications determine the career trajectory and salary of a professor. The freedom to organize their non-teaching time to meet these employment objectives and the lack of serious oversight of the content of courses and the methods of teaching are key elements in the current debased meaning of "academic freedom" for many public university faculty members.

The Research Subsystem

The research subsystem is differently structured because it centers around entrepreneurial activity mainly supported by external grants. Acquiring these grants involves meeting a series of both topical and procedural requirements. The grant cycles are less predictable than are the cycles of applications, admissions, course offerings, and curricula in the teaching subsystem. To complicate things, it is well known that developing a research question or making a discovery is not rooted in a linear analytical process (Levin and Greenwood 2007). Rather, developing and pursuing good research questions depends on creativity, luck, hard work, and the ability to be a reflective practitioner (Schön 1983). A successful and coherent research process depends on organizational ability, work discipline, analytical capacity, and on making the research process transparent to others researching the same issues.

Most research groups are team-based. Like other entrepreneurial activities, research depends on the ability to come to agreements with stakeholders in the problem area, determining who would be interested in the results and who would fund the research process. These conditions demand professorial ability to combine multiple organizational elements and behaviors successfully. Research involves leading and organizing others to achieve common goals, finding and managing financial resources, and finally being able to perform scientific analysis, write research reports, and present the results at professional meetings and in other venues.

Though administrators wish that research could be made more predictable so they could manage the income flows, research is not and cannot be organized through a top-down bureaucratic structure. Organizing the handling of the research money brought in, creating and maintaining research infrastructures, and managing contracts can be and are dealt with by hierarchical administrative bureaucracies in universities. But research itself is fundamentally a bottom-up process. Research initiatives and engagements, while potentially suggested by others in particular fields and stakeholders external to universities, ultimately must be enacted in the heads and hands of the practicing researchers.

There also is differentiation among research leaders, participants, research assistants, etc., meaning that not all participants in a research project have to be entrepreneurs. Still there is a team-based character in most research activities. The necessary organizational relationships and networking activities are mostly self-organized. This is true even when the researcher is working alone, since the proposal submission, funding and grant management, and organizational requirements have to be met through the university's organizational and legal system for supporting research.

Many universities create staff to support research, and these administrative systems operate according to hierarchical, bureaucratic logic. However, this hierarchical system has to interact effectively with spontaneous and network-based research organizational praxis. This often produces frictions in values, norms, and praxis in the encounters between researchers and administrative staff, and constant, occasionally acrimonious, encounters between the research and administrative subsystems. It also sometimes works reasonably well because of the organizational abilities of all the parties to work through a process of give and take.

Typical of the issues that come up in this relationship are ethics and liability in research, the importance of academic freedom, integrity of the researcher versus the needs of the university (as when a research finding contradicts the interests of a big corporate funder, university board member, or university donor). There are also conflicts over the allocation of the acquired research funding between the actual research activities, taking some of the funds for the maintenance or construction of infrastructures, and reallocating some of the funds for more general use and contributions to general university physical and administrative infrastructures. Arguments about public goods and private goods come up directly in this context.

There can also be other important conflicts within the research subsystem. There are conflicts between colleagues competing for the same resources, conflicts between the interests of the university administration and the faculty that may be both pecuniary and diplomatic, and, not the least, conflicts between clashing personalities. There is no bright line between the outcomes of research and the personal abilities and qualifications of researchers. The integration of work and personality makes it difficult to separate judgment of the personal qualities of researchers from their concrete research outcomes.

The Student Subsystem

Despite their obvious importance to universities, the many volumes about students and their education, and the scores of new advisors, enrollment management specialists, residence hall coordinators, and more, students are rarely conceptualized as components in a larger system that they necessarily interact with. The diversity of views about who and what students are dramatizes how the stakeholders in the other subsystems view these key stakeholders through their own optic.

Some administrators view students as customers to be satisfied. Others view them as sources of prestige and national ranking to be recruited selectively from the most competitive and best-reputed secondary schools. Still others regard them as immature youngsters to be managed and guided into meaningful career paths. Another part of the system views them as a source of tuition revenues needed to keep the institution viable. An important percentage of students in the United States also form a part-time university workforce and finance their education by performing infrastructural tasks for the university for low pay. Finally, a small number of administrators treat students as a younger generation to be formed and developed into the next generation of corporate, community, and political leaders. Some faculty view students as a necessary evil that underwrites the important business of universities—their own research. Others see them as a potential community of learners, a new generation that can improve society, and individuals who can be fashioned into a learning community if treated properly and skillfully.

The diversity of takes on who and what students are shows up in the often divergent systems students face. In some parts of the administrative structure, students are paying customers to be courted and to be billed for services. In other areas, they are potentially unruly kids to be controlled and managed. In still others, they are sought-after recruits to be directed and assisted in meeting their life goals. Student experiences range from bureaucratic and authoritarian encounters to formative and enabling ones. Gradually students get used to moving between these uneven and irreconcilable social roles because they have no choice except to interact with different parts of the university system. They come to accept this institutional incoherence as a "natural" condition of university life. If they employ the wrong behavioral role in one of these venues, the difficulties that result for them can be major.

Faculty members also diverge in their views of students. For those who find teaching fulfilling, students are a welcome and precious presence in their classes and young companions on important intellectual trajectories. A few students are viewed as the potential next generation of professors and given particularly close attention. For faculty members who do not like to teach, students are a bother to be avoided to the extent possible or even a burden to be offloaded as much and as often as possible onto teaching assistants and junior faculty. For those faculty members, the university is about their research or other dimensions of their careers and time spent with students is time lost to more "important" activities. For faculty who view university education as a kind of process of broadening and forming independent adults, students are both an opportunity to promote meaningful social improvement and an avenue for carrying the faculty's knowledge forward through the generations. All of these positions exist simultaneously on most campuses.

Not surprisingly, then, from the vantage point of students, the university is a very complicated and diverse place. Some students situate themselves resolutely as customers and insist on the freedom to choose what they want to do according to their own interests and the right to expect that the university will comply. They choose their courses, majors, curricula, and job goals themselves and look to use university resources to reach these goals. In this, given the increasing costs of university studies, they often have the ideological support of their parents and neoliberal policymakers urging them on to be smart "consumers."

Other students understand themselves as learners who know relatively little and want and need advice from faculty and administrators about the various options before them. These students are heavy users of both academic and administrative advising, orientation sessions, and workshops. They are often not sure about their career interests, have multiple interests and have not yet been able to prioritize them, or are simply in an exploratory mode, looking to use the diverse resources of the university as a source of experiences and eventual inspiration about their own path.

These different kinds of students define their university experience quite differently. Some see themselves as having arrived with their wants and tastes well formed and they want to pursue them directly. Others see themselves as having arrived with a need to form their tastes and set their priorities and they want the university to provide experiences that help them make these choices.

Under current circumstances, the student subsystem has certain unique features. The curricula that are set up and required of students are not necessarily those that any particular student would choose. They have a great deal of choice, but within arbitrary constraints. For example, in the case of a U.S.-style liberal arts education, students are given a set of distribution requirements to meet—a few courses in the sciences, in the social sciences, in the humanities, in quantitative reasoning, in history, and often in language. They take these courses in different departments and from different professors with different groups of students. Few of the professors interact with their other professors or care to learn about what the others teach. Students then select a field of specialization and spend their last couple of years focusing more on acquiring specialized knowledge in their chosen field.

While this may sound quite reasonable, the actual distribution requirements are often set by the faculty in politically self-interested ways to maximize enrollments and reinforce calls for more university resources for their unit. These courses are only revised every so often through laborious and rarely deliberative processes and then they often are offloaded on junior or adjunct faculty. The fact that courses fill the requirements does not mean that the faculty offering them take an interest in what is taught in any of the other fields that form part of the students' required distribution of courses. As we pointed out earlier, what professors actually teach in the classroom is mainly up to them.

As a result, students walk from building to building, department to department, year after year taking courses. They are told that taking these "walks" adds up to "getting an education", even though the only link between the pieces is the student, the choices they have been able to make, and the energy they have spent walking from building to building. Building a car from subassemblies designed independently of the other subassemblies will not create a vehicle that will function on the highway, just as the academic equivalent of education by walking around does not result in an "education" in any meaningful sense of the term.

Similar practices occur within a particular discipline in which the professors in subdisciplines do not necessarily consult or even know much about the content and teaching strategies used by their colleagues. The departmental curricula are set through internal struggles among the subdisciplines and political struggles among the faculty. Rarely do the core intellectual issues of the discipline and its relation to the education of students form part of the discussion.

Considering that most real-world jobs and problems actually require the ability to mobilize and integrate many kinds of knowledge and practice and the ability to work in team-based organizations, this kind of "education by walking around" is a poor fit with most students' future employment and community membership needs. However, the students have already learned the rules and take them pretty much for granted, while the faculty and administration treat these rules as if they were natural laws of university life. Any deviation requires petitions, permissions, and invokes many parts of the bureaucratic apparatus, making student creativity and originality a high-cost approach to education.

One of the authors, some years ago, while walking across the campus, overheard a conversation between two professors who were saying that the university would be a great place "if it were not for the presence of the students." Aside from showing that professors are not necessarily intelligent, this statement reveals a failure to understand that students are an intellectual and financial sine qua non of universities as systems. Not only do the student fees and government allocations to cover their costs form a cornerstone of university budgets, but the intellectual life of a university is radically different from that of a free-standing research institute or a knowledge-intensive industry precisely because of the student presence. Teaching and learning, research and teaching, thinking and acting can and should form a positive interactive cycle that generates new ideas and actions for all parties.

Faculty are not the only actors to have non-empirical conceptions of their organizational lives. A significant number of students, administrators, policymakers, and entrepreneurs fantasize about a university that does not need to have students physically present. Online education is here to stay. Even in residential universities with physical infrastructures, information technology-assisted instruction increases all the time.

Only a convinced neoliberal can fail to recognize that group processes of learning are fundamentally different from individualistic, off-site learning. The processes of learning in a group setting, engaging in critical reflection and discussion with peers in real time, exploring subjects at a distance from parents and other adolescent controlling figures, and the possibilities of social mobility through accessing new ideas, skills, and attitudes are all integrally related to physical presence on campus. If current universities do not recognize this and fail to emphasize it, their replacement by online training programs is reasonable and likely.[3]

Administrative Subsystem

The third subsystem identified and mentioned more than once in prior sections is administration. This subsystem is presumed to be present to coordinate teaching, research, the non-teaching and research aspects of the university including the buildings, secretarial staff, budgeting, enrollment management, scheduling, research administration, and many other functions necessary to running any university. In an idealized model, administration is a coordinating link between teaching, research, and the surrounding world. The importance of administrative functions to contemporary universities is not debatable. However, whether or not the kinds of administrative systems most universities have now are suitable to the task is another matter.

As we alluded to earlier, Christopher Newfield (2004) pointed out that despite romantic and self-serving myths about faculty-run universities in the twentieth century, faculty long ago made a Faustian bargain with the administration, in which the faculty let go of the administrative work to free themselves for teaching and research. This choice freed administrators to manage the institutions, albeit with differing amounts of faculty input and steering. The political consequences of this bargain were long obscured up by the extended period of university growth from 1950 onward but eventually these consequences have become clear (Gerber 2014).

The present story of university administrations and the de-professionalization and deskilling of the faculty is anticipated historically by the prior subjugation of doctors and lawyers to administrative managers and to for-profit firms structured by "just-in-time" principles to maximize income while disciplining and controlling the professional practitioners. The problem now in the administrative subsystem is that most university administrations have become separate realms unto themselves. They routinely confuse themselves and their position at the apex of the organizational charts they create with the "university" itself (Ginsberg 2011).

This is clear in the massive worldwide expansion of administrative positions in universities and the tendency of senior administrators to speak as if they were speaking for everyone in the university. While most administrators argue that administration is necessary in order to run a transparent, efficient, and "business-like" institution, it is important to understand that, in the private sector, there has been a fundamental, economically necessary shift towards more participative models, giving more influence to the individual employees and work teams. These changes are known as "lean production", "just-in-time", or "team based" operations.

Introducing the history and diversity of lean production approaches to organization exceeds the ambitions of this book and so we will be brief. Basically, lean production emerged from the same desire to eliminate waste and shorten process time that gave rise to Taylorism, but it differed, from its first major implementation at Toyota, in making all members of the organization aware of and responsible for the elimination of waste. This, of course, can be quite coercive and authoritarian and often was. However, a second way to implement the lean production idea is based on the argument that one of the major sources of waste in most organizations is the failure to use the skills and knowledge of the whole workforce fully. This has resulted in combining the initial ideas of lean production with the promotion of team-based, multi-skilled workgroups in a larger matrix model of organization.

Waste in excessive oversight and administration is just as much of a problem to address as is waste in the direct production of goods and services. The lean production changes involve significant decreases in administrative positions and hierarchies and moving decisions closer to the locus of value production. That is to say, decisions are moved to where the productive work (teaching and research, in this case) is actually being done.

At present, public universities exhibit a massive increase of administrative and support staff at the expense of resources devoted to teaching and research, the primary organizational functions. Key organizational decisions are being moved farther away from the point of value creation in classrooms, laboratories, libraries, and studios. In other words, we are in an era of academic administrative "fat production" that bears no relationship to the best practices in the private sector. If it is understood that the sites of value creation in universities are the classrooms, faculty offices, libraries, and research laboratories, then the reallocation of a significant percentage of university budgets to administrative salaries is unjustifiable and economically irrational waste.

University administrations, in defending their positions and extending their control, have also become significant importers of "management fads" (Birnbaum 2001) putatively drawn from the private sector. Far from being leading-edge corporate practices, these fads usually arise from indiscriminate borrowing from the latest mass-market management literature or from "hired gun" consultants. These imported fads rarely account for the fact that the "products, production processes, and markets" for higher education bear little resemblance to those found in most private sector manufacturing or service industries.

As Birnbaum shows, the implementation of these fads does not take into account internal nor external conditions, is always incomplete, and usually forms part of a succession of half-implemented and rarely successful change processes (Mickletwait and Woolridge 1996; Bradley et al. 2000). What they do accomplish, however, is the consolidation of the power of some administrators, and they serve as a launching pad for these administrators' national and international careers. They list their implementations of these fads on the resumes they give to the university administrative headhunting firms that most universities now rely on for senior appointments (Tuchman 2009).

We accept that administrations must take care of a host of important functions including establishing the teaching schedules and structures;

research grant management; receiving and allocating tuitions, research monies, and gifts; recruiting students and faculty; managing hiring and promotion decisions; determining compensation structures; managing contracts and legal liabilities; managing buildings and properties, insurance systems, retirement and healthcare programs; and many other things. None of these activities is trivial and some are responses to external mandates that cannot be ignored. However, administrative growth is not only extremely costly, occurring at the expense of other possible allocations of resources, but it greatly reinforces the dysfunctional neo-Tayloristic organization of administrative structures. It also reinforces their increasing disconnection from the actual value creation activities in universities and contributes to the out-of-control cost increases in public higher education.

The Complex Integration—Multiple, Opportunistically Connected Networks

Our portrait of universities as systems shows that the functional organization of the subsystems is fragmented, diffuse, and even internally contradictory. The four subsystems have different structures, foci, and dynamics. They often compete for control of decisional authority. Legal and hierarchical authority is located in the administration with the administrative leaders who claim to and often actually do "represent" the institution as a legal entity. Having authority and being unproductively authoritarian are in tension. Many administrative leaders report to a board of trustees or a ministry of education and can be reprimanded or fired from above. While they have great power looking down, it is not infinite, and mishandling key issues, particularly those with symbolic salience on a campus, can make it impossible for them to operate effectively. In the United States, there are occasional "no confidence" votes that result in the ouster of senior administrators. Opportunism and political entrepreneurship can make certain connections and create some power positions but these links are always in flux.

In teaching and research, it is less clear who is in control of what. Certainly salaries, departmental structures, personnel policies, and the like are under administrative control, but the content of curricula and courses, teaching methods, and research priorities are generally set by the faculty. If the students don't come to the courses or if the funders don't support the research, then faculty discretion is also limited. Within the faculty and among the departments, there are hierarchies based on enrollments, scholarly profiles, and *realpolitik* in the local context.

Students both have a great deal and very little power, depending on the part of the system they are interacting with, under what circumstances, and the kind of power involved. A student revolt can bring a university to a halt. Student course choices influence the structure of departments, disciplines, and curricula. Student behavior affects the residential system, the social life of the university, and ultimately its attractiveness as a place to enroll. Yet students have to compete for admission to universities, choose from a preselected set of options for courses of study, choose courses, majors, and choose among a set range of extracurricular options. They are both political protagonists and political subjects of the same system.

Policymakers can and do create a wide variety of accountability and accreditation schemes, set targets, and manage funding allocations to try to force universities as a whole to adjust to their demands. Perched high above campus administrators, who are themselves disconnected from daily university value-production activities, policymakers have almost no concrete understanding of the implementation or impacts of their policy abstractions and the other blunt instruments they use to discipline institutions. From above, they cannot see the resistance and subterfuge that prevent many of their aesthetically pleasing and politically designed schemes from altering campus landscapes much. They often explain the repeated failures of their policies by blaming the faculty for being hidebound and or lazy and to characterizing the students as spoiled or feckless rather than accepting the failure of their ill-designed impositions on academic life.

Universities As "Loosely Coupled Systems", "Organized Anarchies", or "Garbage Cans"

What we have presented above is not what Karl Weick (1976) called a "loosely coupled system." Weick deployed the conceptualization of loose-coupling (ibid.: 3) to show that the linked subsystems in universities are responsive to each other, but that each also has an identity and logic of its own. According to Weick, this makes tight coupling impossible and perhaps even undesirable. In loosely coupled systems, the lack of a straight chain of command supposedly shapes a situation where the leader has little authority to command and has to rely on the good will and judgment of subordinates to get things done.

For Weick, the chain of authority from the president or rector down to the individual professor or to the individual student is long and faces many obstacles because of the fundamental disconnections among the subsystems. No one subsystem can effectively order the others around and so most processes of adaptation and change require various kinds of negotiations and mediations among all the subsystems that make up a university. Coordination of the actions of the parts is especially challenging because their key productive activities in the different subsystems are so fundamentally different.

The other popular organizational metaphors, deployed by Cohen, March and Olsen (1972), are an "organized anarchy" or a "garbage can" model of decision making. They describe universities as organized anarchies because of what they take to be their way of making decisions:

> The garbage can process is one in which problems, solutions, and participants move from one choice opportunity to another in such a way that the nature of the choice, the time it takes, and the problems it solves all depend on a relatively complicated intermeshing of elements. These include the mix of choices available at any one time, the mix of problems that have access to the organization, the mix of solutions looking for problems, and the outside demands on the decision makers. (Cohen, March and Olsen 1972: 16)

While elements in Weick's analysis and in Cohen, March and Olsen's model sound similar to the position we take, they both treat university politics as benign, and neither view leads to an action plan to improve universities. Other than emphasizing loose-coupling and organized anarchy, they take no clear position on the organizational dynamics that create contradictory power relations and they offer no insight into the way these systems could or should be reorganized to create a better overall university. As a result, these metaphors become ways to not take a position on these issues rather than being a proactive position of their own. Perhaps their apolitical bent is what has made them popular. This is a case of analysis leading to paralysis.

Neither framework notes that these systems provide fertile ground for certain consistent larger power dynamics in contemporary universities. Meritocracy in all the subsystems we have presented is one such dynamic. All the subsystems are meritocracies but the meritocratic ladders different sets of actors are climbing are not directly linked. The "meritocrats" on each ladder use each other and the other categories of university stakeholders instrumentally to further their own meritocratic trajectories. Weick's and Cohen, March and Olsen's schemes are now distinctly out of date because neoliberalism and neo-Taylorism work to substitute authoritarian control for loose-coupling and organized anarchy.

As we said earlier in this book, we know from the extensive literatures on the social and cultural production of the person (Berger and Luckmann 1966; Levinson, Weis, Holland and Foley 1996; Holland and Lave 2009) that different organizational systems and regimes encourage the actors to remake themselves as persons to be proper subjects of these systems. To fail to conform to the meritocratic system of which they are a part places them at significant risk. So, despite their differences, the subsystems of universities do similarly construct individuals as individualist actors in competition with other individuals for scarce resources (financial resources, respect and prestige, power, etc.).

To operate successfully in any of these subsystems, actors must understand themselves as competitive individualists and understand others as potential competitors for the same resources. Administrators compete to rise within the administrative systems and to rise in the prestige of institutions where they can acquire jobs (Tuchman 2009). Faculty compete for appointments, tenure, promotions, favorable working conditions, space, research money, etc. They only support each other under quite specific circumstances, when group solidarity serves their personal interests. Students compete for grades, attention, honors, to enter particular fields, and for jobs or postgraduate placements afterwards (Douthat 2006; Kirn 2009). Staff compete for positional improvements in the hierarchical staff job systems.

All this meritocratic effort only integrates the system by viewing everyone in it as a striver who competes by using everyone else as an instrument in their own meritocratic advancement. The system is both loosely coupled and highly competitive. Given this, such a system is profoundly inhospitable to collaborative learning and research processes. It promotes anti-*Bildung*.

This is not to say that altruism and solidarity are entirely absent. They exist but are neither called for nor strongly rewarded. The "hidden curriculum" of contemporary public universities is that we all live in a competitive free-market society and everyone should look out for their own interests. Add to this the subjection of universities globally to regimes of neoliberal accountability and their configuration as competitive, meritocratic arenas is clear.

We now turn, in the next chapter, to the organization of work processes in these neo-Taylorist organizations.

Notes

1. In the context of United States public universities, especially the "land grant" universities, an additional subsystem, "service," would be included. This involves the explicit mission to be of direct service to the people, communities, and policymakers of the state in which they reside. As this does not have a direct analogy in the public university systems in Europe, we will not deal with it here. Excellent works have been written about this service system, such as Peters, Jordan, Adamek and Alter (2005).

2. Currently, this does take place within the increasingly narrow bounds of the censorship of academic speech that makes anyone "uncomfortable" (Lukianoff 2014).

3. We acknowledge the arguments for the cost effectiveness and convenience of on-line education but our own experiences make us quite dubious about the possibilities for a *Bildung* centered educational process to be carried on in the absence of sustained real time interactions with faculty and peers.

CHAPTER 6

Processes in the Work Organization of Universities

Socio-Technical Systems Design, Networking for Power, and Neo-Taylorism

◆◆◆

Universities, whether they are called "knowledge organizations," work organizations, or institutions for higher education, are places where participants cooperate and compete while furnishing society with new knowledge, new professionals, or educated future citizens. In this sense, university work organization can be understood as a set of processes that create "outputs" for the surrounding society. These processes and how they are structured have direct consequences for the behaviors, norms, sense of purpose, and identity of professors, students, and administrators.

Organizational analysis is a necessary step in preparing to envision how to move to participative structures and change processes in re-creating public universities. To facilitate the organizational analysis it is necessary to construct a well-delineated perspective to anchor the analysis. First, attention is focused on what is called "socio-technical systems design" (STSD) and then later the focus shifts to networks, power and, neo-Taylorism. Since the STSD model might be unfamiliar, especially to United States audiences, we provide an introduction to this approach below (see pages 114–18). STSD supports participative change while addressing a comprehensive set of organizational variables that must be dealt with for successful change in any organization to take place. Following this, we put the components in motion by applying Actor Network Theory (ANT) to the study of universities.

The previous chapter laid out a systems view of universities as organizations. Now the focus shifts to analyzing the operational characteristics of university work organization. What follows is not an analysis of any specific university, though extended organizational ethnographies are clearly needed to move this research and reform agenda forward. Here only some general organizational models are laid out to help the analysis of the processes that dominate contemporary university landscapes. The next chapter takes up the complex issues of leadership, steering, and corporatization to round out the organizational analysis.

The Organizational Dynamics of Universities

In the previous two chapters, the focus was on the structural and systems dimensions of the work organizations that constitute universities. Applying a systems theoretical perspective, four different interacting subsystems were identified: teaching, research, students, and administration. An important lack of symmetry in the span of institutional engagement of the various subsystem members was apparent.

Only a handful of texts have been published dealing with this subject. Early attempts include Burton Clark's book, *Places of Inquiry* (1995), where he developed an international comparative analysis of universities. He basically applied a macro-oriented analysis that only dealt with fragments of campus-centered organizational issues. Bousquet and Nelson's book with the promising title, *How the University Works* (2008), is actually a study of the political economy of universities and not an analysis of how everyday work is done. Closer to our focus is Tuchman's *Wannabe U* (2009) where she analyzes the change process that takes place in a university where the senior administrators aspire to improve the institution's ranking while maximizing their own career trajectories nationally. Her analysis deals with the administration without connecting administrators to the faculty and students.

Recently, some works having the much needed focus on university organizational structures and dynamics have begun to emerge. Three important contributions are Kathleen Manning's *Organizational Theory in Higher Education* (2013), Mitchell Stevens and Michael Kirst's edited volume *Remaking College* (2015), and Susan Hyatt, Boone Shear and Susan Wright's edited *Learning Under Neo-liberalism* (2015). Despite J.V. Baldridge's pioneering attempts to examine the politics of higher education (Baldridge 1971) and Ginsberg's anti-administration book (Ginsburg 2011), political science work on higher education mainly has focused on the policy level rather than on universities as work organizations (McLendan 2003; Neave 2003; Pusser 2003).

Manning, Stevens and Kirst, and Hyatt, Shear and Wright as well as Weick (1976) and Cohen, March and Olsen (1972) all focus on campus organizational dynamics. They emphasize complexity and the use of multiple frames of reference as ways of getting at the organizational dynamics we have been discussing and they reward a close reading. Unlike the effort here, however, none of these studies moves from organizational analysis to change praxis. They rest on the familiar academic idea that better understanding will somehow produce reforms. We have been engaged with these problems too long to believe that better models and analyses will produce the needed changes without strategies for acting directly on campus organizational structures and dynamics.

Despite the neoliberal takeover, no one should forget that there are limitations on administrative power that even neoliberal administrations have been unable to overcome. The neoliberals have learned little from history about the limitations to authoritarian power in all Tayloristic organizations. The consolidation of power and decision making at the top of the organizational system distances those at the apex from the daily realities lived by those engaged in the value-creation processes. As we mentioned earlier, this distance often results in administrative behavior that Argyris and Schön (1996) would identify as a Model O-I effort to increase regulation and control of the system. They try to close what is an open system by exerting authoritarian control over it. In doing so, their own behavior creates unproductive organizational dynamics and conditions for poor decisions.

Their impositions often make the system even more resistant to change. In addition to political resistance, there is resistance to what may well be poor policies or counterproductive schemes that are impossible to implement. Because of the hierarchical structure, top administrators' decisions and policies are often based on poor information about actual work processes and motivations. They often result in defensive or passive-aggressive reactions by those below, behaviors including hiding or misrepresenting information. Over time, this dynamic either demoralizes the value creators or causes them to develop a variety of resistance strategies that include "soldiering" (pretending to obey while not obeying), subterfuge, sabotage, and even open defiance.

All of these dynamics are currently visible in different institutions of higher education. They are the result of shifting the structure of university organizations from a kind of craft and collegial model in which faculty and administrators both participated (not necessarily efficiently) in governance (along with students in some European systems) to an administrative, bureaucratic, hierarchical model. In the current system decisional power is increasingly moved upward toward the administrative apex of the institution. They are simultaneously managed coercively in some areas and yet loosely coupled in actual value-production activities.

Such systems will not yield to simple analytical models or metaphors. We need a more differentiated understanding of the integration between system components in university work organizations. Power is enacted in the ways faculty and staff operate, in the way students obey or resist plans made for them, and in the way administrators attempt to extend their control over all other actors. And yet, in no case is the power of any one group sufficient to obliterate the power of the others. Thus these systems are unstable and dynamic. The "blame game" offers very little in the way of insight about how to move beyond this situation.

Socio-Technical Systems Design

Moving beyond the "blame game" and addressing the challenges of integrating university subsystems and functions in positive ways necessarily involves systems thinking. We have introduced systems theory very generally in the previous chapter. There are many different systems frameworks used for specific purposes. For us, the most effective and actionable approach to systems thinking in organizational theory is socio-technical systems design (STSD).

This approach to organizational systems rests on the idea that the operation of an organization is influenced by social and technological (in the broad sense that includes "techniques") variables and by a high degree of permeability between the organization and its environment. STSD recognizes the importance of the technologies, including the organizational designs and structures in use, and the linkages of these to the external political and administrative landscape.

The STSD approach is an offspring of the work of the London-based Tavistock Institute of Human Relations (Trist 1981). The core members of the Tavistock research group were Eric Trist, Fred Emery, Philip Herbst, and Einar Thorsrud. Social psychology, psychoanalytic theory, and work organization were key components in their theories and their practice focused on the reconstruction of British industry after the Second World War.

The general idea in socio-technical systems design is that while both technology and the larger political economy set constraints, these also can be managed to support the achievement of desired goals within organizations through thoughtful and collaborative organizational behavior (Emery 1959). Significant improvements are possible because of the important local knowledge and experience the members of the organization have. When this is made sense of effectively and put to use collaboratively, it can result in significant improvement in the quality of products, services, and of working life processes themselves.

A central feature of STSD is its focus on supporting participative change processes (Elden 1979). Because organizations necessarily are dynamic but rarely make constructive use of a great deal of the human potential found within them, only through the active engagement and participation of the local stakeholders can organizations continue to adapt and develop effectively. STSD argues that the authoritarian structuring of Tayloristic organizations is ineffective in dynamic environments and reduces the knowledge available for successful adaptations. Such organizations can only do more or less of what they initially are structured to do by those at the apex, who treat the organizations as closed systems whose boundaries they control. By combining technical and participative features in a systems framework, STSD generates methods and models for creating and revising the design of an organization in an ongoing, participative, and coherent process.

Influential papers by Trist and Bamforth (1951) and by Emery and Trist (1965) point to the mutual dependence between technology and organization in what are always open systems. Subsequent developments in STSD created a more nuanced view of the unique integration between structural interdependence, processes of leadership, and the processes of dynamic transformation in organizations. The overall result was a new conceptualization of work organizations as open technological and social systems integrated by collaborative human activity. This kind of understanding of organizational dynamics is hardly to be found in the literature on higher education, but has been deployed extensively in manufacturing and service industries in many countries.

Technology

From a STSD perspective, technology creates constraints on human activity, but it can also facilitate and support activity that otherwise would not have been possible. Thus technology can limit some actions and support others: for example, "informating" versus automating, as laid out by Zuboff (1984) regarding information technology. Underlying the STSD perspective is the knowledge that what is being done in any organization at any one moment is only a small subset of the things that are possible within the constraints of technology, staff, and the political economy.

Another STSD aim is to design technologies purposely to enhance working conditions rather than to worsen them. This requires technical design to be informed by an understanding of the realities of the ways social and technological factors impact work processes and organizational dynamics. These conditions are rarely met in the imposition of technologies on university operations. In STSD, the aim is to engage the work organization participatively in a search for technologies, alternative deployments of technologies, or in the design of technologies and processes that facilitate the existence of desired organizational structures, dynamics, and results. Rather than the organization being forced to adapt to the technology, the organization and technology are co-designed and managed.

Leadership in STSD

Leadership emerges as a system function, not as any particular position in a hierarchical organizational system. Leadership is necessary in all work organizations, but it need not be exclusively linked to one person nor necessarily be at the apex of an organizational hierarchy. Leadership takes many forms, depending on the issues being faced and value-creation processes taking place in the organization. The "semi-autonomous groups" (later called teams) that were routinely created in the early days of STSD efforts usually had no permanent leadership. Rather, the participative processes required all members to take part in a range of different aspects of decision making, reducing the need for a single authoritative leader.

It is clear by now that STSD is both a perspective on organizational analysis and a normative "theory" about the ways organizations should operate collaboratively, with respect for all the stakeholders. The idea of leadership as an organizational support function emerged from Emery and Thorsrud's (1976) work in the Norwegian "industrial democracy" program. They pressed to move leadership from an individualistic perspective toward leadership as a collective and shared responsibility.

A key element in this process was to create room for participative approaches by not over-specifying processes and structures that did not need to be specified. For example, it is not necessary for a leader or an expert to determine how a team should work. What matters is the expected output and the quality of the services or commodities produced. Team members are encouraged to organize in ways that work best for them as a group to achieve the agreed-on goals. The system relies on their pride, solidarity, and expertise to achieve good outcomes.

This approach is called "minimum critical specification," a concept originally developed by Herbst in his book, *Alternatives to Hierarchies* (1976). His argument is that good organizational practice specifies as few constraints on organizational development as possible because this gives greater freedom to create alternative and possibly better models in the process of problem solving. Only the functions vital to the survival of the system are specified. The rest are worked out by the teams.

Redundancy of Tasks

In Taylorism, the essential idea is to create specialized jobs that optimize productive output. Each employee is only trained to perform one specific job. If a co-worker gets sick, the only option available is to call in a substitute worker to take over the job. Hopefully the management will have trained other employees to take on this specific job but this often is not the case.

Using the concept of the redundancy of tasks, Emery and Trist (1965) argued for a strategy that trains each employee to handle more than one job. This creates flexibility because if a worker gets sick, local co-workers can step in. In addition, everyone in a particular area has a good understanding of the specifics of everyone else's job and thus they are able to participate knowledgably in group decisions. It creates a redundancy of functions, not a redundancy of parts.

Participation

STSD approaches integrate perspectives on structure and change by showing that the need for coordination does not automatically imply hierarchical leadership. Instead, STSD shows that coordination is a system trait that can either be democratically handled or given over to a hierarchical management system. However, STSD has shown that participation in decisions about daily work processes is essential to shaping efficient operations in any organization. Those doing the work are the most knowledgeable about what is necessary for their particular responsibilities to be properly met. Distant leaders at the apex of a hierarchy lack this knowledge.

Participation also means that the local knowledge of those actually involved in the value-production processes can be used to change and improve the operation of the organization. Often those working in a particular area have detailed ideas about how to improve the work processes and results based on their experiences. In hierarchical organizations, they are rarely consulted when work processes are redesigned. In this respect, participation is practically beneficial. In addition, of course, this emphasis on participation reflects the underlying democratic value system that accompanies STSD. The approach aims not only to contribute to the improvement of work processes but also to the ongoing formation of democratic citizens through participatory processes in their daily working lives.

In most successful organizations in the contemporary economy, the involvement of the members is considered vital. In healthy organizations, most members see themselves as directly implicated in the creation of good quality organizational dynamics and outcomes. This goal cannot be met through lectures and directives from hierarchically positioned leaders. STSD has shown that this kind of high member involvement is only possible when organization members participate in the design of the organization and work processes directly. Years of failure to achieve these high involvement goals in hierarchical, meritocratic systems using carrot-and-stick incentives to engage workers should have convinced organizational leaders that neo-Taylorism is no longer the organizational "best practice." Despite the evidence, many public university leaders persist in their Model O-I, single-loop carrot-and-stick behaviors, thereby contributing to the downward slide of their institutions.

Following van Beinum (Eijnatten 1993: 3), we can summarize the contrast between Tayloristic and STSD approaches to work organization as follows:

Taylorism:	*STSD*
• Redundancy of parts	• Redundancy of functions
• External coordination and control	• Internal coordination and control
• Autocracy	• Democracy
• Fragmented socio-technical system	• Optimization of socio-technical system
• Technological rules, labor as a commodity only	• Humans are a resource and complement to technology
• Organizational design based on total task specification	• Organizational design based on minimum critical specification
• Maximum task breakdown, skills as narrowly defined as possible	• Task grouping based on multiskilling
• Building block is one person, one ask	• Components are self-managing social systems
• Alienation	• Involvement and commitment

Universities in Operation—Networking for Power

In addition to strongly believing in the importance of STSD as an approach to follow in the re-creation of public universities, our combined teaching, research, and administrative experiences working in university systems for nearly seven decades lead us to highlight another dimension of universities as organizations: the extensive construction of networks. Looking at networks as key parts of organization is not new, but taking a network perspective on university organization highlights some important features that need to be understood if reform is to be possible.

One key feature of network analysis is that it requires examination of the way a wide variety of institutional decisions are influenced by the power positions of actors in networks that are generally invisible on organizational charts. Examining networks also shows how power positions can be created by establishing networks among actors who have overlapping interests and perspectives. This networking for power involves developing communication processes that bring involved actors' interests and intentions to light and enable the recruitment of other actors. In addition, our approach to network analysis includes material elements like technology, buildings, and other infrastructures as supporting elements capable of increasing the network's power (e.g., control over space or research facilities). Studying university organizations from a network perspective can yield actionable insights about their overall structural, systemic, and power dynamics.

There is an enormous array of network theories. We have elected to organize the following discussion around Actor Network Theory (ANT) as made popular by Callon and Latour (1981), Law (1986) and Latour (1987), because it gathers the power and technology elements that we focus on. While applying it does not provide a full mapping of universities as organizations, it is a productive step toward understanding the actual dynamics in a university without introducing too much theoretical and methodological baggage into the analysis.

Actor Network Theory

Actors and Actants

According to ANT, a network consists both of actors and actants. The actors are the human members of the networks and the actants are the material elements that are employed to reinforce networks. Actants are not considered merely contextual elements, because these non-human elements are designed and used in accordance with the interests of sets of actors accessing them. For example, information and communication technology is not a neutral system. The values of those who design the system, who is allowed to use the system, who inputs the data, and who controls the outputs, show how actants can reflect or reinforce broader organizational values and practices.

Transformation of Interests

A network is a dynamic social structure where learning, strategizing, and acting are key inputs into the ongoing knowledge generation and networking process. At the beginning of the process of creating a network, values and interests generally are not fully aligned. Thus processes must be created by which interests and values are negotiated among the actors until they share them sufficiently to act on them. This is a voluntary process in which actors interact to create shared or at least mutually agreeable perspectives. Such network formation does not always exemplify the art of compromise. It can also involve strategic choices by a potential network member in which they accept the current situation in the network. Further down the road, they may believe that, at another decision point, other values and interests can be negotiated.

Obligatory Passage Point

The actors and actants that become members of a network must have a legitimate reason to be linked in its development. The obligatory passage point refers to the criteria that determine that the actors and actants are legitimate members. An example from university life can be seen in the fight over who should design and run particular teaching programs. One group that can mobilize for this network construction is composed of the professors responsible for the particular teaching. An obligatory passage point for deciding how and what should be taught and how the teaching should be organized is to hold a teaching position in the field in dispute and thus to have the right to participate in decisions.

Decisional Power

The ultimate goal of the network is to have an impact on the institutional decisions made, to have power. This makes it important to understand the kinds of power that are at stake in these processes. Steven Lukes (2005) lays out three dimensions of power. The first is having "power over," and this is the simplest form of power because who has power is visible and evident to all actors. This kind of power, as Weber (1947) saw it, could be linked to a position in the organizational hierarchy, past history, to charisma, and to the legitimacy of institutions and actors. Control of the agenda is another source of power. What is not open for debate is as important as what is discussable. Finally, control over the development and articulation of one's own interests is a fundamental element in power. Gramsci (1975) argued, for example, that the working class adopted the ruling class's construction of what was important in a society and therefore, the ideology and interests of the ruling class had "hegemony" over the working class, i.e., power over them.

A core feature of work processes in universities is created by the many overlapping areas of interest and responsibility. These overlaps may be key features of the organization, but because universities do not revolve around one hub alone, the overlaps can be very complex. A proper organizational analysis in universities necessarily must deal with multiple hubs and then trace the networking for power within and across many subsystems. Stepping back to take an overview, the suggestion is that core operational characteristics of most university processes are determined by the ways faculty, staff, administrators, and students construct enough power and assemble enough resources through networks to prevail in decision-making processes in different areas. The nodes of these power networks may either exist by organizational design or come into being through the skillful actions of particular stakeholder networks. Together these networks can result in a flexible and adaptable system or one that is mired in opposition and strife. Their key operating characteristics center on the actors' ability to create subsets of stakeholder groups that have enough power to further their interests.

For us, ANT has the virtue of adding power and strategic actions to Herbst's (1976) earlier conceptions of networks as socio-technical systems. This ANT perspective shows the way actors operate strategically to build enough support for their own interests but always in the context of the other groups of actors who are doing similar things. Networks for power are created by a process of translating and reconciling interests to achieve an operational consensus, even if temporary, among the members of the network. Some of these networks may become integral parts of a socio-technical system in an organization and be understood to be an important feature of the organization by most members.

These networks are dynamic because the strategic preferences of the actors shift, resources decrease or increase, and new agendas emerge from the external political economy or from internal competition between strategic power networks. Given the various subsystems in universities and their different spans, there are multiple networks throughout the whole system, an organizational reality obscured by organizational charts or authoritarian leaders that view these networks as undermining their "power over." Neoliberal imaginaries about transparency and accountability in the "new public management" are especially incompetent at capturing the functions and value of such networks.

Networking for power is a situated power dynamic within the larger organizational environment and contextualized by the dynamics of external and internal political economies. Among the important contextual elements conditioning these processes are societal perspectives on academic freedom, employee rights to participation in organizational decision making, how national work life is structured, and the goals and challenges faced by the institutions in question. This list could be multiplied, but all networks are affected by these external environments precisely because universities are open systems, even if university leaders and policymakers try to treat them as if they were not.

Financial impacts on networks

Financial Structures

Not surprisingly, financial structures and transactions are very important. Universities are pushed towards becoming market operators when government and private sector funders expect them to "sell" services in order to make money to cover their operations. This change in the funding of public universities has had enormous impacts on the internal networks described above. Neoliberal policies have disarticulated and otherwise threatened many of the more collaborative and collegial processes that were integral to university networks and work organization in the past. In addition, actants in the form of changes in available technology impact operations, including the cost and character of the apparatuses in use, the sources of the funding for them, and the costs of maintaining them, which also affect many networks and drive organizational change. Calls for transparency (e.g., the opportunity for employees to be informed about the economic status of the organization and the demands of external constituencies to be informed about the efficiency and effectiveness of the organization) also influence the decision-making processes and power networks. Often senior administrators attempt to capture and privatize the data on finances as a way of maintaining or gaining "power over" these networks.

Corporatization and Marketization

The processes of seeking unilateral financial control are often called "corporatization" or "marketization." These vague concepts conflate and confuse many discussions and so we now stop the argument briefly to provide an analytical approach to them. The issue with these terms is not that they are meaningless but that they mean too much, too many different things to different stakeholders.

Corporatization and marketization have two kinds of meanings, negative and positive. For neoliberals, they can mean at least three things. They can refer to taking an organization run according to a mix of social and economic principles (e.g., a family business) and shifting it to run according to economic maximization principles only. They can also refer to converting an organization that provides a human service into a service commodity provider that minimizes costs in service provision and maximizes incomes for the leaders and for stockholders or political operators outside the organization. Finally, they can mean rescinding the rights to deference and respect for autonomous craft professionals (academics, doctors, lawyers) and converting them into fee-for-service employees.

For neo-Taylorists, corporatization and marketization involve claiming to run an organization according to economic maximization principles while actually running it for the benefit those in power positions and perhaps their external constituencies. They can also mean adopting the language of business to reconceptualize all functions of a service organization as if it were a commodity manufacturing company. Another approach is adopting the language of business to hide internal reallocations of resources in the organization that serve political interests of key leaders rather than the collective interests of organization members.

For the "casino capitalist" university administrators and policymakers who want to manage universities as if they were hedge funds, corporatization and marketization involve converting an organization that manufactures objects or generates services into an organization whose sole objective is to maximize income for the leaders, subcontractors, and for stockholders over the short term. Another part of the casino capitalist agenda is taking an organization that provided a mix of goods and services and shifting the balance of activities to minimize those goods and services that do not add to the bottom line. This includes outsourcing, short-term contracts, and converting management into capital accounting. Casino capitalist university leaders and policymakers often invite external economic interests into the organization and give them the dominant voice in management decisions. In effect, for them, corporatization and marketization mean treating a non-financial organization as if it were an investment bank focusing on liquidity, cash flow, bond ratings, leveraging capital, and building income sources.

Corporatization and marketization are not inherently negative concepts, despite the fact that many authors use them as epithets in the blame game. In well-managed organizations in the private and public sector, corporatization and marketization can refer to structuring the organization according to the contribution of each participant to the creation of value relevant to the organization's mission. We fully support this approach as consistent with best practices in STSD. However, most contemporary administrators and policymakers fundamentally contradict this meaning of corporatization and marketization by allocating resources away from the value creators and toward the upper ranks of management, their projects, and their external constituencies.

Therefore, the negative and positive meanings of corporatization and marketization should be distinguished carefully. When they appear, readers should ask exactly what is meant and whether or not the authors know what they are talking about.

Neo-Taylorist Network Destruction

In our view, most recent university administrative and policy efforts to enforce a neo-Tayloristic approach toward faculty, staff, and students are a systematic effort to destroy the networks of university actors outside the senior administration. They try to force existing networks to report only upward and to force faculty to report individualistically to the administration. These efforts aim to limit the organizational spans of the faculty and students and thereby convert them into subjects of administrative power.

This process goes on while the administrators themselves constantly network for power within the administrative structure and the external political structures of the public and private sectors. Their competition in these arenas is often quite cut-throat and careerist and they are held accountable by boards of trustees and political authorities as if they were the CEOs of publicly traded stock corporations.

Networking for Power and University Subsystems

Returning to our arguments in the previous chapter, universities have four main subsystems: teaching, research, students, and administration. One of the complexities is that spans of the four systems are unequal. Faculty are the only group who can be members of three subsystems, while the administrators and support staff are only allocated to the administrative system and students are mainly involved in the teaching system. The lack of symmetry means that faculty are the only ones that can participate across most of the functions of the university system, making them a vital link and also a target for administrative efforts at authoritarian control.

Being mainly rooted in one subsystem gives rise to quite different strategies in networking for power within the larger institution. One option is to design a work situation that tries to build a "wall" around a subsystem to protect certain privileges or rights. This plays out differently in the different subsystems. When professors to try to do this, they currently either unionize to protect themselves as a group or they mobilize as a collectivity in a particular discipline to oppose changes they do not want. Alternatively, many professors operate as loners, staying remote from responsibility for common problems and interests. Only under duress can such isolated individuals be mobilized for collective action to protect their own positions.

Similar strategies can be seen among students, who can either mobilize collectively or operate as solo actors seeking to protect their self-interest. Administrators face similar choices between allegiance to their leaders or to their functions and to the constituencies they serve. Some administrators make the choice to go with the bosses and others remain loyal to the stakeholders in the functional areas they administer. These choices give rise to very different career paths and to different forms of strategic networks.

Thus, students, faculty, and administrators all have a variety of ways to occupy and utilize the elements in the social field available to them. We will concentrate on faculty here but similar arguments can be made for students and administrators.

Faculty Networking

The faculty have a legitimate position and responsibility in three subsystems of universities. In principle, this offers them a broad space for engaging in strategic networking activity, but few faculty are aware of this potential. Even fewer are good enough at managing this kind of organizational process to build networks for "power" that can influence decisions in favor of their interests, e.g., new buildings, new faculty positions, or new programs. For the faculty to carry this kind of development forward, two different forms of power are available. Here we return to Lukes' (2005) definitions of power.

The first form is the simple "body weight" kind of power. If many members signal that they have a common interest, they have a chance to impact the decision process because angering a large group has a high cost for administrators and could even result in a "vote of no confidence." The second important form of power is the power to set the agenda. This strategy builds on the intention to control which issues actually become "issues" that must be dealt with by the organization. Putting items on the agenda or keeping them from coming on to the agenda is a key way to exercise power. In Wright and Ørberg's study (2009), steering is a way of trying to stop the faculty from having the ability to put items on or take items off the agenda. We will take this topic up in detail in Chapter 7.

Another example can be given that comes from an unnamed U.S. university where a recent very large donation was given to promote "engagement." This donation and the attendant publicity has meant increased academic attention to and support for community engagement and service learning. It involves nearly $150 million dollars, new administrative positions, grants for the faculty, etc. The administration undertook this, announced it, appointed the administrators, and set the terms of reference for the work all without consulting the faculty, the students, or the community partners. Yet, according to the bylaws of the university, any matter affecting academic policy must be reviewed by the faculty legislative body. Even though this kind of faculty review has been understood mainly as a courtesy in the past twenty years, even such a token gesture for faculty "input" was not made. In response to a faculty challenge about this, the senior administration responded that engagement was "not a matter of academic policy." By defining engagement as non-academic, despite the mission of the engagement grant to change the academic priorities and practices at the university, the central administration excluded the faculty. Examples of controlling the university agenda this way could be multiplied endlessly at this and other universities.

Strategic networking can also mean that external actors can be enrolled to support local university networks. This is often a powerful strategy. Local actors use arguments from external stakeholders to support their internal efforts to change organizational structures and priorities. Such external actors can be peers, public agencies, industry, or even existing legislation that is being ignored by campus actors. These strategies work best when the external actors either have lots of money or political power.

Since a university actually is an open system, a smart strategy for faculty is to include external actors within their own networks who are considered to be significant to many of the stakeholders across the university, including the administration. Doing so actually blurs the line between insiders and outsiders in a productive way. External persons can be highly involved in internal university affairs and will often engage because they are already significant social actors, or see personal economic interests being satisfied, or are simply flattered to be involved in a university in an important way. This strategy is equally available to students and administrators who can line up with external constituencies against their internal opponents and use the external pressures to further their own internal networks and agendas.

Operating in such strategic actor networks raises fundamental questions about the role of leadership in universities. In STSD, there is no formal hierarchical position for leaders and leadership emerges from the organizational structures and operational processes themselves. Under those circumstances, a person who takes on core coordinating activities generally emerges as a leader and engages in liaison activities with other such leaders.

There are limits to this kind of leadership since, in a strategic network, actors will continue to operate as members only as long as it is in their interest to remain in the network. As a result, leadership in networks must work to create consensus on what to do in a way that brings the network members into processes where they have a voice that will be heard by other members and where they can hear the voices of others. Habermas' (1989, 1992) discourse ethics provides a view of the way these communicative processes might operate.

These "informal" networks often operate in complex partnerships with the existing management echelons. Neo-Tayloristic senior administrators generally experience these strategic networks as a threat to their ability to control the university and they often try to encapsulate them, buy them off, or destroy them. Such administrative strategies may work for a while but they are unstable. For example, these strategies can cause the faculty networks that have built up real creative energy for knowledge construction to rebel and repudiate the administration. Academic knowledge construction (research and teaching) depends on faculty involvement, creativity, and engagement in collective efforts to enable research and teaching on issues that they see as important and valuable. As a result, senior administrators cannot easily control these processes or effectively tell the faculty what it is "important" for them to do, no matter how much they would like to.

Student Networking

At this point in the analysis, we have to separate our experiences in Norway from those in the United States because the regimes affecting students are very different. To a certain extent this represents a key differentiator between Europe and the United States regarding public higher education.

Students in Norway

Currently no tuition is charged at Norwegian universities and students can also obtain state subsided loans to cover the cost of living. Students are in a different position from both the faculty and administration. They usually operate within a representative democratic structure of their own. The leadership of student organizations is elected by peers. In addition, students are often represented on university decision-making boards and through these, they are able to impact institutional decisions. The influence of students is also a result of their being invited to participate in different strategic networks for power, either networks emerging from the management echelons or those that are faculty-initiated. In such networks, they play an important role because they present informed views about the way the students judge the merits of particular issues. The situation in Norway is interesting because the university boards consist of insiders (university employees, faculty, and students) and outsiders, and the students represent a block that can shift the weight of decisions between insiders or outsiders. This means that students have real power.

Despite this, Norwegian students are not expected to have any significant impact on teaching. Only on rare occasions and at the initiative of a professor whose courses they attend are they involved as learning partners. Democracy can be taught in abstract intellectual terms in the classroom, but giving students the concrete academic experiences of democratic organizational behavior is rare. The students have a very limited ability to promote this approach to teaching.

Students in the United States

Because of the size and diversity of higher education, meaningful generalizations about the United States are quite difficult. Students at the community colleges and in "for profit colleges and universities" are basically customers and behave as such. The faculty are mainly fee-for-service employees, that is, contracted education providers.

Students in liberal arts colleges, state universities and colleges, and private universities generally compete to be admitted to the best ones and often pay high tuitions and fees. Some of these costs are offset by financial aid and by work-study opportunities that lessen the burden. Much of the required money comes from loans and in cash from families. Students' indebtedness has become a crisis in recent years. Under these conditions, students who compete to enter the institutions have little or no expectation of being included in significant governance decisions. On rare occasions, they might mobilize to protest some particularly salient problem (e.g., buying institutionally branded clothing from overseas sweatshops, sexual assaults or racist behavior on campus) but this is rare and often narrowly focused. Otherwise, students mainly have the power to vote with their feet by choosing particular majors, professors, or colleges within the university, or moving to other institutions, thereby forcing resources to be reallocated by administrators. Since the students are being socialized to be "excellent sheep," in the phrase of Deresiewicz (2014), these forms of resistance are rare.

At the postgraduate level in universities, most students are on full financial aid in the arts and sciences and also work for salaries as teaching assistants and research assistants. Many attempts to organize this labor pool have occurred. A few have succeeded, causing strong mobilizations by senior administrators to try to put a stop to this movement. The difficulties in organizing these students show the fragmented powerbase among even students whose services are crucial to the operation of the institution. In addition, many are admitted to graduate programs because they are needed to teach sections of undergraduate courses and to staff laboratories and other research facilities. They are admitted even though the faculty know that the demand for these very students, after their advanced degree is completed, has all but evaporated in many fields. That is, many graduate students being admitted to then be thrown away.

Post-graduate level law, medicine, and business students largely pay their own way and have somewhat more power but even self-financing students must compete hard to get in. The institutional prestige attached to the credential they are getting is part of the value they are looking for but they also seek to maximize their access to broader professional networks through their universities. They typically are less interested in gaining power and influence within the institutions themselves. They expect their institutions to provide them with connections to future employers and networks of alumni as a condition of their paying such high tuition costs, and they don't want to risk being ostracized.

Administrator Networking

Administrators network for power and we lack needed organizational ethnography on their power plays and strategies. The scene is diverse and there are fractures from top to bottom of administrations and also according to functional areas. These fractures create competitive power dynamics that can become quite aggressive and nasty. Careers are made and destroyed in this environment of administrative entrepreneurs, their dependents, and the constituencies they can mobilize. It would be tedious to rehearse the ways they operate in the abstract, mobilizing each other, staff, other university stakeholders in the other subsystems, and external constituencies. What is clear is that this is a highly fluid, competitive and often cut-throat arena. In these battles, the interests of the students, faculty and staff and even the long-term viability of the university are often treated as "collateral damage."

What Are the Actual "Corporate" Organizational Models in Use outside of Universities?

As stated, what is claimed to be corporatization in higher education is nothing of the sort. Successful private sector firms, especially those in dynamic high tech areas and in service industries, look nothing like current neoliberal universities and university systems. Most firms now are flexible matrix organizations (Herbst 1976) with product or area teams that cross boundaries of expertise from design to production to distribution and sales. These teams usually have a team leader and a set of goals to meet within the larger strategy of the firm. The teams are coordinated and supported by a relatively small number of administrators and the teams and administrators are held responsible to each other for their success or failure.

Details vary greatly from one organization to another, but usually these teams engage in a good deal of dialogue and collaborative problem solving. In many companies, they are free to seek help and advice from other teams, from outside the firm, and from the central administration. One goal is to lessen hierarchy and to put decision making in the hands of those who are doing the work, not because of fairness only but because those who do the work are in the best position to know what is needed to reach the desired goals. This is also a faster adaptive process and often less financially costly. These team-based matrix organizations make better use of the knowledge and human potential of their members than any hierarchical organization ever can. This is why they are coming to dominate the innovative areas of the private sector.

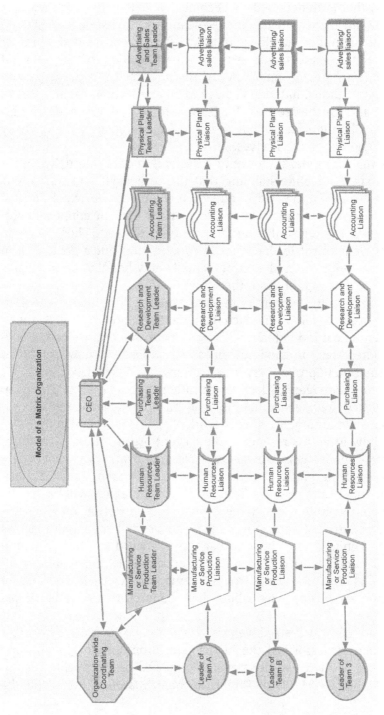

Figure 6.1 One of the Many Possible Variants of Matrix Organizational Structures

When this is understood, it becomes clear that the very features of successful matrix organizations—teamwork, autonomy in making decisions based on knowledge of the work at hand, facilitative rather than coercive leaders, and extensive participation of the relevant stakeholders—are the hallmarks of *Bildung* itself. To participate in such organizations, individuals have to be intellectually acute, able to criticize and synthesize knowledge, able to share knowledge and argue critically but with civility, and to be able to cooperate effectively with people unlike themselves.

This matrix model is not only a systems model internally, but it is also based on understanding that the firm itself and its various product lines exist in a world outside the company to which it must adapt proactively. Actions inside the company must be connected productively to the relevant external conditions as well. These links do require some apical leadership and coordination but a great deal of the linkage with external environments is now handled by the teams within a matrix organization themselves.

We know from working with such organizations that, in a short time, an ethos develops in which team members no longer view themselves as radical individualists. They come to see themselves as having a shared stake in good outcomes and understand how exchanges of information improve everyone's working life. They also come to see leaders and managers as facilitators rather than as bosses. The commitment to quality, accountability, and transparency emerges very often from such an organization of work. This is *Bildung* in action.

Just how little this resembles the current organizational structures in universities is clear. University work organizations violate nearly every one of the practices described above. Hierarchy prevails; decisions are made at a distance from the point where they will have to be applied, multiskilling is actively discouraged, external relationships are often controlled and censored from above, and cooperation across fields and units is actively discouraged and viewed as a loss of central power. Nothing about such a system is accountable, transparent or efficient. It is high time critics stopped demonstrating their ignorance of contemporary business by calling these counterproductive behaviors "corporate."

Beyond its local destructiveness, this parody of corporate behavior has actually transformed the higher education system globally into a radically divided two-tier system composed of a few elite institutions—Oxbridge, Harvard, Princeton, Yale, Stanford, etc.—and the rest.

Models for Change

Clearly universities are not static organizations. While some change processes are planned, many key processes are spontaneous and driven by the active involvements of stakeholder groups, separately or in various networks. Despite the existence of suitable and much fairer alternative approaches like STSD, we have argued that the dominant change model in public universities now is neo-Taylorism. The upside of this process for the administrators is that they can pretend to control the change process simply because they control key financial resources. While operating this way may satisfy their image of themselves as powerful, it is neither an efficient nor productive way to utilize the available talents and resources of faculty, students, and staff. It discourages individual creativity, critical thinking, and shackles constructive energy.

Top-down processes in organizations generally waste energy because stakeholders are both ignored and then provoked by top-down processes and easily become resisters, whether active or passive resistance is their strategy of choice. Failure of senior university administrators to understand the university as a socio-technical system activated through actor networks results in administrative failure, inefficiency, a negative organizational climate, and a failure to fulfill the mission of the institution. Neo-Taylorist behavior often only works to polish the curriculum vita of the top administrators who, if successful in that system, then move on to positions at "better" institutions or to the presidency of a foundation, think-tank, or other institution.

Organizational research shows that any lasting and meaningful organizational change requires broad employee involvement because significant organizational change requires work to be done in new ways. In top-down processes, these new ways are called "implementation." The higher echelons have determined both what the problem is and what the solution should be, usually without consultation with the local stakeholders and often through the use of paid external consultants. The task for central management is both to make all the other stakeholders at least to pretend to agree that the senior administrator's way is a desirable way of working. Senior administrators then train the other stakeholders to perform the mandated new functions or discipline them for not complying. This approach to administration engenders stakeholder strategies that often involve changing as slowly as possible, making as few of the ordered changes as possible, or becoming a local cheerleader for the senior administration and alienating themselves from the rest of the local networks. Making threats and disciplining workers to achieve compliance is costly and undermines morale. Frustrated and negative employees are an expensive presence in any organization. The alternative is to create change processes built on the employees' active involvement, and we now begin the turn in this direction that takes us to the final arguments in this book.

Neo-Tayloristic systems involve significant redundancy of "parts" because they require large numbers of people, each one doing a single or relatively simple task. This is visible in the enormous and increasing administrative bloat in public universities. These redundant "parts" have to be coordinated and controlled from above because the redundant "parts" only have their own skills and specific areas to work in and are not allowed to interact with other parts of the system outside of their boxes. The result is a fragmented set of socio-technical activities, the imposition of machine metaphors on work behavior, high specification of tasks by breaking them into the smallest areas of expertise possible, the alienation of the labor force from work process improvement, and the distancing of decision makers from the empirical realities of the processes they are making decisions about.

By contrast, the STSD is based on all necessary functions being able to be performed by multiple actors, internal and collaborative control and coordination in a team environment, and treating human capacities for change and improvement as a centerpiece of successful operation. It involves the design of tasks that balance production goals and a sustainable work environment. It requires developing broad skills and competences in all workforce members, counting on their involvement and commitment to the organization, and, of course, a genuinely democratic ethos.

Despite the presence of highly educated people in all of the subsystems within higher education, STSD has never been systematically applied in university contexts. Rather, inappropriate, costly, and unproductive neo-Tayloristic management continues to expand. In Chapters 8 and 9 we will show how organizational change can redevelop public universities as organizations designed by and for the organizational stakeholders. Before that, it is necessary to discuss the topics of leadership and steering as they apply to contemporary universities.

CHAPTER 7

Leadership and Steering in Public Universities

◆◆◆

The previous chapter dealing with Socio-Technical Systems Design, networking for power, and neo-Taylorism prepared the ground for our advocacy of participatory, team-based, open systems organizational structures and processes in public universities. *Bildung* for students and faculty and valuable research for service to communities and organizations beyond the university are not possible without participatory democracy and team-based structures as the core organizational features of public universities.

A standard counter-argument employs the same set of excuses made by the power holders to legitimate their authoritarian behavior everywhere over the past two hundred years. The typical claim is that democracy is "inefficient," that urgent decisions must be made efficiently, and that, therefore, the imposition of hierarchical authority is necessary. Another claim often made against democracy is that after a decision is made, it is not possible to hold any particular individual to account for bad results or reward anyone for good ones.

The popularity of these arguments does not make them correct. In Chapter 3, multiple views of democracy were reviewed. The links between democracy and *Bildung* were established, and we also made the claim that democracy is the best decision model for organizations and for society as a whole. Democracy has direct ethical and political value, but we also emphasized that the deliberative dimensions of democracy, well pursued, are capable of producing better, fairer, and more sustainable results. This is because democratic processes incorporate the knowledge and interests of the stakeholders. Various generations of experience with STSD have shown the efficiency and effectiveness of participatory approaches to organizational development and management (Klev and Levin 2012a, 2012b).

Another dismissive stereotype about democracy is that it prohibits the exercise of leadership. This too is wrong. The systemic complexity and multiplicity of activities that compose public universities mean that effective and practical coordination and cooperation among all levels of institutional actors is required. Team-based organizations do not make leadership disappear. Rather, they require multiple kinds and locations of leadership and coordination throughout the organization. This kind of participatory leadership and coordination is now in very short supply in the neoliberal world of public universities. In its place, the authoritarian leaders of neoliberalism are busily consolidating their grip on "power over."

Leadership as Steering

Leadership in neoliberal universities is located at the apex of the organizational hierarchy and is legitimated by authoritarian ideology. Claiming that this position provides a panoptic view of the organization, the apical leadership monopoly is justified on the grounds of efficiency and transparency (Scott 1999). We have pointed out the flaws in this argument in Chapters 5 through 6. Precisely because of their apical position, such leaders have little empirical knowledge of work processes and innovation. They do not have a nuanced understanding of value creation in their own organizations. Knowing so little about the real work processes, they are in no position to make informed decisions.

In addition, for many neoliberal leaders, no amount of power over others is sufficient. Many complain about their insufficient control over the subsystems in universities, excusing the failures of their leadership with references to "loosely coupled systems" and "organized anarchies." Attempting to solve the problems their own authoritarianism creates, they often advocate further concentrations of authority and apply increasingly coercive administrative technologies. This is another example of a Model O-I dynamic in which the unexamined behaviors that create the problem are intensified and thereby make the problem worse (Argyris and Schön 1996).

Some university stakeholders are aware of this problem even though it is obfuscated by the extensive use of rhetorical justifications of unilateral apical authority. The neoliberal rhetorics and practices of accountability, transparency, efficiency, and steering make it appear that the faculty and the students are unruly and need to be controlled. The non-compliant behavior of these supposedly unruly stakeholders is used to explain a stream of administrative failures and subsequent new administrative impositions.

These points do not need to be argued in the abstract. An excellent ethnographic analysis is provided by Wright and Ørberg in their study, "Prometheus (on the) Rebound? Freedom and the Danish Steering System" (2009b). In this study and in another entitled "Paradoxes of the

Self" (2009a), they show how neoliberal policymakers and senior academic administrators in Denmark have used these rhetorics and devices to overcome the relative autonomy of the faculty and student subsystems. In so doing, these leaders have created havoc in the whole public higher education system.

The policymakers began by declaring that the national universities were "self-owned" and therefore autonomous units, free to act as they wished. Then the Danish policymakers imposed a series of non-negotiable requirements these universities had to meet. The policymakers pretended that the "self-owned" universities had complete autonomy to address these requirements as they saw fit. While the requirements were seen as irrational, non-negotiable, and destructive to the mission of public universities, these universities were basically forced to abide by authoritarian impositions while being told they were "free" to do as they wished.

Wright and Ørberg have called this a "steering" model. This refers to a system in which the administration adjudicates to itself the authority to set the goals and imposes accountability downward on the universities, while all the time claiming that it is up to the universities how to respond. This is analogous to Henry Ford's classic response to a question about the possibility of having different colors for his early Ford automobiles. Ford is reputed to have said that customers could have any color they wanted so long as the color was black.

Key to understanding this coercion is that the top administrators and policymakers themselves are not held accountable to the university stakeholders for their steering strategy or for the functionality of the requirements they impose. Universities that fail to respond appropriately to the steering lose national resources. In addition, disobedient local administrative leaders find themselves at immediate risk. They must either obey or leave. Few open avenues exist for faculty, students, and staff to question the targets, dimensions, or logic of the schemes to which they are being held accountable. This is, in effect, a coup using the buzzwords of self-ownership and autonomy to hide a systematic process of stripping resources from universities. It also supports the reallocation of public university budgets toward ever larger numbers of administrative staff, higher administrative salaries, and lucrative business deals for private sector actors given contracts to perform services for the universities.

Denmark is not an exception. These processes are taking place worldwide. Accountability, management by objectives, zero-based budgeting, and steering all sound rational, but when they are unilaterally imposed from above, they are technologies of coercion. The indicators of coercion are non-negotiable demands imposed from above without prior discussion, the development of goals outside the institution, and imposed rather than collaborative implementation processes.

This version of steering is a key element in a larger strategy of "neo-Taylorism." We use "neo" with the term "Taylorism" because F.W. Taylor would never have used the fictions of self-ownership and autonomy to describe the hierarchically imposed work systems he designed. He would have been unapologetic about advocating the unilateral authority of the "bosses" over the "workers."

We do, of course, understand that leadership is a necessary function for any organization to operate effectively. The intelligent coordination of operational activities and strategic action based on authentic understandings of the value creation processes and organizational systems involved is the basis for effective leadership and properly functioning organizations. However, neoliberal steering is not intelligent coordination; it is authoritarian coercion.

There are meaningful alternatives to this coercion. In well designed, successful organizations, both formal leaders and local stakeholders are collectively responsible for the daily operations. These responsibilities include setting goals and determining the best practices to meet them. Some of the local leaders may coordinate this, but every category of stakeholder actively contributes to development and management of the organization's efforts. Leadership emanates from many parts and levels of the organization.

Leadership

All work organizations involve leadership structures and functions, but there are many options in structuring leadership. It is not a "one size fits all" function and must be attuned to the members, structures, functions, and environments of an organization and its broader context. This requires reflexive ways of making sense of the organization, its technologies, and dynamics as an open system nested in a larger, dynamic environment.

The STSD framework introduced in Chapter 6 conceptualizes leadership as a system-specific quality rather than as an individual and personal trait or as a position at the apex of a hierarchy. This contradicts popular views of leadership as an entirely personal talent and activity. In our experience, the reciprocal relationships between leaders, subordinates, and the working teams that operate the organization are central to successful and sustainable organizational processes and outcomes.

On a student visit to a production plant in Western Norway, one of the students asked the CEO what good leadership was. He answered: "Tell me who your colleagues and subordinates are and I can tell you how good you are as a leader." For this CEO, a leader is judged according to how well he or she relates to colleagues and subordinates to reach important goals. In his perspective leadership is relational. This is also in line with our understanding of leadership. It should help set the direction for the work to be done, and leaders also must be able to listen to the local stakeholders and change modes of operation when necessary to facilitate their success. Doing this relies on the ability of leaders to make sense of how organization members experience and can contribute to current work procedures and requirements. A good leader helps coordinate these work realities with the demands of the external environment in a way that the local stakeholders understand and support. The key is the leader's ability to encourage a participatory organizational system where everyone is expected to take part and to contribute knowledge and effort to creating a dynamic, flexible, and well-adapted organization. Participatory leadership does not eliminate a leader's responsibility to achieve agreed upon goals, but requires leaders to involve the whole organization in joint activity to reach objectives.

In a participatory approach, leaders and organization members cooperate to create a participatory leadership function that is not monopolized by a few top people. In a university, this would mean that the goal is to enable every stakeholder to have "space" enough to realize their own potential in administration, research, teaching, and learning. These actions range from leading a small research, teaching or service group to being in charge of a multi-site university. They involve exercising coordination, engaging in effective and constant communication, strategizing, and synthesizing information in actionable ways.

Very little has been published that focuses on detailed analysis of leadership in institutions of higher education. Aside from a few senior administrators' autobiographies after retirement (Duderstadt 2000; Rhodes 2001; Bok 2004), there is little to read that takes account of the particular dynamics of university organizations. The promising analytical effort begun by Clark Kerr (1963)—whose background was in industrial and labor relations—was not followed up by the development of a significant literature. Two useful more recent works are Birnbaum's *Management Fads in Higher Education* (2001) and Tuchman's *Wannabe*

U (2009). Despite this work, anyone interested in meeting leadership responsibilities effectively in universities will not find much of value to read. Most academic administrators, to the extent they try to develop an analytical grasp of their roles, end up accepting the latest management fads, most of which are poorly adapted to work in university environments (Birnbaum 2001). The dearth of analytical discussion of the organizational dimensions of higher education leadership also permits abuses like neoliberal "steering" to go unchallenged and inhibits the development of better understandings of the complex roles of university administrators.

Steering and Leadership Contrasted

Steering and leadership are different but related functions in any organizational system. If we rid steering of the neoliberal meaning it has acquired, steering remains a relevant concept because such functions are important responsibilities in organizations. In public universities, steering implies articulating and championing the general goals for the education, research, and service systems, while leaving it to the university stakeholders at the operational level to work out how these goals can best be accomplished or if they may need to be reconsidered and revised.

The general literature shows that an enormous span of behaviors are called leadership (Lawler 1986; Vroom and Jago 1988; Kotter 1996; Stagic 2003; Northouse 2004; Stech 2004). This is a large and diverse literature. By contrast, the current neoliberal steering approach to leadership originates elsewhere. It comes directly from studies of public administration and recent decades of neoliberal reform in the public sector. This neoliberal public administration origin is revealing. In Norway, current legislation in higher education is often paralleled by laws on municipal politics and public administration. The problem is that public administration is not an appropriate venue from which to draw management technologies for public universities. Universities are constituted of a complex mix of private and public goods and deal with multiple internal and external constituencies. Ignoring the public/private mix in public universities has been a recipe for disaster and has permitted the stripping of public goods from universities to deliver them to private sector actors.

The "new public administration" in particular shows a fundamental distaste for any and all public goods (Behn 2001) and for stakeholder participation. Given the current public policy climate, in most national university systems the steering function is made the responsibility of a ministry of education that sets the general goals for the public university system. These goals are created by those authorities in negotiation with other government officials and then they are communicated down to the individual campuses. In some strongly unionized national systems, union representatives may also participate in these processes. In Norway, where the social partners collaborate in setting policy to some extent, employers, unions, and government together work out policy agendas. At the local unit level, these expectations create goals and frame the space for their concrete deployment and development activities. If this function is handled badly or cynically, the consequences are disastrous, as has been shown by Wright and Ørberg (2009a, 2009b, 2011). In other words, the situation in national university systems varies a good deal from union and employee pushback on ministerial decisions to authoritarian ministerial implementation without significant opposition.

But even in countries like Norway now, the apical actors (boards of trustees, ministries, etc.) decide on the general goals of universities in isolation, without direct connection to the daily operations of universities. They do not have detailed knowledge of the local consequences of trying to implement their imposed goals and they treat problems of implementation that emerge as the fault of the university stakeholders. There are few options for direct feedback between the steering level and daily operations, unless the situation becomes so dysfunctional that there are protests or strikes.

In the U.S., the situation is structurally more complex and yet the outcomes are strikingly similar. There is no ministry of education but rather a U.S. Department of Education with limited legal powers and a modest budget and accreditors who are private sector organizations rather than governmental agencies. Education is a specific responsibility of state departments of education and so the U.S. has 50 mini-ministries of education. While this could have the advantage of permitting a diverse system, most state governments are as fully in the throes of the neoliberal coup as are the national ministries in Europe. The boards of trustees of most U.S. colleges and universities are dominated by wealthy business people from the private sector and their support for neoliberal policies in education is well known. Some states, like Wisconsin, are known for their extremism in neoliberal educational doctrines but the effects of this ideology are seen across the U.S.

Leadership, as we understand it, does involve steering functions but these must be anchored in the context of the relevant local value creation activities. Properly handled, steering is a shared function based on routine interactions and cooperation among the stakeholders and a focus on achieving the larger organizational goals. It may require developing dialogues and new arenas for cooperation, including new subsystems, taskforces, commissions, and working groups. Steering always requires engaging in prioritizations of activities, an often conflictive process that necessitates dialogue and cooperation to sustain the work organization and morale.

Thus local leadership is a complex of behaviors and attitudes, an amalgam of variable roles and activities ranging from participation to coordination and even some disciplining activities. Neoliberal steering shortcuts all of this and holds local apical leaders accountable to externally imposed standards. Such a system discourages any attempt by local administrative leaders to play a participatory, coordinating role in collaboration with local stakeholders.

The explicit aim of neoliberal steering is to force universities to demonstrate that they have spent the funds they have received properly to accomplish goals the external authorities have imposed on them without consultation. Local administrators are treated as the surrogates or enforcers of the demands of the policymakers and budget allocators. In our view, this means that they are not organizational leaders at all.

There is an in-built policing function in this approach. The receivers of the funds are treated as not being worthy of trust. Indeed, the underlying ideology of the new public management is that the receivers of funds are never worthy of trust; they are guilty until they prove they are innocent. They therefore must be disciplined to perform their duties under threat of losing their financial support. Thus the "steerers" adjudicate to themselves the right of speaking for the funders (that is, they claim to speak for the "public" whose tax monies they are allocating and who they also propagandize by claiming that public universities are wasteful and untrustworthy). The public pays the taxes that support higher education but they have no say in these matters (Behn 2001). The steerers set themselves up as the defenders of the taxpayers when in fact they are key actors in the process of privatizing the public resources paid for by the citizens through taxes to benefit private interests.

To summarize, one set of leadership concepts and practices has emerged from organizational theory in which team coordination and acting as process champions are central features and are central to best practices in contemporary dynamic organizations. Another set of concepts centering on the authoritarian use of the concept of steering in public universities has emerged from practices in public administration under the aegis of neoliberalism.

The current situation of contemporary public universities is influenced by approaches drawn both from best practices in creative businesses and from neoliberal public administration. Both approaches are being applied in to public universities simultaneously and indiscriminately. We regularly observe public higher education administrators evoking coaching and participative leadership postures in their public rhetoric while operating behaviorally by means of neoliberal coercive steering and accountability. They issue homilies on education, diversity, community and transparency while behaving toward faculty, students, and staff as authoritarian bosses.

This duplicity is exacerbated in multi-unit systems such as the state university systems in the United States and in national public university systems in Europe. Neoliberal steering radically simplifies the job of state departments of education and national ministries of education. They can set standards and create policies independently of the universities and then allocate funds competitively according to a coercive accountability model with little or no knowledge of academic work or the local consequences of their actions. Their ignorant decisions are backed by their budgetary control and their ability to promote legislation supporting their actions, regardless of the consequences for the stakeholders in universities (see McGettigan 2013).

Just because neoliberal steering is a widespread practice does not mean it is a competent approach to university management. Widespread phenomena, like air pollution or global warming, are not good merely because they are broadly distributed. We agree that all organizations need explicit standards, quantitative and qualitative, to measure performance and to identify areas for improvement in their operations. But in neo-Taylorist steering schemes, the goals and indices for measurement are decided solely by the policymakers and local senior administrators without meaningful contextual knowledge or consultation. The local actors who know the local situation and understand what is possible and what may not work or at least needs to be modified play no role in the process. Their local knowledge is treated with disrespect and suspicion or even as an obstacle to the perfect marketization of their institutions. Steering without participation in developing the indicators by which performance is steered is an authoritarian coup over universities. It further consolidates the grip of financial elites over the resources and functions of public institutions.

Forces for Change in Higher Education

In the current era of free market authoritarianism, the concept of freedom is widely used in public discourse to legitimate reforms in the public sector. It is claimed that organizations are "freed" from overburdening and presumably economically irrational governmental and internal regulation. Users of the institutions are "freed" to be rational consumers of services whose quality is guaranteed, transparent, and the value of which the consumer decides. At the same time, tough leadership is constantly praised and so-called leaders are paid a king's ransom to follow neoliberal schemes. The image of market freedom is used to cover up this authoritarianism and exploitation.

This neoliberal dream of a "stark utopia" (Polanyi 1944) is impossible. Leadership can support people's freedom but only by supporting organizational units and dynamics based on significant and regular high degree of participation and the freedom to make their own choices about how to accomplish agreed-on goals. This is because the local stakeholders are the only ones with sufficient knowledge and experience of their working conditions to be able to devise, critique, and implement functional plans. In organizations with strong values for stakeholder engagement, authoritarian governance is ruled out.

The current public university world is based on distrust and disrespect for the public sector, disdain for the integrity of public sector actors, and the repudiation of a notion of society as more than a marketplace with a few winners and an army of losers. These practices set up policymakers and local administrators as the referees who hold the stakeholders to account. They are the police. The system now is adversarial and competitive, evoking a vision of the market not unlike that of the nineteenth century ideologues who appropriated a false view of Darwinism to legitimate their exploitative activities as capitalists. For us, this is inimical to the management and development of public universities in which authentic participation and *Bildung* are core features.

The Struggle for Control over Higher Education

The above analysis is not new. Neo-Marxist perspectives have been applied to higher education reform already (Shumar 1997; Slaughter and Leslie 1997; Giroux and Giroux 2004; Slaughter and Rhoades 2004; Bousquet and Nelson 2008; Canaan and Shumar 2008, and many more). We do not ignore these analyses. Rather, we seek to add dimensions to them by making it clear that universities remain contested ground where democracy and authoritarianism are clashing head-on. This struggle is not only about social class in general but also about organizational dynamics that support different class positions in public institutions like public universities.

Earlier in the book (Chapters 3 and 4), the meritocratic competitions as they apply to students, faculty, staff, and administrators were the focus. Competitions simultaneously alienate actors from one another, instrumentalize all relationships, and produce conformist behavior in all stakeholder categories. This fragmented situation matters in various ways. It provides ready scapegoats outside the self to blame mediocre personal results on. It encourages each stakeholder group to ignore the role of their own behaviors and attitudes in perpetuating situations that are prejudicial to themselves and others.

From our perspective, there are no real winners in this competition because all the stakeholders are victimized in different ways. To be sure, some are much better paid victims than others, but they remain victims of the destruction of the meaning and value of the public universities they are charged with managing, enacting, learning in, and improving. Even the less well-paid victims like the faculty and the often-indebted victims like the students bear some responsibility for the decline of public universities by acquiescing to these meritocratic competitions. They all experience the ills personally.

Well known conservative "rants" about tenured radicals, lazy "deadwood," and good-for-nothing faculty who have never done an honest day's work remain popular but they are basically insulting stereotypes perpetrated by people who have no understanding or engagement with academic work. There are a few no-good faculty in this world, just as there are some no-good administrators, incompetent and lazy staff, useless students, and stupid politicians. These drags on the system are a distinct minority. In our view, the problems are more serious and difficult to deal with. Rooting out a few malingerers would be relatively easy.

For us the central problem is that, over a number of generations, faculty have converted themselves into members of disciplines, departments, professional associations, into editors of disciplinary journals, reviewers of disciplinary grants, and so on. In Ellen Messer-Davidow's term, they are now "disciplined" (Messer-Davidow 2002) to accept the boundaries of their academic discipline and department, to color inside the lines, and to fend off any and all attacks on their space, resources, and subject matter. The mandated noncooperation among academic departments gives deans and higher administrators all the power they need because they only have to manipulate university resources and make departments and disciplines compete for them and their power at the apex of the system is assured.

This is not to say that within the disciplines, faculty are particularly cooperative. When frontally attacked by others, they may rally together out of self-interest but, in our experience, within department competition for gaining higher merit raises, faster promotions, bigger offices, and more graduate assistants trumps the kind of supposed intellectual solidarity that is a consistent founding myth of most disciplines and departments. Many academics are one-person businesses building their own "brand" by means of a curriculum vitae, national and international standing, the ability to get external support, invitations to be on editorial boards, grant review boards, etc.

When such people speak of academic freedom, they often mean freedom to be an entrepreneur in whatever way they see it fit in their department, college, university, and national and international arenas. They feel entitled to speak their minds on most subjects and expect to be listened to but they only rarely rally in defense of colleagues whose rights to free speech have been abridged either within or beyond the university. Given this, we think it is disingenuous for radical individualist academic entrepreneurs to disparage academic administrators who are similarly entrepreneurial or students who are trying to make pragmatic educational and economic decisions on their own behalf. The moral high ground that many academics claim to occupy does not seem quite so high to us.

For students to complain about the self-serving and self-regarding behavior of faculty is common and occasionally the complaints are legitimate. But students, especially now that they are told to behave as customers, are capable of intensely self-regarding, competitive, and hostile behavior toward each other. They often show a startling lack of interest in the fates of anyone but themselves and their personal goals.

Staff are locked in hierarchical competitions with each other and to keep their positions in the system secure. Solidarity and cooperation is rarely rewarded; more often it is punished. Administrators are under the gun from above, compete with each other, and often are intensely disliked and disrespected by those below them, hardly a joyful working life.

It is hard to believe that the world we have just sketched out is actually "good" for any of the stakeholders. All are playing defensive or aggressive human roles, operating in a world in which everyone else above is a threat, those on the same level are competitors, and those below are to be exploited. The main actors, policymakers, university administrators, faculty, staff, and students, all think they know what is going on, all understand the situation differently, and few have much of an idea how the system as a whole is working. Most ultimately become victims in someone else's game. This is the opposite of the premises on which democracies, *Bildung*, and participation are based.

Leadership revisited

State-of-the-art leadership involves the local functions of coordination and external liaison as well. This requires knowing the stakeholders, understanding their work situations concretely, and being at their disposal for support, advice, and coordination. To function this way, local leaders must be in daily interaction with the local organization members on all levels. Goals have to be negotiated, human resource issues must be worked out, markets for their students and research products need to be understood and articulated with.

From the outset, we argued that universities should be democratic institutions because *Bildung* cannot be produced in authoritarian organizations. This means that participative management is not just the best option. It is the only option for public university leadership. Properly practiced, as in STSD, participative management builds on stakeholders' capacity to participate in making good decisions and to be involved learning and developmental activities that lead to even better future decisions (Klev and Levin 2012a, 2012b) and more skillful enactment of agreed-on solutions. This is participatory democracy in action (Pateman 1970, 2012).

Participative management, however, does not arise on its own. It has to be learned through active and engaged processes that are themselves participative. These processes must be participative in structure and operation, and so an essential task for participative leadership is to create good learning opportunities for all the stakeholders. The goal is to shape learning situations that enable participants to learn to handle tasks without being directed by someone in an authority position.

As STSD shows, doing this results in redundancy of competences and increases the capacity of the organization to handle unplanned incidents. Over time, this competence building enhances the whole organization's ability to react flexibly and effectively to future challenges. Stated another way, creating these learning opportunities is also a step up the ladder to creating a learning organization (Argyris and Schön 1996).

Another key dimension of leadership in university organizations is direct engagement in the current discourses and debates on campus. There are always important issues at stake for some group of actors on every campus. There are many campus debates about issues of national and international importance and about the bulwarks that support civil society. Many of the issues that arise deal with problems of uneven interest to different groups of stakeholders but this does not mean they can be dismissed. For anyone who believes in civil society, addressing issues of importance to particular stakeholder groups is a core process in the ongoing development of democracy. It involves sharing of experiences and learning about the situations and interests of others. A living democracy depends on continued discourses that include everyone's issues, which helps create an understanding of the different and even competing goals and interests of different groups. It is a living portrait of what we have to do to maintain civil society. It requires an active practice of the harmonization of interests and needs if good decisions are to be made and implemented. Issuing white papers and op-ed pieces is no substitute for promoting and participating in these debates in an open and knowledgeable manner.

Lest we be misunderstood, we want to emphasize that we do not believe that democracy in public universities should be built on creating consensus among the stakeholders. The interests of stakeholders may be in real conflict and often require complex negotiated agreements. Consensus can be the enemy of respect for real differences and can coerce minority positions into silence. Organizational democracy does not mean that everyone will experience that her or his points of view will always "win" in decision-making processes. Accepting participative decisions for the common good is part of what it means to live in an organizational democracy and in civil society. What legitimizes the decisions is the transparent participative process by which decisions are reached and the openness of the process to diverse positions and arguments.

Operating in a democratic public university requires avoiding two extreme positions. A poorly led democratic system can end up with every stakeholder group blocking the actions of every other group. The result is no change at all. This is a road to disaster since a democracy that survives needs proactive and pragmatic engagements that find smart new solutions both to new and old problems. Facilitative leadership skills are vital in avoiding stalemates.

Another danger is manipulation of the processes in the ways Sherry Arnstein (1969) laid out in her famous "ladder of participation."

Arnstein's ladder included various levels of participation starting with manipulation and therapy, which she classified as "nonparticipation." Moving up the ladder, she placed informing, consulting, and placating, which she classified as "tokenism." Finally, she moved upward to partnership, delegation, and citizen control which she called "citizen control." Whether or not one accepts the details of this ladder, it is clear that a most of what happens to faculty, students, and staff at public universities now takes the form of "tokenism." We are asked to provide "input" or we are "consulted" and then we are ignored while senior administrators claim to have provided a participatory process. It takes very few such experiences to bring democratic processes to an end. The kind of participatory democracy found in STSD and that we advocate for public universities is built on "citizen control," not on "tokenism."

This closely matches the argument of Robert Flood and Norma Romm who in, *Diversity Management: Triple-loop Learning* (Flood and Romm 1996) argue that, in addition to participation and social reorganization, processes of this sort are not complete until the way power changes hands has been assayed and the resulting arrangements satisfy the stakeholders.

Conclusion

Throughout Part II, we have infused the discussion of public universities with arguments about organizational structures and operations based on socio-technical systems design, actor network theory, and arguments about leadership and steering functions. We have also criticized the loose use of terms like corporatization and marketization and replaced them with a more detailed analysis of the structures and operations of dynamic creative organizations.

We have kept a constant contrast going between these STSD and dynamic participative systems and the neoliberal, neo-Taylorist approaches to the organization of public universities that currently dominate the world scene. We have rejected neoliberal claims that the authoritarianism they impose is either good business practice or economically rational. In place of this, we have advocated the creation of STSD organizational dynamics based on collaboration, respect, and coordination. We argue that only in collaborative, respectful democratic universities can competent, respectful democratic citizens be nurtured.

Now the question is how such an ideal future could be accomplished. We turn to this in Part III.

Part III

◆ ◆ ◆

The Road Forward: Action Research for *Neue-Bildung* in Public Universities

In the final part of this book, we bring the components of our argument together by linking *Neue-Bildung*, organizational change and development, and action research. We argue that action research is the most promising approach to re-create public universities as a core element in democratic civil societies. Because action research is not well known in academia and in the policy literature on higher education, we introduce action research, its approaches, and history in Chapter 8. Following this, we present ways action research could be deployed to re-create authentically public universities and to exile neoliberal neo-Taylorists from these vital social institutions.

Action Research as a Strategy for Organizational Change

◆◆◆

This book points inexorably to the need for a radical change strategy to re-create public universities. We argue that universities must become organizations that systematically learn and improve their own structures and operations to promote processes of collaborative knowledge production and democratic citizen development. In Part II, we argued that the ways these organizations are structured, how the work processes are organized, and the kinds of leadership exhibited are the core features affecting knowledge generation and transmission processes at universities. In Part I, we argued that a key purpose of public university education is to prepare students in the practices of democratic citizenship.

For these functions to be performed, participation in learning processes must be properly structured and cannot be restricted to students and faculty. They must include the administration and staff because administrators must play a role in creating and protecting learning opportunities on campuses and in coordinating the many different learning structures across universities. The staff members must support these processes and understand their purpose and meaning and importance.

Most university faculty now are encouraged to view research as their main "learning" activity because research is so fundamental both to their individual careers and to effective teaching. This is partly because research accomplishments are emphasized in all kinds of professorial evaluation schemes. However, fewer faculty and very few administrators seem to understand that teaching also is a form of new knowledge generation both for students and for the professors. We hasten to point out that this only holds when teaching is done by applying interactive pedagogies. We affirm this because we understand teaching to be a co-generative process (Greenwood and Levin 1998b; Levin and Greenwood 2001b) capable of creating new insights through social interaction in the classroom between professors and students, among students, and between students and professors both inside and outside the classroom. This has been our experience over decades of teaching and we are in good company in understanding teaching this way (Freire 1970; Dewey 1990).

It has been clear for at least a century, since John Dewey formulated the model clearly (Dewey [1938] 1991), that learning through direct engagement with concrete problems in a collaborative learning environment improves learning, retention, and the quality of academic life for everyone involved. Because this learning is a result of cooperation among the parties, it already involves the practice of some of the skills required for democratic life. In this case, they are skills aimed at solving salient academic problems or puzzles, but they are suitable for use in many other arenas. This kind of learning is directly connected to the evolutionary development of individual work trajectories and maturation, as well as to improving the quality of cooperation with other learning partners (Nelson and Winter 1982).

Earlier we argued that current university organization models are dysfunctional and need to be changed. We see the long-term survival of today's public universities in their current form as quite unlikely. They are stressful, economically unsustainable institutions that generally are unsuccessful at meeting the promises they make to most stakeholders. They are ripe for fundamental change.

The key question is how such a profound transformation of universities into genuinely participatory learning organizations could take place. Transformations in the opposite direction have already occurred and are experienced around the world. We have seen how Danish higher education is changing dramatically for the worse as a consequence of centralized political decisions (Wright and Ørberg 2009a, 2009b, 2012). There, the top-down processes create a new bureaucratic, authoritarian structure for the public university system. By the use and abuse of ministerial power, the formal structures are being changed to create a hierarchical neo-Tayloristic system that only intensifies the worst features of what we already see today in universities. Employees in that system are learning that the best survival strategy is to follow the old power-play rules within the context of the new bureaucracy. It seems that the emerging Danish public university will have all of the faults of the previous system and none of the benefits it once produced. This is not university reform. It is the demolition of public higher education. The Danish story, unfortunately, is not unique.

Building a New Public University

The new public universities we want to create have the central mission of contributing to the building of a democratic society through a central emphasis on individual and social *Bildung*, through research, teaching, service, and social mobility through higher education. This university transformation must be broadly participatory because a democratic organization producing democratic citizens cannot be created by authoritarian processes. We have looked in vain to the current organizational and management consulting literature for models of such participatory processes in public university reform.

Conventional Change Models versus Action Research

The conventional organizational change models, leadership change strategies, and consulting strategies that have been deployed in general do not work in public universities. These conventional strategies have had their day and made lots of money for "expert" consultants and executive search services. The results are public universities that are more inefficient and costly, more poorly managed, produce worse educational outcomes, produce more irrelevant research, and are increasingly unpleasant places to study and work. Clearly it is time for a fundamental change in organizational development strategy.

Our own experiences in organizational change center on action research (AR). AR's focus on participatory change processes and the expertise developed in managing these processes makes it viable for developing democratic change processes in public universities. To be an AR strategy, it must engage students, faculty, staff, and administrators collaboratively, control costs, ensure high quality educational experiences, improve research strategies and outcomes, and provide relevant public service at a cost affordable to the working and middle classes. The cost is relevant because a university not affordable to working- and middle-class students is not a "public" university.

Both of us are long-time practitioners and proponents of AR. We have written various books individually and collaborated on two editions of a well-regarded introduction to action research and we have written numerous articles on action research and higher education.[1] We have worked as change agents applying action research in the private sector, public sector, and in educational institutions. We have published peer-reviewed articles based on our AR projects, on our teaching experiences, and on our university reform efforts. All of these experiences point us toward AR as the best feasible option we have identified for the transition of public universities away from neoliberal pseudo-corporate structures and toward collaborative teaching, research, and service to democratic societies.

Many others agree that fundamental change in public universities is needed. The problem is that few have explored how to accomplish it concretely. Partly, this lack of concreteness arises from a combination of pessimism and a misjudgment that neoliberalism will collapse under its own weight. We also think this stems from the phenomenon we have explored in Part II of this book. Very few of the affected stakeholders have developed a differentiated, actionable understandings of universities as organizational systems. Too many critics accept the power of the neoliberal managers and their seeming immunity to resistance. We are optimists about the possibilities but not we are not naïve. We see and understand that AR has its own limitations in dealing with entrenched authoritarianism. Conducting AR in the context of hegemonic neoliberalism is a daunting task. Still, we have concluded that no other course of action remains open that could promise a meaningful future for public universities.

Accepting the power of the neoliberals has converted too many critiques, including some of our own, into nostalgic commentaries and jeremiads rather than projects for change. Despite our criticism of the present state of affairs, we think these catastrophist views are wrong. Following Gibson-Graham (2006) and generations of action researchers, we think that solutions are to be found only by stepping outside conventional thinking about the economic and political determinants of the decline of organizations and institutions in advanced capitalist societies.

Why Armchair Research Will Not Solve These Problems

Most research on higher education is armchair research, using databases, some observations, and existing conceptual frameworks for analysis without making recommendations about how to change the current course of history and without direct engagement in the needed change processes. An important strength of AR is that it connects research to the change process by combining cycles of action, reflection, and reformulation. This makes the change process itself the practical experimental arena and simultaneously the centerpiece of research learning. As Kurt Lewin said, the best way to understand something is to try to change it (Lewin 1948). So to change the university, you must operate in it and struggle with the powers that be on their own fields of action. We want to take an AR step toward exploring ways to initiate and sustain democratic change in these institutions.

Why Change Is Possible

We believe that fundamental, meaningful change is possible because public universities are failing too many categories of stakeholders at all levels. Students are receiving an impoverished and largely useless "education" at a very high cost. Faculty are being occasionalized and subjugated. They rapidly are losing academic freedom, job security, and decent salaries. Staff members live on the knife edge of obedience to superiors while attempting to satisfy increasingly imperious student consumers and to implement administrative systems that are unworkable. Many of their functions could be outsourced at any moment in the current climate.

Administrators find themselves operating as adversaries to the constituencies they are supposed to manage. They are subjected to the non-negotiable demands of boards and policymakers. All but a few "fat cats" in this system are getting cheated, impoverished, and manipulated. Most of the stakeholders know this on some level. We believe that any institution that satisfies so few stakeholders is ripe for fundamental change. In any case, unless we fight for fundamental changes of direction, leadership practices, and organizational dynamics, we are complicit in permitting the ongoing expropriation of public universities for private gain.

It is worth remembering that this expropriation is a theft of facilities and capacities paid for mainly by society through their taxes. The taxpayers pay for public universities either indirectly because because public universities have tax-exempt status in most countries or because a portion of their taxes are used to fund public universities. The neoliberal coup thus steals from the public what the public has bought and paid for over and over again. This expropriation of public goods is similar to the privatizations of the public goods in the countries of the former Soviet Union, privatizations that created vast new fortunes for the few and significant poverty and loss of opportunities for the majority.

Since AR is not widely taught and is unknown to many who have passed through universities, we begin this final section of the book by explaining what AR is and then we show how AR is relevant to the reform of public universities. We close this chapter with a discussion of the strengths and weaknesses of AR as it approaches public university reform.

What is Action Research?

Action research involves bringing action and research into an integrated, interactive relationship. Action research creates new knowledge by initiating actions aimed at solving recognized problems for and with the stakeholders who have a legitimate interest in those problems. For action to be well directed and designed, it must be based on in-depth understanding and information about the existing situation and this requires solid research data and proper analysis. In action research, this research process involves the stakeholders directly as co-researchers and interpreters of the research throughout the process. This is not a democratic gesture. Action research requires it because only the legitimate stakeholders have sufficient experience and understanding of their own work situations to be able to provide meaningful data, analysis, and to have realistic understandings of the implications of choosing particular pathways for change.

Action research is based on the premise that all organizations can best be changed through developmental phases built around collaborative organizational learning processes (Bateson 1972; Argyris and Schön 1996; De Gaus 1997; Senge 1990; Scharmer 2008). An action research team is a "learning organization" and learning organizations are characterized by adaptability, flexibility, and dynamic change. They respond opportunistically to create adaptive responses to complex and differentiated internal challenges and external environments. Anyone who knows about universities knows how unlike learning organizations current universities are (Greenwood 2009) and thus is it not surprising that AR is very rare in university environments.

Concrete collaborative social experimentation creates learning opportunities. This learning builds the capacity among the collaborators to identify what to do next in an ongoing process aimed at achieving collaboratively set goals. Among other things, this means that the design of learning arenas is vital to such processes.

AR also brings us back to the concepts of public and private goods, because all stakeholders in an organization have both personal rights and mutual responsibilities. Balancing rights and responsibilities in a sustainable way is essential for the development of open and fair learning organizations. Maximizing personal gains regardless of the impact on others destroys the social fabric and the public good.

Who Participates?

In action research, all relevant categories of stakeholders are invited to participate in the process. This is because action research requires both local participants and professional researchers to take part in the co-generation of new knowledge. AR is also a democratic research procedure because it leaves space for members of the organization to participate both in the practice of research and in the creation of new knowledge.

This is not merely an ethical or political choice. Local stakeholders know far more about their life and work situations than any outside researcher can. They have years of experience to contribute along with their own analyses of the situation. They also have a good understanding of the consequences (including the risks) of taking particular courses of action in their local context.

Professional researchers help coordinate the process and have methods and facilitation techniques to assist in creating this collaborative learning community. They also have knowledge of other possibly similar situations elsewhere and the successful and unsuccessful strategies in those situations. So their role is also important. Together the researchers and local stakeholders participate in the same co-generative learning experience.

In AR, the design of learning arenas is usually the responsibility of the professional researcher who functions as the process coordinator and who provides supportive input to keep the research process up and running. This places a premium on the facilitator (researcher) being able to manage the change process by having the necessary skills and knowledge to construct productive learning situations.

Who Takes Action?

Once the problems are collaboratively defined and researched to the satisfaction of the collaborating stakeholders, actions to improve the situation are jointly designed. These designs too require the experience and expertise of local stakeholders. Expert outsiders often construct elegant change processes that are dead on arrival when attempts are made to put them into practice locally.

The collaboratively designed actions then are taken by the stakeholders. Implementation is not a matter of an expert outsider or a boss telling the local stakeholders what to do. They act on the designs they have co-created because they understand and believe in their practicality. The collaborators then evaluate how well their actions functioned in producing the desired outcomes. If the results were not satisfactory or if new issues emerged as a result of the process, further cycles of research, action, and evaluation are undertaken until the stakeholders are satisfied with the outcomes.

Action Research as Scientific Research Practice

Action research, thus, is a form of in-context experimentation based on application, evaluation, redesign through lessons learned, and future cycles of application. It is fundamentally different from the conventional social sciences that emphasize taking an objectivist, "spectator" position and theorizing the results of the research. Conventional research draws conclusions without designing action to ameliorate the problems studied and thus does not "test" the viability of the analyses in practice. Action research, in contrast, follows the scientific method of testing knowledge in relevant settings and learning from the failures and successes in order to design new and more effective courses of action. In this regard, action research is a more "scientific" practice than armchair social science.

Successful action research projects produce practical and relevant outcomes (solutions to the pertinent issues as defined jointly by the stakeholders and researchers). They also must produce publications that analyze and explain the experiences gained in the work and the methodological learning created in the project. This enables others to learn from each project. A variety of public reports for the stakeholders and broader constituencies may also be produced. Some projects cause more change on the ground than publications and reports. Others reverse the emphasis. There is no general rule but both action and research must be present. If a process is action without research or research without action, then it is not action research.

To synthesize these points, we provided the following brief definition of AR in our book, *Introduction to Action Research*:

> Action research is social research carried out by a team that encompasses professional action researchers and the members of an organization, community, or network ("stakeholders") who are seeking to improve the participants' situation. AR promotes broad participation in the research process and supports action leading to more just, sustainable, or satisfying situation for the stakeholders. Together, the professional researcher and stakeholder define the problems to be examined, cogenerate relevant knowledge about them and, learn and execute social research techniques, take actions, and interpret the result

of actions based on what they have learned. (Greenwood and Levin 2007: 3)

Action research necessarily takes a long-term perspective because the solutions and innovations are evaluated in the light of the sustainability of the processes being developed and their fairness to all categories of stakeholders. Doing this depends on long-term vision, shared human experience, and mutual respect. By contrast, the short-term pseudo-maximizing imposed by neoliberal models of organizational change emphasizes the hierarchical authorities' perspectives on change processes. They involve the imposition of change from the apex of the organizational pyramid. Most of the benefits arising from decisions accrue to administrative bosses, boards of trustees and governors, and external investors. The daily consequences of their decisions for the legitimate stakeholders are largely ignored or considered irrelevant because pseudo-economic arguments are used to justify the pain of the many for the benefit of the few.

Action Research and Public Goods

We argued in Part I that, despite current neoliberal dominance, it is essential to recognize that public universities produce both private and public goods. It is a core mission of public higher education to produce both kinds of goods in a sustainable balance. This balance is never perfect and must constantly be calibrated. The sustainability of public universities depends on this constant calibration.

Many of the stakeholders in public universities produce public goods without which these institutions cannot function. Key components of these public goods are cooperation, loyalties to the larger institution, work that permits the institution to sustain itself even though the work does not generate an immediate financial profit, etc. Jettisoning functions that do not generate immediate "income" for someone in a position of power or an external constituency is an expropriation of public goods. Failing to redistribute incomes to units that are necessary to the institution at large and produce teaching, research, and support without producing financial profit for the institutional leaders attacks a core meaning of the concept of a university. These financializations of public university management have led to the current collapse of public universities and the exploitation of students, faculty, staff, and junior administrators. It also is one of the main causes of the massive annual cost increases of these failing public institutions.

The History of Action Research

We assume that most readers are not familiar with the history of action research and so we now provide a brief introduction. AR has a long history but has been repeatedly ignored during the development of the authoritarian models of public higher education and in the hyper-development of conventional social research in the neo-Tayloristic disciplinary model.[2]

Action research can be traced back to the early 1940s. At Cornell University, the University of Illinois, and ultimately at MIT, a Polish-born German refugee to the United States, Kurt Lewin, worked as a social psychologist on the promotion of social change processes. How to accomplish significant and socially valuable social change was his central research question. Unlike many others at that time, Lewin had developed participatory strategies for bringing about change. In one famous project, Lewin focused on the efforts during the Second World War to have housewives utilize cow, sheep, and pig tripe as meat for the family. Meat was scarce because of the war and tripe is both nutritious and abundant. However, tripe was, in most U.S. and European diets, unpopular and even made some groups squeamish.

Rather than ordering the housewives to cook tripe, Lewin gave the women the resources and training to practice preparation of tripe-based dishes. By doing this, they acquainted themselves with this food item, innovated recipes that created flavors to their liking, and they began to use these dishes at home. This strategy contrasted starkly with the typical approach of a nutritional expert or government authority telling the women that tripe would be good for food and that they should use it. Lewin's participative approach worked and gained attention for this action research approach to social and behavioral change on subjects far afield from tripe.

Parallel developments took place at the Tavistock Institute of Human Relations in London. A research group led by Eric Trist was working on the reindustrialization effort after the end of the Second World War. In a famous study of British coalmining practices, Trist and Bamforth (1951) developed some of the ideas of what came to be called the "socio-technical systems design (STSD)" perspective. The Australian and Norwegian psychologists, Fred Emery and Einar Thorsrud, eventually joined the Tavistock group and became central figures in this action-oriented socio-technical work. STSD subsequently became one of the foundations of AR.[3]

Trist and Emery collaborated to show the existence of a strong connection between the production technology in use and the social and psychological welfare of the workers using it. To create a good working environment, Trist and Emery learned that the technology in use, to be effective and to enhance workers' capacities, must enable the creation and maintenance of a desirable quality of work life for the production teams. To accomplish this, Trist and Emery engaged the workers in dialogues about their work and the technologies they used.

Eventually, Trist and Emery realized that the workers should have significant impact on the actual design of work if effective work systems were to be created and sustained. They learned that worker involvement was not just an equity question but one of being able to generate and apply the relevant knowledge of all the stakeholders to the change processes in an effective way. Thus, broad participation became central to this kind of developmental work. Because the relevant stakeholders had participated in the developmental process as genuine partners, the design and implementation belonged to them, matched their interests, and respected their experiences.

AR is always connected to change processes. It aims to bring about concrete, fair solutions to important stakeholder problems. The problem-solving process produces the research and the research helps produce designs for future actions aimed at improving the situation for the stakeholders. This is why we say that an action research project integrates problem solving with development of scientific knowledge in cycles of discovery, redesign, application, evaluation, and further discovery.

The Role of Research–Based Knowledge

Research-based knowledge does feed into AR problem-solving processes. Existing research is regularly deployed to assist in generating insights and strategies that can be transformed to practical action to solve the problem at hand. Researcher experience from other cases can often help local stakeholders winnow the possibilities they generate collaboratively or assist them in thinking of new strategies stimulated by experiences from beyond their local areas of experience. Data sets and relevant statistical studies on problems of interest to the AR group are regularly utilized as are a variety of sampling, interviewing, and data analysis techniques.

Personal Participation

An important feature of AR is that participants, both stakeholders and professional researchers, are convoked in a way that requires them to embody their roles. They are encouraged to inhabit their existing roles as particular kinds of social persons with their unique backgrounds, skills, and commitments. They enter the process as authentic participants who have certain basic human and social rights and valuable knowledge and experience to share.

This openness and respect for the knowledge and interests of others means that action research participants are unlike neoliberal meritocratic strivers who seek to game all processes for personal benefit or for the benefit of their supporters. Participants in action research have rights only insofar as they take on obligations to others. This kind of social person is the key building block in any democratic civil society.

Developments after 1960

After the founding era, in the 1960s, significant new AR developments took place in Norway. A national project to redesign industrial work emerged from negotiations between the labor unions, the employer federation, and the government. This project aimed both to improve productivity and enhance democracy in work life. Over the years, this collaboration created some quite successful approaches to finding new, smart and effective ways of organizing production in ship manning, oil platform design and safety, hospital organization, social service provision, and manufacturing.

Team-based production strategies emerged as a centerpiece of these efforts and these teams were initially called "partially self-determined groups." These team practices spread worldwide with surprising speed, but, unfortunately, the focus on the work life democracy remained mainly limited to the Nordic countries. It is now on the wane there too under the neoliberal assault. Many organizations have come to use team strategies and the language of participation cynically to exploit their workers more effectively rather than to transform their organizations. They have devalued the practice into fake participation, into tokenism.

The biggest groups of action researchers now are to be found in poor countries. Participative action research (PAR), or participatory research, or community-based participatory action research are the names these practitioners give to some of their modes of practicing action research (Freire 1970; Hall 1975; Fals-Borda and Anisur Rahman 1991; Chambers 1997; Gaventa and Cornwall 2001; Oppenjuru and Jaitli, eds., 2015). In their context, the core focus is to develop democratic structures that permit local people to gain better control over their own lives. Making necessary changes in agricultural practices, the provision of social services, and putting people in the position to determine their own fate rather than being subjected to political bosses, absentee power holders, or international agencies are all central processes and the goals. Many of these projects are staunchly liberationist and involve oppositional social action and even civil disobedience.

Action Research Opposes Taylorism

Despite the significant differences, it should be clear that AR everywhere opposes Taylorism (bureaucratic, authoritarian organization) in all its guises. This is no accident since Taylorism is an anti-systems and inhumane model. It relies on backward-looking problem identification, command-and-control systems built on fragmentation and management control, hierarchy, the prevalence of authority over situated competence, and hermetic organizational levels and organizational units. It operates with active bosses and passive workers. The bosses give orders rather than generating the capacity for team-based problem solving. Taylorism is the antithesis to AR-based learning organizations committed to the production of public and private goods.

Neo-Taylorism and its current neoliberal proponents have created a system that optimizes inequality and waste, imposes impossibly short time horizons on action, and creates unsustainable practices. From the perspective of action research, this is a dysfunctional and incompetent management model because it locates decision-making authority at the greatest possible distance from those engaged in the processes of value creation on which the survival and further development of the organization depends.

Critiques of Action Research

Voices critical of action research focus mainly on three different issues. One perspective basically claims that participation is impossible because power holders in organizations will never release their grip. Holders of this view criticize AR as engaging in false participation because the people in power limit the problems they will allow stakeholders to deal with based on their own interests. Participation is fine as long as the "lowers" don't challenge the "uppers." The "uppers" are satisfied so far as participation generates energy for solving small problems without raising broader and more fundamental questions related to the political economy of the organization or location (Cooke and Kothari 2001).

We reject this critique because we know from experience that participation, once unleashed in co-generative learning organizations, is very difficult for power holders to control. Power is generated in participation itself and the illegitimacy and selfish interests of the existing power hierarchies are often revealed as the process proceeds. Foucault knew this well (Foucault 1973, 1977) as did others of his generation.

Action researchers occasionally have been accused of becoming insiders, a sin according to the armchair positivist view of social science. It is asserted that action researchers' preoccupation with local changes makes it impossible for them to develop the critical distance needed for taking broader critical, scientific positions on the issues at hand (Levin 2012). Put more baldly, this claim states that action researchers are poor social scientists because they are not objective. While this may be true in some cases, the proliferation of poor, boring, and irrelevant conventional social science research projects in academia is evident. So too are the incentives to produce this kind of work created by the imposition of neoliberal accountability on researchers' publication and systematically severing the link between research and action. In addition, these critiques reveal ignorance of the work of Lewin, Fals Borda, Freire, Gaventa and subsequent generations of well-regarded and academically celebrated action researchers.

Another version of this critique points to the sparse academic accomplishments of many action research professionals. We agree with this criticism. Many AR practitioners are rightly accused failing to develop strong academic profiles, either because they write narratives that lack analytical depth or because they simply do not publish good analytical accounts of their work (Greenwood 1999; Levin 2012). Many action researchers fail to work on the problem of developing generalizable knowledge from their work or exploring the "trans contextual" applicability of their findings. The failure to take these steps is not inherent in action research. They are a failure of the practitioners rather than of the approach.

With this brief background, we are ready to put forward our views on the use of action research to re-create public universities.

Notes

1. Greenwood 1991, 1999, 2007, 2009, 2012, 2013; Greenwood and Levin 1998a, 1998b, 1999, 2000a, 2000b, 2001, 2005, 2007, 2008; Levin 2002; Levin and Greenwood 1998, 2001a, 2001b, 2007, 2011.
2. For a more comprehensive overview of the history of action research and the current diversity in approaches, see Reason and Bradbury 2001, 2008; Greenwood and Levin 2007; Bradbury 2015; and Coughlan and Brydon-Miller 2014.
3. See our full discussion of STSD in Chapter 6.

CHAPTER 9

Practicing Action Research in Public Universities

◆◆◆

This chapter provides illustrations of the ways action research can be used re-create public universities that produce *Bildung* for the stakeholders and the surrounding society. We do not subscribe to a naïve belief that action research practice in this context is easy or unproblematic. We do not promise that it will provide perfect solutions to these complex problems. Our goal is to bring forward ways to proceed toward AR's deployment in these institutions. These scenarios, accompanied by our reflections on some of problems and pitfalls, are ones likely to arise in the process. A brief inventory of some examples of their use and various projects deploying AR in higher education innovation and reform follows.

Pragmatic Action Research

There are many ways to approach these issues using AR because, as shown in Chapter 8, there are many different approaches to AR (Heron 1996; Reason and Bradbury 2001, 2008; Greenwood and Levin 2007; Coughlan and Brannick 2009; Coughlan and Brydon-Miller 2014 and Bradbury 2015). We have learned valuable lessons from many of these approaches, but we mainly work using socio-technical systems design and an overall approach we have called "pragmatic action research" (Greenwood and Levin 2007). The term "pragmatic" is an intentional reference to John Dewey's pragmatism and educational practices.[1]

Pragmatic action research is built around the co-generative model presented in Greenwood and Levin, *Introduction to Action Research* (2007). The co-generative AR model creates learning structures that enhance the developmental capacity of organizations by enabling democratizing changes. This process is participative and is structured and supported by a facilitator responsible for designing learning opportunities and creating and facilitating spaces for communication and collaborative reflection.

We begin by discussing what is a common opening cycle in an AR-based organizational change activity. This is called a "search conference" and we include a brief presentation of this process of AR-based organizational development. In the following sections, we present examples that show how AR can be carried out in university settings. Among these examples are curriculum development, setting the research agenda, organizing the research process, developing speech and behavioral codes, doing evaluation and reviews, and engaging in strategic planning.

Search Conferences

Problem identification

It is common to hear action researchers say that: "You never know exactly when the AR process started and you do not know when it will end." This is because the momentum that builds to the point that local stakeholders are ready to take a bold step in reorganizing their working lives comes from many locations and often arises by idiosyncratic means. It can be evoked by a financial crisis, a visionary organization member, a small group of stakeholders that manage to gather enough power to put change on the agenda, a national program funding such work, etc. It is not possible to order an AR process into existence. What can be structured are the opportunities to engage in developmental activities. Before steps can be taken to create favorable conditions for participation and collaboration, the local stakeholders must decide collectively to move forward in sufficient numbers to make action research possible.

Once there is a decision among the stakeholders to initiate a change process, the change effort necessarily begins by developing a detailed and shared understanding of the problems to be addressed. Typically, this starts with a preliminary identification of the key problems. Often the problem is brought forward by a subset of the relevant stakeholders who are actively sponsoring the change effort. This problem identification and group of stakeholders serve as a point of departure, but theirs is not the final word on which problems are to be addressed or on stakeholder inclusion. Unless an initial problem formulation resonates with a broader subset of organizational stakeholders and with the facilitator, there is nowhere to start. This means that the first step is to get beyond this starting point by refining the problem statement and including more stakeholders.

Stakeholder Inclusion

The initial subset of stakeholders is rarely knowledgeable about the needs and interests of all the relevant stakeholders in the process. The action research process begins with an exploration of the organization with the initial knowledgeable insiders to identify additional categories of stakeholders with legitimate interests in and knowledge about the problem. In action research the knowledge of the initial participants about the organization and its members is used to identify and include stakeholders who should have a say in this particular problem area because their interests are directly affected.

This stakeholder identification process is vital. It demands and is worth lots of effort because so many change processes are begun with assumptions about, rather than knowledge of, the different stakeholders and their views on which problems matter and why. It is also important to design the change process in a way that allows for new stakeholders to become involved when it becomes obvious that they are necessary to its success.

This contrasts with the typical ways organizational leaders and their consultants operate. They often try to define the organizational problems for all the stakeholders, select a few stakeholders for token input, and then impose their own preferred solutions. They rarely touch the ground where the problems are experienced and understood. Or they create a "taskforce" to study the problems and propose solutions, reserving to themselves the definition of the problems and the choice of solutions. Solving problems "for" others is routine. AR opposes these cooptive practices directly, viewing such manipulations as incompetent and unsustainable.

Creating a Co-generative Learning Arena via "Search Conferences"

Once the stakeholder categories are well identified and representatives from those categories have been found and sorted according to their level of interest and their ability to participate (including figuring out which obstacles might prevent certain stakeholders from participating and what can be done to remove those obstacles), this newly configured group is convened in what is called a "search conference" to address the problem.

Search conferences are intensive, usually two-day participatory strategic planning processes often undertaken in a retreat setting. This approach, developed by Fred and Merrelyn Emery originally (Emery 1999), has been widely used in Scandinavia, Australia, and the United

States. We describe the process and its structure in Greenwood and Levin, *Introduction to Action Research* (2007: 136–150). Another account of the approach can be found in Weisbord and Janoff (2010).

In the retreat setting, a collaborative process of issue identification and process initiation begins. There are many ways to handle this but it never involves the facilitator imposing a problem definition on the group. The facilitator's role is to advise and support the creation of good learning arenas and to keep the dialogue open and moving ahead. In the initial phase, the facilitator has heavy responsibilities for modeling and supporting inclusive learning opportunities for all the participants. As the AR process continues, the facilitator must see to it that the responsibilities for the process shift gradually and fully into the hands of the local stakeholders.

Developing a Problem Focus through a Shared History

The initial development of a focus for the search activity is crucial. Having convened a diverse set of the legitimate stakeholders in the problems to be addressed, to begin the search conference, the facilitator must create a common ground for discussing the key issues. An effective way to accomplish this is by developing a shared history of the issues. There are good organizational reasons to start this way. All participants, including the facilitator, need to develop a shared understanding of the issues to be addressed based on the stakeholders' knowledge of the local context and practical issues and the facilitator's previous experience and knowledge of participatory processes that work.

Thus, the AR process does not start from the first rendering of the problem that initially brought the stakeholders together. That formulation is used to convene the search conference. However, once the full set of relevant stakeholders is identified and convened, the initial problem focus is presented to the broader assembled group of stakeholders and they enhance, refocus, or fundamentally change it through shared dialogue using examples drawn from their direct experiences.

In a shared history process, given the general problem focus that brings them together, all the participants are asked to reflect on their personal experiences of the issues and then share them with the rest of the group. This is done by placing a long sheet of butcher paper on a wall and providing markers to the stakeholders. The sheet is divided into the more distant past, immediate past and a line is drawn at the present. Beyond the present, there are two segments, one called the probable future and the other called the ideal future.

The stakeholders are encouraged to write or draw their experiences of the central problem up on the sheet in all the different locations where they feel they have an important experience or observation to share. This can and should take a good bit of time with the facilitator encouraging people and checking to be sure they feel free to express themselves. When this process is completed, the facilitator goes to the beginning of the timeline and points to each successive item on the paper, asking the person who placed it there to explain it to the group. That person explains to the rest of the stakeholders what their item means and why it is important to them.

This process often produces significant surprises and new knowledge. Everyone knows their part of the problem and their key concerns but they rarely know much about what others think. This happens because there are few venues in hierarchical organizations to share such perspectives. Local knowledge and concerns generally are boxed into a rigid frame of reference. As a result of this initial sharing, everyone present emerges with a more differentiated and complex sense of the problems. The participants also experience some initial sense of the ways the same issues may be experienced differently by others.

The Probable Future

The facilitator then asks the group to imagine the probable future associated with the problem at hand if no changes are made in current structures and practices (including their own behaviors). Usually the probable future is not very desirable. If it were, there would be no stakeholders group meeting to discuss changing the situation.

The Ideal Future

After this process is complete, and it may or may not take long, the facilitator asks the members of the group to lay out for themselves and then write on the wall their notions for the ideal future regarding the issues being addressed. The ideal future encourages the expression of their hopes and wishes. These often are suppressed by pessimism and negative experiences with the problem. It also shows the stakeholders that what is ideal for some of them may not be the highest priority for others. Together, they gain a general picture of how the future would have to be different to satisfy those participating.

Creating the Co-generative Learning Arena

From this point forward, the group has a shared frame of reference about the past, present, and future and begins the analytical work involved in understanding what makes the ideal future less than probable under current conditions. This is the point of departure for the configuration of a co-generative learning arena. Now that the participants have assimilated the wealth of information the various stakeholders brought to the problem definition and have examined the probable and ideal futures, they need to sort out the obstacles to changes they desire.

There are many ways to do this. It is possible to spend some time in plenary discussion making a "keep, drop, create" list. This simply means listing which activities need to be kept because they are making positive contributions to solving the problem, which activities are obstacles and need to be stopped, and what things are not being done that should be done to improve the situation. From this emerge a number of topics or areas of work that need to be addressed.

At this point, the stakeholders can be divided into groups to engage in more detailed analyses of particular problems or needed initiatives. One common way to do this is to use "force-field analysis" (Lewin 1948) to sort out forces that hold change back and forces that promote it. SWOT analysis is another option.[2] There are many more processes available for doing this. The aim with any of these methods is to make the emerging analysis of the obstacles faced in creating a more ideal future more specific and more fully shared. These analyses open up the demanding process of thinking through strategies and resources that can be mobilized to move the obstacles aside.

Small work groups permit more detailed discussions that often encourage new ways of thinking that might result in innovations. Depending on the topic of the search, these groups can be composed of stakeholders from the same areas or across the range of stakeholders. This is decided based on the kinds of problems being addressed. The value of grouping similar stakeholders is that they may have detailed local knowledge about particular problems and solutions. The value of the multi-category groups is that the differences in their experiences and locations in the organization may help them to come up with previously unimagined strategies for change.

This kind of work moves between teams and plenaries and back a few times. In plenaries, the working groups share their results with the other groups and learn from each other's ideas. Eventually, a few major foci of work emerge from these deliberations. Each of these major work areas is named and written on separate flipchart at front of the room. At this point, the action turn is taken.

The Action Turn

The assembled stakeholders are asked to volunteer to join a team to deal with one of the identified problem or work areas. Often some problem areas will attract many participants and others won't attract a single person, even though everyone recognizes the importance of the issues. This sorting is important because in any change effort, there are always more issues and problems to solve than energy and commitment available to solve them.

The action teams created this way hold an initial meeting at the search conference, appoint a temporary convener, identify other stakeholders they will need to involve, and plan future actions and meetings. After some time, the teams are asked to present their action plans to the assembled plenary and the initial meeting draws to a close.

After a period of work (weeks or months) in teams, the entire stakeholder group is reconvened to hear and evaluate the results of the actions they have taken. If the results are partial or not what were hoped for, processes are begun to analyze what happened and to reformulate the action design with an eye toward further work on the problem. The cycles of presentation, analysis, action design, action, evaluation of results and new action designs continue until either the problems have been addressed to the stakeholders' satisfaction or until the energy that gathered them initially has dissipated.

These are the broad outlines of a search conference process. There are many other ways to do this kind of participatory strategic planning and action design. The *Handbook of Action Research* (Reason and Bradbury 2001, 2008; Bradbury 2015), *The Encyclopedia of Action Research* (Coughlan and Brydon-Miller 2014) and the manuals by Chevalier and Buckles (2008, 2013), Klev and Levin (2012a, 2012b), and Senge (1990) lay out alternatives. It is the responsibility of the facilitator to select approaches they are competent to use and that suit the kinds of problems and stakeholders they are working with.

Using Action Research on Core Organizational Processes in Existing Public Universities

To bring this into university environments, we now show how pragmatic action research processes could be applied to some of the key arenas of existing public universities. Doing this highlights how different the dynamics of these participatory processes are when compared with existing neo-Tayloristic approaches to academic administration and management. Since we believe that public universities can only operate effectively by engaging in participatory decision making and collaborative action, we argue that AR-based processes must be integrated into their daily operating procedures on a permanent basis.

Action research effectively turns the conventional understanding of university organization on its head to reconceive universities as participatory learning organizations. In the popular press on leadership and management, processes like this have become known as turning the organizational pyramid upside-down. In the case of universities, this means that participatory curriculum development, course delivery, research processes, management of infrastructures, financial management, and service to external constituencies take precedence over imposed organizational behaviors generated by a few senior administrators on their own or with the help of external consultants and boards.

We do not argue that strategic planning is irrelevant. Rather we claim that strategic planning only yields results when all the stakeholders have contributed their knowledge and experience to the design of those plans and understand together the challenges to be met. Senior administrators lack both the expertise and knowledge to develop meaningful strategic plans on their own. The kind of plans they develop mainly serve their own interests, not those of the other legitimate stakeholders, and are rarely implemented successfully (Birnbaum 2001).

Our point of departure in the following discussion is curriculum development. Following this, research and then community engagement are discussed. This provides the context for an examination of strategy and leadership development as it is understood in AR. This discussion is completed by showing why freedom of speech and academic integrity are fundamental to the activities of students, faculty, staff, and administrators and why these rights and obligations must not be limited to faculty and student codes of conduct.

Curriculum Development

Curriculum development and change is a key feature of any university. The contents of a curriculum involve decisions about diverse matters including the broad meaning of an "education" and the role of accrediting agencies and professional societies in insisting that certain topics be covered and in certain ways. These decisions also involve the reconciliation of the interests of the many departments, academic professional societies, and units (for whom curricular decisions mean more or fewer students and more or fewer faculty); the actual content of courses; and coordination of curricular requirements across units.

This is a complex process. Even admitting this, the state of the art in curriculum development at most universities is shameful. One of the authors, Greenwood, is a graduate of a United States liberal arts college that actually had an integrated curriculum. In that college, during the 1960s, the faculty collaborated in the overall design of the core required courses covering the first two years of undergraduate work, and they collaborated across departments in offering them. The college also held a third year examination on the general liberal arts as a capstone to the core requirements. It was not a perfect system, but it contrasts so radically with the university curricular processes with which Greenwood and Levin are familiar at research universities that it provides a useful point of reference.

The typical research university curriculum involves a menu of required courses agreed on by the faculty or a combined administrative or faculty committee. The curriculum is arrived at through debate and often through power plays aimed at strengthening the hand of particular departments at the expense of others. This is because the selected courses provide student numbers that are converted into income to finance other dimensions of individual department life. This course menu generally ends up being nothing more than a checklist for students to complete. It often involves large introductory courses in various departments, courses rarely taught on a continuing basis by senior faculty. They generally involve backward-looking summaries of past views of each discipline in isolation from other disciplines. They are also a lot of work, involving grading, supervising teaching assistants, managing a website, etc. A few exceptional senior professors take such courses on as a civic commitment to teaching, but they are rare. Generally they are offloaded on junior faculty and graduate student teaching assistants.

The leading-edge work in each field rarely finds its way into these courses. There is little attention paid to updating these courses on a routine basis, except in some science and engineering fields where accreditation requirements force the issue. Usually the courses are revised whenever someone new wants to teach them or when significant numbers of students refuse to take them.

These courses generally belong to individual departments, are developed within the departments by some subset of the faculty, are often taught without regular consultation with the rest of the departmental faculty and without their input into the content and methods. To compound the lack of integration across departments, almost no one has a clue about the contents and possible linkages among the required courses offered in other departments.

The result is a dated curriculum in checklist style composed of unrelated and unlinked courses taught by faculty who often do not know each other and could not care less about what other departments are doing, except as it affects their student numbers. There is no integration, no meaningful content or quality control. It is anti-*Bildung* in action.

Since this is the current system at most universities, even small changes could bring about major improvements. But changes are extremely hard to make. Accreditation standards set by disciplinary, state, national, and international agencies are in the way. Departmental boundaries also obstruct changes. Authoritarian administrative management generally pits departmental units against one another as a way of optimizing central power. Rather than rewarding interdepartmental dialogue, collaboration, and innovation, these administrative structures stifle attempts to build an educationally meaningful change of the curriculum across units. Those collaborations would affect political arrangements in departments, colleges, and across the institution as a whole.

How Could this be Different if Action Research Were Applied to the Process?

Taking on curriculum change as an AR process involves a fundamentally different approach. All of the stakeholders would have to stop pontificating and start opening up the space for a different kind of curriculum development and planning process. This would begin, as does any AR process, with stakeholder identification. Among the relevant stakeholders are the students from different degree programs; their potential employers in the public and private sector; faculty members from all ranks and representing a good cross-section of all the academic units; accrediting agency representatives; staff who manage the rooms, facilities, enrollments, and myriad practical arrangements; and the administrators who must facilitate the execution of the plans arrived at. A process that looks very much like this has been in operation within engineering departments at the Norwegian University of Science and Technology (NTNU) for some time. It has become the standard approach for revisions in the teaching program. The process there is a successful strategy for curriculum development and certainly a better one than the default alternative elsewhere.

We would use search conferences as a work form. Most of the stakeholders almost never interact with each other about the curriculum because of the neo-Tayloristic structure of universities. Thus, the first step has to be the development of a shared history in which all the stakeholders are able to document and explain their experiences with curriculum issues (good, bad, indifferent) and to share what for them have been pivotal moments in their experiences. Once this information is widely shared and the participants are more aware of the experiences and frustrations of the other stakeholders, they can proceed.

From here, the stakeholders can move to projecting the probable future of the curriculum at the institution in the event that nothing much is done to change the current system. They can then lay out their ideal future for a changed curriculum and it benefits. Looking back at the shared history, the group can then identify the forces that seem to cause the outcomes the stakeholders least like and most want to change.

Armed with this list of forces, the stakeholders can break up into multi-stakeholder groups to examine the restraining forces and to begin to strategize about possible ways to relax those restraints. After a round doing force-field analysis (or SWOT, or similar techniques), the working groups can reconvene and share their results. From this plenary discussion will emerge a set of organizational issues that have to be addressed to improve the curriculum in the direction of the ideal future. From here, voluntary cross-stakeholder teams can continue working on them. They will hold a first team meeting to decide who else to recruit to their teams, to select a convener, and to set a date for their next working meeting.

After some time spent working, the teams can be reconvened and can share the results of their work to that point and mentor each other regarding problems encountered. They then will continue to work as a team for some period into the future. Ultimately, these teams will convene again to design an overall action plan to change the institution's curriculum development and management process as a whole. They then will either put the plan into action or engage the academic administrators, accreditors, and policy makers directly in the process of changing the curriculum based on the real experiences of the knowledgeable and legitimate stakeholders. After some period of this kind of work, the stakeholder group can reconvene to examine progress, perhaps engage in some action redesign, and then continue the work.

Just how radically different this process is from university "business as usual" is clear. The new plans use the personal knowledge and the needs and interests of all the stakeholder groups rather than having institutional designs imposed on them from above and from without. Such an approach is *Neue-Bildung* in action.

Development of a University Research Agenda

Public research universities and their accreditors, and the educational policymakers at the state and national level now place considerable emphasis on their research agendas and accomplishments. Despite this, the idea of having a well-developed, coherent university research agenda would appear far-fetched to most current research administrators. It also would be threatening to many individual faculty researchers who want to do what they want to do with university support and without any interference from anyone else.

Various granting agencies (governmental, foundations, and private sector funders) develop priorities with little consultation with university faculty members who will do the research. They send out requests for proposals based on their priorities, and faculty either respond or do not. Some agencies change priorities abruptly, others fund particular activities for long periods, others demand deliverables of various sorts, etc. The university administration tries to support efforts to get grants that either bring major money or significant prestige to the institution, and compete with other universities regarding these grants and their institution's position in the research university rankings. Out of this swamp emerges a pattern of research activities that is mostly opportunistic and entrepreneurial on all sides.

Calling this outcome a research agenda obscures that is it mostly unregulated and unrelated activity. It is also prejudicial to many fields. Because it is opportunistic, where fewer funded research opportunities exist (e.g., the humanities and the less positivistic social sciences), there is little attention to supporting faculty research at all. The mix of research support heavily underwrites the physical and biological sciences, medicine, and engineering. But these fields have high infrastructural costs, with laboratories, research assistants, etc. that have to be paid for. These facilities and groups are expensive to build and maintain and so there is a strong tendency to resist taxing them to support the less well-financed humanities and social sciences. The university leadership supports the existing patterns because that is what the funders want, a posture that certainly cannot be called leadership in any meaningful sense. Thus the so-called research system really amounts mostly to fee-for-service research. Within the campus, the global dynamic of the few rich researchers and the many who are impoverished is reproduced.

This is a non-rational system that creates a competitive zero-sum environment that is difficult to sustain economically. By not having a real research agenda, most universities end up chasing money and adapting to the consequences of the decisions of outsiders rather than taking responsibility for setting a research agenda, for supporting a reasoned mix of infrastructurally expensive and less expensive forms of research, and encouraging positive sum forward planning. To develop a research agenda that is respectful of the differences among the various university fields and the integrity of a university as a broad array of disciplines and activities would require university administrators to operate in collaborative, open, and participatory way. This would involve dismantling the organizational structure that has turned public university research into what it currently is.

To change this, we would begin again with stakeholder identification. Doing this alone changes the scene because many faculty members who are never engaged by the research administrative structure of the university do in fact have knowledge of and ideas about research agendas. However, their experiences and views have been ignored for so long that they have given up thinking about these issues institutionally. They tend their own gardens as best they can. Their experiences and what they have to say about a different future would surprise many of the other stakeholders who have been the beneficiaries of this unfair and unregulated system of haves and have-nots.

The have-nots would be surprised to learn that many of the successful and well funded scientific researchers are deeply frustrated by funding that demands so much of their time to be spent in grant getting and grant administration. These researchers also are often frustrated by the insistence of external funders on applied research and their unwillingness to support the basic research that many university researchers see as the key to future developments. Many funded researchers feel that this overemphasis on application is undermining the future of science.

Students too are stakeholders. Many attend research universities in hopes of being mentored by faculty researchers, being trained in research, and learning the skills of being successful in a research environment. Of those students, few actually get this chance. Most never work closely with researchers on important projects, and end up seeing this emphasis on the value of being at a research university as admissions recruitment hype, not an academic reality.

The academic administrators who currently try to manage research operations mainly end up chasing and managing research contracts and infrastructures while they are hectored by their bosses to increase the research output, grants won, and patents gotten at the university. Forcing researchers to meet university rules often puts university staff in adversarial relationships with the research faculty. Their task, as currently set, is, at the very least, unrewarding.

The funders of research, rather than entering the scene mainly by sending out requests for proposals, need to be engaged as partners in defining meaningful public university research agendas that are in civil society's interest. These funders need to learn to engage with each other rather than trying to outdo each other in their own meritocratic and reputational games. Joining forces to secure quality research in socially important areas would be better than following idiosyncratic funding fads. They too must to be convoked, along with the extra-university users of university research, to understand how reasonable or unreasonable their demands are and how their procedures are also part of the problem to be addressed.

To avoid repetition, we just review briefly the sequence of actions that need to be followed to use AR processes to develop and manage university research agendas: identification of all the relevant types of stakeholders and the selection of representatives to develop a co-generative dialogue with collaborative issue identification; and the development of a shared history of the research-related experiences of all parties, the probable future without major changes, the ideal future and what keeps it from being realized through force field analysis. In the process they would find out that the current situation is negative for nearly all the stakeholders. Following this would be strategy development, team formation, action design, evaluation, redesign, and further actions.

Research Processes

Research processes are different from the development of a university research agenda. Research processes refer to the ways research is conducted and given institutional support. Through proper stakeholder identification, it is possible to learn quickly how little voice key stakeholders have. Principal among the excluded are the many postgraduate students and research associates who are relied on for much of the day-to-day work of research, but whose control over their contractual and working conditions is extremely limited. There is evidence in the United States that many universities keep dead-end graduate programs going (that is, programs where future employment in the field is a dubious proposition) to have cheap labor for the research system they already have in place. [3]

Many undergraduate students want to have research opportunities, but they are often limited to a select few who are rarely "democratically" elected to receive these opportunities. Many secretaries, accountants, and infrastructure staff whose activities are vital to the research system have little voice in designing these processes.

On the European side, national funding patterns for research are decided both nationally and impacted heavily by the decisions of the scientific and educational policy bodies of the EU. A key EU political game is to create university consortia including important countries that are powerful enough to win the battle for funds. Researchers complain quite a lot about this bureaucratization of research and the unfairness of the resulting allocations of funds.

It is clear that including the relevant stakeholders in the development of a new set of research processes would result in a different research system from the one in existence now. Collaborative issue identification emerging from a shared history among these stakeholders would dramatize how few are being well served by the current system and precisely who the major beneficiaries actually are. The probable and ideal future exercise would highlight the institutional constraints, and the problems with the research system would center on how to democratize the research process and its financial benefits for the good of all the stakeholders. From this would follow team formation, strategy development, the design of new institutional processes, action, evaluation, and redesign.

Other Areas of AR Intervention

Rather than repeating what by now should be a familiar strategy of AR program development and action design, we will concentrate on listing some of the other key issues that could be addressed by AR means if public universities were to be transformed to produce *Bildung*.

Service to Local Communities

Service is now often called "community engagement" in the new public relations rhetoric of most universities. It is widely trumpeted as one of the important functions of the university, including faculty work on issues of community interest, and student "service learning." Despite this, service is ill-defined and often ill-rewarded.

Defining a service mission for faculty, students, and staff is now typically done by central administrative pronouncements in the form of "white papers" and strategic plans elaborated without consultation with those who must do or receive the service. These documents often imitate similar documents from other, more prestigious universities. Their recommendations typically are not linked to the university financial or professional reward structures. For example, engaging in community service at the expense of building a research profile is highly problematic for most younger faculty members. These "white papers" generally end up as public relations pieces for the university public relations office, the university fundraisers, and the recruitment/admissions staff to use.

Bringing the relevant stakeholders together to educate each other about their situations regarding service would produce something different. Having them engage in the probable or ideal future contrast leading to the identification of the problems that prevent service from developing in a meaningful way for most stakeholders is central. Developing proper systems for documenting and rewarding the service in ways stakeholders find meaningful would likely become central activities. This is distant from vague talk about a service mission coming from senior administrators who are themselves remote from the realities of university service activities.

Creation and Enforcement of Speech and Behavior Codes

One of the most troubling developments currently taking place in United States public universities centers on free speech. In our earlier discussion of academic freedom in Chapter 3, we argued that academic freedom, free speech, academic integrity, and *Bildung* are interrelated. As handled now, free speech tends to be equated with academic freedom for faculty and perhaps for some student advocacy groups and little more.

While research and writing are important dimensions of university life, speech acts are the very core of academic work: speech in teaching, speech in responding to questions, speech acts in formal presentations and disputations, staff speech about work conditions, policies, and practices, speech in debates about institutional matters, and speech practices as learned by students as a key skill for their future lives.

Despite freedom of speech being constitutionally guaranteed in the United States, there has been a heavy suppression of freedom of speech on campuses. Faculty and student speech is now closely regulated by speech codes and obedience is enforced by penalties, dismissals, and expulsions. Faculty find themselves in trouble whenever they say or write something that upsets some constituency of the university, be they powerful private sector companies, Zionists, the lesbian, gay, bisexual, or trans-gendered community, evangelical Christians, women,

African-Americans, etc. Nothing resembling free speech for all parties exists (Kors and Silverglate 1999; Lukianoff 2014). Guarantees of free and open debates on institutional and academic matters are suppressed now by required "trigger warnings" or political correctness on the left, right, and in the center.

This is the opposite of a participatory, democratic organizational environment, and, as a training ground for younger citizens, it undermines the foundations of a democratic society. In Norway, free speech has a stronger position. First, it is grounded in the Norwegian constitution and it is enforced by stronger unions than exist in the United States. Every now and then attacks from far right and far left are experienced, but these groups have rather limited power to challenge the praxis of university free speech.

To address free speech, we would return to stakeholder identification. Who are the relevant stakeholders to be considered in any attempt to manage speech in a university? Surely students, faculty, staff, and administrators belong on the list and probably representatives from the surrounding communities and funders. To our knowledge, the question of academic speech has never been addressed by such a group anywhere. The time to do this has come, because granting limited freedom of speech to some stakeholders and imposing speech restrictions on most other stakeholders undercuts the basis of public university life. It is a source of institutional duplicity and manipulation and sends students out into the world prepared to keep their mouths shut and let civil society wither.

It is hard for us to imagine what collaborative issue identification would produce as a set of issues, what the shared history of these issues would be, and how such a group would visualize a probable future and ideal future. This is because so little attention has been given to the key issue of protecting free speech in public universities that it is actually difficult to imagine what issues and priorities would emerge. We believe this is precisely why such a process is required. We must move toward a university based on *Neue-Bildung* rather than on static speech codes and hierarchical code enforcers who silence the majority. That we are so far from this ideal future in public universities should be profoundly unsettling. Once these issues were clarified, the subsequent force-field and/or SWOT analyses, problem-solving team formation, action designs, and evaluation could take universities into territories that might make them functional contributors to democratic societies rather than sources of cynicism and disenchantment.

Review, Evaluation, and Promotion Standards and Procedures

No organization functions without standards for hiring, evaluation, and promotion. Public universities are no different from other organizations in this regard. However, the systems are drastically different for faculty, lecturers, staff, and administrators, with the added barb that the administrators rarely apply the standards they impose on everyone else to themselves.

There is no question that review, evaluation, and promotion standards and processes have a major influence on the way people behave in any organization. We know that at most public research universities, for example, lip service is paid to evaluating teaching and to appreciating administrative service. Still, most faculty members know that neither of these counts much for promotion or salary increases. The lack of alignment between the "espoused theory" and the "theory-in-use" in these areas not only produces stress but alienates faculty from their own priorities and intuitions about the kind of work that suits them best and makes them the best kind of contributors to the institution.

An AR process to develop fair and meaningful standards and practices for tenure, promotion, and salary decisions for faculty, for staff, and for administrators would take universities into unknown territory regarding a system that currently only senior administrators and a few political operators among academics and staff benefit from. Substituting coercion with meaningful evaluation, on dimensions and with processes the parties agree are fair and transparent, would be a step in the direction of democratizing universities through the actual practice of democratic dialogue and debate.

Strategic Planning

In the current world of universities, strategic planning is monopolized by senior administrators. They hold on to strategic planning as a key dimension of their crucial role in the university and as a justification for their large salaries. Most university stakeholders are the victims of strategic plans imposed by others rather than being themselves contributors to the development of well-designed strategies and plans. This is not how strategic planning is done in dynamic, learning organizations.

For this to change, stakeholders from all major categories on a campus would have to engage in collaborative issue identification regarding the strategic planning topics that could affect their present conditions and futures. Doing this would require the development of shared histories of the frustrating experiences of being subjected to the plans of others, the sequences of dysfunctional and counterproductive strategic plans they have survived, and their experiences of subjection to administrators' ideal futures rather than democratically developed ideal futures belonging to the institutions' stakeholders.

Force-field analysis would be particularly important here because many participants would quickly discover that they themselves are understood by many administrators to be obstacles in the way of good strategic plans rather than the sources of workable ideas and practices to improve the strategic directions of the institution. This kind of participatory strategic planning has happened in some major cities around the world and in a number of businesses and voluntary organizations. To our knowledge, it has not taken place at universities except at the Mondragón University that we will discuss later in the chapter.

Budget Development

Budget development is another sector where the senior administrative monopoly combines secrecy and the use of financial flows as a way of controlling the university faculty, staff, and students. Letting go of budget development is a key basis for a fundamental reorganization of universities. All parties are actually stakeholders.

Budgets, when made open to the stakeholders, generally cause major inequities, irrationalities, and special interests to surface and require them to be explained. The way budgeting creates disincentives for cooperation and solidarity is directly related to senior administrative domination of universities and to the hegemony of a few faculty "heavy hitters" with big research budgets, international prestige, etc. Where budgets are shared with all stakeholders, as in the case of the Mondragón University, budgets not only look different but the stakeholders can occasionally be called on and are willing to make sacrifices of their own economic interests on behalf of the institution.

Participatory budgeting enforces a greater priority for sustainable decisions because sustainable and livable work situations are important to most stakeholders. The exceptions to this are the senior administrators, who parachute in and soon move on to the next highest-bidding university, and a few faculty "stars", who are bid for by other institutions in the academic equivalent of the "free agency" of professional athletes. These administrators and stars are the only winners in current budget systems.

Employment and compensation structures fit into this discussion, since everyone is subject to them but only a tiny segment of the current university system controls them or is even allowed to see the information. Those now in control also happen to be the highest-paid people in the system and the ones whose pay is rising fastest. This is an unacceptable dynamic in terms of fairness and also socially regressive in view of the rising cost of public higher education and increased indebtedness of the students.

The AR process here could be energizing because it would require opening the university's books. Doing this would promote understanding the budget allocations and then requiring explanations, including justifications for the current systems of compensation. While some parts of that system may be reasonable, others will be seen as indefensible, including differential tuition costs, subsidizing research operations with student tuition increases, differential financial aid, different salary structures for disciplines, pay hierarchies based on an indefensible ranking of staff services (ranking that usually reinforces gender and class discrimination), and pay and bonuses for senior administrators. Many of these allocations may turn out to be hard to justify when confronted by the employment and compensation conditions faced by everyone else.

Physical Plant Development, Maintenance, and Redesign

Physical plant development and maintenance is just as amenable to these AR processes and would put another cross-section of stakeholders into relation with each other who currently have almost no idea about the nature of each others' lives in the institution and how these dimensions affect the well-being of everyone else.

This is not an exhaustive list of the arenas for the application of AR processes to democratizing existing public universities. We have selected these areas to model the general contours of such AR processes and to highlight how different they are from current institutional behavior.

How Can these Socio-Technical Design Processes Fit Together into an Overall AR Process?

What we have described above are some of the dynamics that would derive from treating major institutional areas of public universities as participatory and collaborative work systems in which all stakeholders have the right and the obligation to participate. They all would contribute their knowledge to joint problem solving and their efforts would then focus on collaborative action to enact and evaluate the designs arrived at in this way. Following these organizational processes in all the major functional and stakeholder areas of public universities would result in profound changes. The cumulative effect could be the re-creation of the public university as a participatory democracy producing *Bildung* for all.

The AR processes we have presented are what was and is done in the historical development of socio-technical systems design in manufacturing and service industries. Thus the approach we are proposing is not new. We already know a great deal about the positive consequences of such approaches in cost savings, greater commitment to the organization, solidarity among the stakeholders, and the improved quality of the organizations and their products or services.

Employment structures based on performance in a team environment and that reward solidarity, participation, and engagement result in overall improvements in the organization as an economic system and as a place where people live significant parts of their lives. Socio-technical systems based on matrix structures and team organization also cause compensation differences between the top and bottom salaries to be reduced, something that could help a with the runaway processes of tuition increases for students and salary bloat for senior administrators.

Could Such AR Processes Be Practiced in Existing Public Universities?

It probably will be objected that no neoliberal administration would ever permit such AR processes to prosper. We agree that very few of them would permit these processes of their own free will. They are jealous of their power and privileges and insensitive to the pain their privileges impose on others. But these current beneficiaries of this system may not have the choice to ignore these problems for much longer.

Practically everyone examining and writing about public universities sees that we are in the midst of a profound crisis. State funding is drying up. Political hostility to public universities is high. Tuition costs in the United States and the United Kingdom are skyrocketing, while job prospects are becoming more uncertain for students. Student learning at these institutions is being called into question nationally. Faculty tenure or job security is being destroyed. Many staff functions are being outsourced to multinational corporations. The tax exemptions of these increasingly money-oriented institutions are being called into question.

A perfect storm is brewing. Inefficiency, waste, massive cost increases, bloated administrations, and poor student and research results are hard to defend. They are even harder to defend when the authoritarian leaders of these institutions have demanded increased control of every sphere of university life. If they are in control, then they also are to blame. As hard as they are trying to place the blame on secondary schools, governmental mandates, cost increases, immature students, and unruly faculty, having styled themselves as CEOs means they will be blamed for the failures of their organizations.

This provides an opening for the more prescient among these administrators, who would prefer to give up their coercive power in return for their own survival in their jobs, or would like to have a parachute that would float them to the ground rather than finding themselves pushed over a cliff. Being smart about forcing these issues onto the agenda and organizing the local stakeholders to pose these options to imperiled senior administrators may provide the necessary opening for action research processes.

"Greenfield" Universities, Stakeholder Take-Overs, and Cooperative and Trust Universities

At this point in history, there are a small number of universities, none public that we know of, that were either founded and organized using action research principles or that are set up as labor managed and owned cooperatives. We will review these cases briefly and then discuss the various networks and ideas we are aware of to promote the creation of democratically owned and run public universities.

Sabanci and Ozyegin Universities

In Turkey, at least two private universities have been created and organized using action research practices in the process of developing the university concepts and organization. These processes were led by Oğuz Babüroğlu. The best known case is the Sabanci University.[4] It was created using search conference methods and describes itself as a "participatory institution that is financially and administratively self-sufficient and sustainable."[5] The process of creating it began with an international search conference in Turkey and the university opened in 1999. It has nearly 4,000 students and 388 faculty members. It is a private university and provides scholarship aid. Basic tuition stands at about $7,500 per year. Levin participated in this search conference. The story of the search conference that created it is told in Babüroğlu, Emery and Associates (2000). What we do not have is a detailed understanding of its structures, operations, successes, and problems since its founding.[6]

Mondragón University

Mondragón University is a four college, nine-campus, private university in Euskadi in Spain. It is part of the Mondragón Cooperative system[7] and originated in a technical school that was created by the founders of the cooperative system. With nine facilities around the Basque Country, it includes an engineering campus, a business school, a culinary college, and a college of humanities and education.[8]

It is structured as a labor-managed cooperative with the students, faculty, administrators, and staff managing all of its operations. The university has a total of 4,000 students and yet has a central administration of only three senior administrators and three staff members. All regular operations are taken care of by the students, staff, and faculty of the colleges through a variety of structures and processes that emphasize participatory self-management. The pedagogy of the university, called the Mendiberri Project, is an active non-lecture engaged pedagogical model. There are no lecture halls because all classes take place in the form of collaborative working groups.

Greenwood, together with Susan Wright and Rebecca Boden, visited this university. This fieldwork was built on relationships created during Greenwood's three years of action research in the Mondragón cooperatives in the early 1980's. A field report about the university was published (Wright, Greenwood and Boden 2012). This case demonstrates that a labor owned and managed cooperative university with a participatory method of teaching not only can survive and prosper but it can do so without spending much of its budget on hierarchical administration.

Interest in Cooperative Universities

Joss Winn and Mike Neary at the University of Lincoln in the United Kingdom are managing a project and network called "Beyond Public and Private." They focus on the study and promotion of cooperative universities as an alternative to the neoliberal public university system.[9] They are building a significant international network of people interested in this kind of project and are examining the structural, legal, and processual dimensions of a move of public universities to a cooperative model.

Trust Universities

This is a project in its early stages of development and it is led by Susan Wright at the Aarhus University in Copenhagen. Wright has been cited often in this book because she, with a number of colleagues, has done some of the best ethnography of neoliberal higher education policies and practices. Wright, Greenwood, Boden, and a growing team of researchers are examining the English use of "irrevocable trusts" as a way of creating participatory, democratic organizations that are efficient and sustain themselves over time. The business example they began working from is the John Lewis Partnership Trust in the United Kingdom. One of the United Kingdom's most successful department store chains, it has nearly 89,000 partners and is owned and managed by the partners.[10] Wright and Greenwood are coediting a special issue of the journal *Learning and Teaching* in which the trust concept and practice will be explored as an alternative to neoliberal public university business as usual. The project is in its early stages.

Employee Takeovers?

One of the interesting and unanswered questions is whether or not colleges and particular smaller, less prestigious national universities (in Europe) or state colleges and universities (in the United States) might be taken over and run by the employees. There is a long history of employee buyouts of companies in the United States, though the record of success is uneven.

Action research has a significant history of this kind of transformational work in major corporations where action research based reorganization was able to change organizational designs and save jobs and communities (Klingel and Martin 1989; Whyte 1991). This is STSD in action and it certainly could be applied to employee takeovers of public universities.

Many smaller public universities are struggling in these neoliberal times. Public funding has been cut drastically and the world ranking system pretty much ignores these campuses. They are neither rich enough nor large enough to be ranked internationally. It is likely that future neoliberal higher education policies will either consolidate or close many of them. The current system has only a few winners and an army of losers. One of the consequences could well be the loss of many regional campuses that play an important public role in poorer or more remote areas of Europe and the United States. The people in those areas may well depend on these institutions for education, research, and service.

Because of this, another possible line of development would be to convert these campuses into cooperatives or irrevocable trusts, owned and managed by the partners. It may well be that removing the high administrative overheads and other regulatory burdens these institutions currently face and dedicating them to the regions where they are located could create viable, participative, public universities that live by and create *Bildung*.

Concluding Remarks

Taylorism has had since the 1880s to structure public universities as efficient, well-run, fair, productive and transparent organizations. This is more than enough time to evaluate the approach. The result is clear. Academic Taylorism is a failure. It is time to move away from this failed simulacrum of "business" and toward the recreation of public universities as participatory learning organizations that enhance *Bildung* for all involved.

Notes

1. There are many other approaches to practicing AR (See Greenwood and Levin, 2007). In the interest of brevity, we only explore the pragmatic approach we use to illustrate our point. Other AR approaches could be used and we encourage other practitioners to bring them forward and deploy them.
2. See https://www.mindtools.com/pages/article/newTMC_05.htm (accessed 2 May 2015).
3. The situation is different in the Nordic countries. Graduate students working toward their PhDs receive compensation sufficient to support a family.
4. See https://www.sabanciuniv.edu/en (accessed 2 May 2015).
5. See https://www.sabanciuniv.edu/en/about-sabanci/philosophy (accessed 2 May 2015).
6. We hope that information will be forthcoming in future publications. Ozyegin University is another private university created through the use of action research processes and principles. Babürglu was also a central player in that process, but we know very little about the case. Greenwood heard a brief oral presentation about it in Norway in the spring of 2015. It opened in 2008. More information about it can be found on its website at http://www.ozyegin.edu.tr/en/Anasayfa (accessed 1 October 2016).
7. See http://www.mondragon-corporation.com/eng/ (accessed 2 May 2015).
8. See http://www.mondragon.edu/en (accessed 2 May 2015).

9. Their website is found at http://josswinn.org/tag/co-operative-university/ (accessed 2 May 2015).

10. See http://www.johnlewispartnership.co.uk/about.html (accessed 2 May 2015).

Conclusion
What Difference Could Action Research in Public Universities Make?

◆◆◆

We argue that action research applied across the range of university organizational structures and dynamics can produce radical and beneficial change for most of the stakeholders. This transformation process is built on the principles of participatory organization, in which the stakeholders enact the right to impact their own working conditions and the broader issues of organizational decision making. This is our ideal future.

For students, being a co-participant in the management of the institution rather than the passive recipient of training would be a valuable educational process. It would help prepare the next generation of democratic citizens and leaders who would have practiced democracy and citizenship as students. Through this involvement, students would have acquired hands-on knowledge in the practice of participatory processes.

Now, instead, students are pitted against one another in meritocratic competitions within an institution whose other stakeholder groups are opaque and often distant. Students are encouraged to become self-interested, competitive narcissists rather than citizens of a civil society. It would be a groundbreaking experience for students to live in and study in democratic institutions of higher education and subsequently carry these experiences over to their future work life and participation in civil society.

Being a faculty member in such a system would involve knowing the experiences and wishes of the other categories of stakeholders in the university. Faculty would learn to understand their own actions and interests in the context of the rest of the stakeholders. This moves away from the individualist professor competing for promotions, salary raises, grants, and other perks at the expense of other colleagues. The faculty would have to gain an understanding of themselves as active participants in a working community who do not instrumentalize their relationships with students, other colleagues, administrators, and funders for the purposes of personal professional success and mobility.

For staff, understanding the working lives of the other stakeholders would be a significant change. Participating in decisions regarding the aims and structure of their own work would be a nearly unprecedented experience. Many staff members know quite well how the systems they work in could be better designed, but are forced to work in them without protest anyway. Being able to influence these working conditions would be a major step in their development as professionals and as people.

Being a senior administrator would be fundamentally different. The role would be transformed from "boss" to convener, facilitator of learning, and supporter and guarantor of participatory processes. A major effort for the institutional leaders would become creating learning arenas that support the development of everyone in the organization. The leaders' roles would be to prepare the ground for a democratic organization by supporting collaborative experiential learning processes. This role is especially important when the collaborative processes we described earlier raise the ire of some stakeholders who are not used to working in a collaborative way. In addition, the hiring, compensation, and evaluation of these administrators would become a democratic process in which all the stakeholders participate.

Many people currently in senior administrative positions would flee from such roles. They might well abandon higher education for the few remaining business environments where people who behave as they do are still rewarded. We would welcome their departure.

There would be other significant differences. The roles of public sector, private sector, and community stakeholders would change under the conditions we have laid out. The same kinds of processes of stakeholder identification, shared problem definition, participatory design of solutions, and participatory evaluation of outcomes would apply here in developing their relationships to the university as critics, supporters, and beneficiaries of the new public universities.

In such universities, *Neue-Bildung* would be the key element in all stakeholder positions and experiences. Personal growth, self-determination, transparency about actions and interests, and accountability to all other stakeholders based on democratically developed indicators would become central features of the lives of students, faculty, staff, administrators, and external stakeholders. This is organizational democracy in action.

The integrity of the processes would be guaranteed by open and critical dialogue, the openness of the information, the honesty of the participatory planning and decision processes, and the transparency of the evaluation processes of the actions taken. The democratic capabilities of all stakeholders would be moved along a path of development and become part of the daily operations of the institution.

The organizational outcome might be a matrix organization with flattened hierarchies, the proliferation of multi-stakeholder project teams structured by problem area and system features of the issues, and deliberative decision making made by those in most direct contact with the relevant sites of value creation. Regular communication would create opportunities for mutual learning, rather than for engaging in conventional political debates where the aim is to win the debate and defeat the opposition. Institutional leadership would serve at the pleasure of the rest of the organization's stakeholders. These leaders would take the lead in promoting processes to balance the diverse activities and functions of the university and optimize relationships among teaching, research, and service over the long run.

The future scene we have just presented only resembles one university of which we are aware, the Mondragón University described in Chapter 9, and it is a private university. However, that one successful case and the long list of successes in participatory systems in other kinds of organizations makes it clear that such organizational changes are possible and desirable. The relative scarcity of examples does show, however, that the current small minority of major beneficiaries of neo-Tayloristic public universities are in very strong power positions and have a great deal to lose by permitting participatory democracy in their institutions. They can be expected to fight hard to prevent democratic changes.

Thus we are aware that the re-creation of public universities based on *Neue-Bildung* will not be easy. Notwithstanding, we argue that the effort must be made. A system with so few "winners" and so many "losers" is toxic for a democratic society and should not be allowed to persist. The current system, with its high costs, student debt, poor quality education, and bloated administrations, is unsustainable. The choice is to change it to promote *Neue-Bildung*, or to join voices like Kevin Carey's in calling for "the end of college" and the creation of what he calls the "University of Everywhere" run by MOOCS with students at their computers on their dining-room tables, taking courses for free with hundreds of thousands of others on the way to professional licensing (Carey 2015). That dystopian, alienating scenario is another version of anti-*Bildung*. Unfortunately, Carey's future strikes us as a possible future for public universities unless the current public higher education stakeholders wake up and profoundly reform their institutions into collaborative learning arenas committed to the promotion of

Neue-Bildung, social class mobility, and democracy. The choice is ours. We can sit by passively and complain about the current developments. Or, we are free to fight for democratic public universities, if we really want them to exist.

Bibliography

◆◆◆

Abbott, A. 1988. *The System of Professions: An Essay on the Division of Expert Labor.* Chicago: University of Chicago Press.

Abel, J., R. Deitz, and Y. Su. 2014. Are Recent College Graduates Finding Good jobs. *Current Issues in Economics and Finance* Vol 20, Number 1:1-8.

Argyris, C., and D. Schön. 1996. *Organizational Learning II: Theory, Method, and Practice,* second edition. Reading, MA: Addison-Wesley.

Arnstein, S. 1969. Ladder of Citizen Participation. *Journal of the American Institute of Planners* 35(4): 216–224.

Armstrong, E. A., and L. T. Hamilton. 2013. *Paying for the Party: How Colleges Maintains Inequality.* Cambridge, MA: Harvard University Press.

Arum, R., and J. Roska. 2011. *Academically Adrift: Learning on the College Campuses.* Chicago: University of Chicago Press.

Babüroğlu, O., M. Emery, and Associates (eds). 2000. *Educational Futures: Shifting Paradigm of Universities and Education, Fred Emery Memorial Book.* Istanbul: Sabanci University.

Baldridge, J.V. 1971. *Power and Conflict in the University: Research in the Sociology of Complex Organizations.* New York: John Wiley.

Barley S., and G. Kunda. 2001. Bringing Work Back in. *Organizational Science* 12(1): 76–95.

Barnett, R. 2003. *Beyond All Reason: Living with Ideology in the University.* Maidenhead: Open University Press.

Bateson, G. 1972. *Steps to an Ecology of Mind.* New York: Ballantine Books.

Behn, R. 2001. *Rethinking Democratic Accountability.* Washington, D.C.: The Brookings Institution Press.

Berger P., and T. Luckmann. 1966. *The Social Construction of Reality: A Treatise in the Sociology of Knowledge.* Garden City, NY: Doubleday.

Birnbaum, R. 2001. *Management Fads in Higher Education: Where They Come From, What They Do, Why They Fail.* San Francisco: John Wiley and Sons.

Boden, R., P. Ciancanelli, and S. Wright. 2012. Trust Universities? Governance for Post-Capitalist Futures. *Journal of Co-operative Studies* 45(2): 16–24.

Bok, D. 2004. *Universities in the Marketplace: The Commercialization of Higher Education.* Princeton: Princeton University Press.

Bolman, L., and T. Deal. 2013. *Reframing Organizations: Artistry, Choice, and Leadership.* San Francisco: Jossey-Bass.

Bourdieu, P., and J. Passeron. 1979. *The Inheritors: French Students and Their Relation to Culture* (translated by R. Nice). Chicago: University of Chicago Press.

Bousquet, M., and C. Nelson. 2008. *How the University Works: Higher Education and the Low-Wage Nation.* New York: NYU Press.

Bradbury, H. (ed.). 2015. *Handbook of Action Research*, third edition. Los Angeles: Sage Publications.

Bradley, H., M. Erickson, C. Stephenson and S. Williams. 2000. *Myths at Work*. London: Polity Press.

Brown, E., and R. Hodgson. 2012. *The Web of Debt: The Shocking Truth about Our Money System and How We Can Break Free*, 5th edition (revised). Baton Rouge, LA: Third Millennium Press.

Brown, P., H. Lauder, and D. Ashton. 2011. *The Global Auction: The Broken Promises of Education, Jobs, and Incomes*. Oxford: Oxford University Press.

Bruford, W. 1975. *The German Tradition of Self Cultivation: "Bildung" from Humboldt to Thomas Mann*. Cambridge: Cambridge University Press.

Caanan, J., and W. Shumar (eds). 2008. *Structure and Agency in the Neoliberal University*. New York: Routledge.

Callon, M., and Latour, B. 1981. Unscrewing the Big Leviathans: How do Actors Macrostructure Reality? In K. Knorr and A. Cicourel (eds), *Advances in Social Theory and Methodology: Toward an Integration of Micro and Macro Sociologies*. London: Routledge, pp. 277-303.

Carey, K. 2015. *The End of College: Creating the Future of Learning and the University of Everywhere*. New York: Riverhead Books.

Chambers, R. 1997. *Whose Reality Counts? Putting the Last First*. Rugby, UK: ITDG Publishing.

Chevalier, J., and D. Buckles. 2008. *SAS2 Social Analysis Systems: A Guide to Collaborative Inquiry and Social Engagement*. London: Sage Publications.

——— 2013. *Participatory Action Research: Theory and Methods for Engaged Inquiry*. London: Routledge.

Chomsky, N., I. Katznelson, R. Lewontin, D. Montgomery, L. Nader, R. Ohmann, R. Siever, I. Wallerstein, and H. Zinn. 1997. *The Cold War and the University: Toward an Intellectual History of the Cold War Years*. New York: The New Press.

Clark, B. 1995. *Places of Inquiry, Research and Advanced Education in Modern Universities*. Berkeley: University of California Press.

Clark, W. 2007. *Academic Charisma and the Origins of the Research University*. Chicago: University of Chicago Press.

Cohan, W. 2010. *House of Cards: A Tale of Hubris and Wretched Excess on Wall Street*. New York: Anchor.

Cohen, M., J. March, and J. Olsen. 1972. A Garbage Can Model of Organizational Choice. *Administrative Science Quarterly* 1: 1–25.

Cole, J. 2010. *The Great American University: Its Rise to Preeminence, Its Indispensable National Role, Why It Must Be Protected*. New York: Columbia University Press.

Commission on the Social Sciences. 2003. *Great Expectations: The Social Sciences in Great Britain* (edited by D. Rind). London: Transaction Books.

Cooke, B., and U. Kothari. 2001. *Participation: The New Tyranny?* London: Zed Books.

Cooke, M. 2000. Five Arguments for Deliberative Democracy. *Political Studies* 48(5): 947–969.

Corsín Jiménez, A. (ed.). 2007. *The Anthropology of Organisations*. London: Ashgate.

Coser, L. 1956. *The Functions of Social Conflict*. London: The Free Press.

Coughlan, D., and T. Brannick. 2009. *Doing Action Research in Your Own Organization*, third edition. London: Sage Publications.

Coughlan, D., and M. Brydon-Miller (eds). 2014. *The Sage Encyclopedia of Action Research, Vols. I and II*. London: Sage Publications.

Dahl, R. 1962. *Who Governs? Democracy and Power in an American City*. New Haven: Yale University Press.

—— 1989. *Democracy and its Critics*. New Haven: Yale University Press.

—— 1998. *On Democracy*. New Haven: Yale University Press.

Davis, L., and J. Taylor. 1972. *Design of Jobs*. Harmondsworth: Penguin.

De Gaus, A. 1997. *The Living Company: Growth, Learning and Longevity in Business*. London: Nicholas Brealey Limited.

Deresiewicz, W. 2014. *Excellent Sheep: The Miseducation of the American Elite and the Way to a Meaningful Life*. New York: The Free Press.

Dewey. J. [1916] 2009. *Democracy and Education*. Merchant Books., New York: Macmillan Company.

Dewey, J. [1938] 1991. *Logic: The Theory of Inquiry*. Carbondale: Southern Illinois University Press.

Dewey, J. 1990. *The School and Society and The Child and the Curriculum*. Chicago: University of Chicago Press.

Douthat, R. 2006. *Privilege: Harvard and the Education of the Ruling Class*. New York: Hyperion Books.

Duderstadt, J. 2000. *A University for the 21st Century*. Ann Arbor: University of Michigan Press.

Ehrenberg, R. (ed.). 1997. *The American University: National Treasure or Endangered Species?* Ithaca: Cornell University Press.

—— (ed.). 2007. *What's Happening to Public Higher Education?* American Council on Education/Praeger Series on Higher Education. Westport, CT: Praeger.

Eijnatten, F.M. van. 1993. *The Paradigm That Changed the Work Place*. Assen: Van Gorcum.

Elden, M. 1979. Three Generations of Work-Democracy Experiments in Norway; Beyond Classical Socio-Technical Systems Analysis. In C. Cooper, and E. Mumford (eds), *The Quality of Working Life in Western and Eastern Europe*. London: Associated Business Press, pp. 226-257.

Elster, J., and J. Roemer (eds). 1993. *Interpersonal Comparisons of Well-Being*. Cambridge: Cambridge University Press.

Emery, F. 1959. *Characteristics of Socio-technical Systems*. London: The Tavistock Institute of Human Relations.

Emery, F., and E. Thorsrud. 1976. *Democracy at Work*. Leiden: Martinus Nijhoff.

Emery, F., and E. Trist. 1965. The Causal Texture of Organizational Environments. *Human Relations* 18(1): 21–32.

Emery, M. 1999. *Searching: The Theory and Practice of Making Cultural Change*. Amsterdam: John Benjamins Publishing Company.

Fals Borda, O., and M. Anisur Rahman (eds). 1991. *Action and Knowledge: Breaking the Monopoly with Participatory Action Research*. New York: Apex Press.

Finkelstein, N. 2000. *The Holocaust Industry: Reflections on the Exploitation of Jewish Suffering*. London: Verso.

Finkelstein, N., and R. Birn. 1998. *A Nation on Trial: The Goldhagen Thesis and Historical Truth*. New York: Henry Holt and Company.

Flood, R., and N. Romm. 1996. *Diversity Management: Triple-loop Learning*. San Francisco: John Wiley & Sons.

Forester, J. 1999. *The Deliberative Practitioner: Encouraging Participatory Planning Processes*. Cambridge, MA: MIT Press.

Foucault, M. 1973. *The Birth of the Clinic* (translated by A. Sheridan, translator.) New York: Vintage Books.

———. 1977. *Discipline and Punish*. (A. Sheridan, Translator). New York: Vintage Books.

Freire, P. 1970 *Pedagogy of the Oppressed*. (D. Macedo, Translator). New York: Continuum.

Furner, M. [1975] 2010. *Advocacy and Objectivity: A Crisis in the Professionalization of American Social Science*. Piscattaway, NJ: Transaction Press.

Gadamer, H.G. 1993. *Truth and Method*, second edition (translated by J. Weisenheimer and D. Marshall). New York: Continuum.

Gallie, W. 1956. Essentially Contested Concepts. *Proceedings of the Aristotelian Society, New Series* 56: 167–198.

Galtung, J. 1989. *Solving Conflicts: A Peace Research Perspective*. Honolulu: The University of Hawaii Press.

Garland, J. 2009. *Saving Alma Mater: A Rescue Plan for America's Public Universities*. Chicago: University of Chicago Press.

Gaventa, J., and A. Cornwall. 2001. Power and Knowledge. In P. Reason and H. Bradbury (eds), *Handbook of Action Research*. London: Sage Publications, pp. 70–80.

Gerber, L. 2014. *The Rise and Decline of Faculty Governance: Professionalization and the Modern American University*. Baltimore: Johns Hopkins University Press.

Geuss R. 2001. *Public Goods, Private Goods*. Princeton: Princeton University Press.

Gibson-Graham, J.K. 2006. *Post-Capitalist Politics*. Minneapolis: University of Minnesota Press.

Ginsberg, B. 2011. *The Fall of the Faculty: The Rise of the All-administrative University and Why*. New York: Oxford University Press.

Giroux, H., and S. Giroux. 2004. *Take Higher Education Back: Race, Youth, and the Crisis of Democracy in the Post-Civil Rights Era*. New York: Palgrave.

Graeber, D. 2011. *Debt: The First 5000 Years*. Brooklyn, NY: Melville House.

Gramsci, A. 1975. *Letters from Prison* (translated by Q. Hoare and G. Nowell Smith). London: Jonathan Cape.

Greenberg, D. 1997. *The Politics of Pure Science*. Chicago: The University of Chicago Press.

——— 2007. *Science for Sale: The Perils, Rewards, and Delusions of Campus Capitalism*. Chicago: The University of Chicago Press.

Greenwood, D. 1991. Collective Reflective Practice through Participatory Action Research: A Case Study from the Fagor Cooperatives of Mondragón. In D. Schön (ed.), *The Reflective Turn: Case Studies in and on Educational Practice*. New York: Teacher's College Press, pp. 84–107.

——— 2007. Teaching/Learning Action Research Requires Fundamental Reforms in Public Higher Education. In M. Levin and A. Martin (eds), The Praxis of Education: Action Researchers, *Action Research* 5 (Special Issue): 249–264.

——— 2008.Theoretical Research, Applied Research, and Action Research: The Deinstitutionalization of Activist Research. In C. Hale (ed.). *Engaging Contradictions: Theory, Politics, and Methods of Activist Scholarship*, Global, Area, and International Archive, Berkeley: University of California Press, pp. 319—340.

——— 2009. Are Universities Knowledge-intensive Learning Organizations? In D. Jemielniak and J. Kociatkiewicz (eds), *Handbook of Research on Knowledge-intensive Organizations*. Hershey, PA: IGO-Global, pp. 1–18.

——— 2012. Doing and Learning Action Research in the Neo-liberal World of Contemporary Higher Education. *Action Research* 10 (2): 115–132.

——— 2013. Organizational Anthropology: An Analysis of American Anthropology and the Organization of Higher Education in the United States. In D.D. Caulkins and A. Jordan (eds), *A Companion to Organizational Anthropology*. Chichester: Wiley-Blackwell, pp. 27–55.

Greenwood, D. (ed.). 1999. *Action Research: From Research to Writing in the Scandinavian Action Research Program*. Amsterdam: John Benjamins Publishing Company.

Greenwood, D., and M. Levin. 1998a. *Introduction to Action Research: Social Science for Social Change*. Thousand Oaks, CA: Sage Publications.

——— 1998b. The Reconstruction of Universities: Seeking a Different Integration into Knowledge Development Processes. *Concepts and Transformation* 2(2): 145–163.

——— 2000a. Reconstructing the Relationships between Universities and Society through Action Research. In N. Denzin and Y. Lincoln (eds), *Handbook of Qualitative Research*, second edition. Thousand Oaks, CA: Sage Publications, pp. 85–106.

——— 2000b. Recreating University-Society Relationships: Action Research versus Academic Taylorism. In O. Babüroğlu, M. Emery, and Associates (eds), *Educational Futures: Shifting Paradigm of Universities and Education, Fred Emery Memorial Book*. Istanbul: Sabanci University, pp. 19–30.

——— 2001. Re-Organizing Universities and "Knowing How": University Restructuring and Knowledge Creation for the Twenty-first Century. *Organization* 8(2): 433–440.

——— 2005. Reform of the Social Sciences, and of Universities Through Action Research. In N. Denzin and Y. Lincoln (eds), *Handbook of Qualitative Research*, third edition. Thousand Oaks, CA: Sage Publications, pp. 43–64.

——— 2007. *Introduction to Action Research: Social Science for Social Change*, second edition. Thousand Oaks, CA: Sage Publications.

——— 2008. The Reformed Social Sciences to Reform the University: Mission Impossible? *Learning and Teaching* 1(1): 89–12.

Guinier, L. 2015. *The Tyranny of Meritocracy: Democratizing Higher Education in America*. Boston, MA: Beacon Press.

Gulowsen, J. 1971. *Selvstyrte arbeidsgrupper* [Self-managed Work Groups]. Oslo: Tanum.

Gustavsen, B. 1992. *Dialogue and Development: The Theory of Communication, Action –Research and the Restructuring of Work*. Assen/Maastricht: Van Gorcum Publishers.

Gustavsen, B., H. Finne, and B. Oscarsson. 2001. *Creating Connectedness: The Role of Social Research in Innovation Policy*. Amsterdam: John Benjamins Publishing Company.

Habermas, J. 1992. *Moral Consciousness and Communicative Action* (translated by C. Lenhardt). Cambridge, MA: MIT Press.

——— 1984. *Theory of Communicative Action, Vol 1: Reason and the Rationalization of Society* (translated by T. McCarthy). London: Heineman.

——— 1989. *The Theory of Communicative Action, Vol 2: Lifeworld and System: A Critique of Functionalist Reason* (translated by T. McCarthy). Cambridge: Polity Press.

——— 2012. *The Crisis in the European Union, A Response* (translated by C. Cronin). Cambridge: Polity Press.

Hall, B. 1975. Participatory Research: An Approach for Change. *Convergence* 8(2): 24–31.

Herbst, P. 1976. *Alternatives to Hierarchies in Organizations*. Leiden: Martinus Nijhoff.

Hill, D. (ed.). 2009. *Contesting Neo-liberal Education: Public Resistance and Collective Advance*. New York: Routledge.

Heron, J. 1996. *Co-Operative Inquiry*. London: Sage Publications.

Holland, D., and J. Lave, 2009. Social Practice Theory and the Historical Production of Persons. *Actio: An International Journal of Human Activity Theory* 2: 1–15.

Hollingsworth, P. 2000. *Unfettered Expression: Freedom in American Intellectual Life*. Ann Arbor: University of Michigan Press.

Hyatt, S., B. Shear, and S. Wright (eds). 2015. *Learning Under Neoliberalism: Ethnographies of Governance in Higher Education*. New York: Berghahn.

Ikenberry, S., and M. MacLendon. 2009. *Privatizing the Public University: Perspectives from across the Academy*. Baltimore: Johns Hopkins University Press.

Jackall, R. [1988] 2010. *Moral Mazes: The World of Corporate Managers*. Oxford: Oxford University Press.

Kahn, S., and D. Pavlich (eds). 2000. *Academic Freedom and the Inclusive University*. Vancouver: University of British Columbia Press.

Kerr, C. 1963. *The Uses of the University*. Cambridge: Harvard University Press.

Kirn, W. 2009. *Lost in the Meritocracy: The Overeducation of an Underachiever*. New York: Doubleday.

Kirp, D. 2003. *Shakespeare, Einstein, and the Bottom Line: The Marketing of Higher Education*. Cambridge: Harvard University Press.

Kjelstadli, K. 2010. *Akademisk kapitalisme* [Academic Capitalism]. Oslo: Res Publica.

Klein, N. 2007. *The Shock Doctrine: The Rise of Disaster Capitalism*. London: Penguin.

Klev, R., and M. Levin. 2012a. *Forandring som praksis Endringsledelse gjennom læring* [Change as Praxis Change Management through Learning and Development]. Oslo: Fagbokforlaget.

Klev, R., and M. Levin. 2012b. *Participative Transformation: Learning and Development in Practicing Change*. London: Gower.

Klingel, S., and A. Martin (eds). 1989. *A Fighting Chance: New Strategies to Cut Costs and Save Jobs*. Ithaca, NY: ILR Press.

Kors, A., and H. Silverglate. 1999. *The Shadow University: The Betrayal of Liberty on America's Campuses*. NY: Harper Perennial.

Kotter, J. 1996. *Leading Change*. Cambridge: Harvard Business School Press.

Kronman, A. 2007. *Education's End: Why Our Colleges and Universities Have Given Up the Meaning of Life*. New Haven: Yale University Press.

Latour B. 1987. *Science in Action*. Cambridge, MA: Harvard University Press.

Law, J. 1986. *Power Action and Belief: A New Sociology of Knowledge?* Sociological Review Monograph. London: Routledge and Kegan Paul.

Lawler, E.E. 1986. *High-Involvement Management*. San Francisco: Jossey-Bass.

Levin, M. 2002. *Researching Enterprise Development: Action Research on the Cooperation Between Management and Labor in Norway*. Amsterdam: John Benjamins Publishing Company.

—— 2012. Academic Integrity in Action Research. *Action Research* 10(2): 133-149.

Levin, M., and D. Greenwood. 1998. The Reconstruction of Universities: Seeking a Different Integration into Knowledge Development Processes. *Concepts and Transformation* 2(2): 145–163.

—— 2001a. Pragmatic Action Research and the Struggle to Transform Universities into Learning Communities. In P. Reason and H. Bradbury (eds), *Handbook of Action Research*. London, Sage Publications, pp. 103–113.

—— 2001b. Reorganizing Universities and "Knowing How": University Restructuring and Knowledge Creation for the Twenty-first Century. *Organization* 8(2): 433–440.

—— 2007. The Future of Universities: Action Research and the Transformation of Higher Education. In P. Reason and H. Bradbury (eds), *Handbook of Action Research*, second edition. Los Angeles: Sage Publications, pp. 211–226.

—— 2011. Revitalizing Universities by Reinventing the Social Sciences. In N. Denzin and Y. Lincoln (eds), *Handbook of Qualitative Inquiry*, fourth edition. Thousand Oaks, CA: Sage Publications, pp. 27–42.

Levin, M., and Martin, A. 2007. The Praxis of Educating Action Researchers: The Possibilities and Obstacles in Higher Education Action Research. *Action Research* 5(3): 219-229.

Levin, M., T. Nilssen, J. Ravn, and L. Øyum. 2012. *Demokrati i arbeidslivet* [Democracy in Working Life]. Oslo: Fagbokforlaget.

Levinson, B., L. Weis, D. Holland, and D. Foley. 1996. *The Cultural Production of the Educated Person: Critical Ethnographies of Schooling and Local Practice*. Albany, NY: SUNY Press.

Lewin, K. 1948. *Resolving Social Conflicts: Selected Papers on Group Dynamics* (translated by G. Lewin). New York: Harper.

Lucas, C. 1994. *American Higher Education: A History*. New York: St. Martin's Press.

——— 1996. *Crisis in the Academy: Rethinking Higher Education in America*. New York: St. Martin's Press.

Luhmann, N. 1982. *The Differentiation of Society*. New York: Columbia University Press.

Lukes, S. 2005. *Power: A Radical View*, second edition. London: Palgrave.

Lukianoff, G. 2014. *Freedom from Speech*, Broadside 39. New York: Encounter.

Madoo Lengermann, P., and J. Niebrugge-Brantley. 1998. *The Women Founders: Sociology and Social Theory*. Boston: McGraw-Hill.

Manning, K. 2013. *Organizational Theory in Higher Education*. New York: Routledge.

Mansbridge, J. 1983. *Beyond Adversary Democracy*. Chicago: University of Chicago Press.

March, J., and H. Simon. 1958. *Organizations*. New York: John Wiley.

Marshall, A. [1890] 1920. *Principles of Economics: An Introductory Volume*, eighth edition. London: Macmillan.

Mayo, E. 1933. *The Human Problems of an Industrial Civilization*. New York: Macmillan.

McGettigan, A. 2013. *The Great University Gamble: Money, Markets and the Future of Higher Education*. London: Pluto Press.

McLendon, M. 2003. The Politics of Higher Education: Toward an Expanded Research Agenda. *Educational Policy* 17(1): 165–191.

McMahon, W. 2009. *Higher Learning, Greater Good: The Private and Social Benefits of Higher Education*. Baltimore: Johns Hopkins University Press.

Menand, L. (ed.). 1996. *The Future of Academic Freedom*. Chicago: The University of Chicago Press.

Messer-Davidow, E. 2002. *Disciplining Feminism: From Social Activism to Academic Discourse*. Durham: Duke University Press.

Mickletwait, J., and A. Woolridge. 1996. *The Witch Doctors: Making Sense of the Management Gurus*. London: Times Business.

Mills, C.W. 1956. *The Power Elite*. New York: Oxford University Press.

Mintzberg, H. 1983. *Power in and around Organizations*. Englewood Cliffs, NJ: Prentice-Hall.

Neave, G. 2003. The Bologna Declaration: Some of the Historic Dilemmas Posed by the Reconstruction of the Community in Europe's Systems of Higher Education. *Educational Policy* 17(1): 141–164.

Nelson, R., and S. Winter. 1982. *An Evolutionary Theory of Economic Change*. Cambridge, MA: Harvard University Press.

Newfield, C. 2004. *Ivy and Industry: Business and the Making of the American University, 1880–1980*. Durham: Duke University Press.

——— 2011. *Unmaking the Public University: The Forty-year Assault on the Middle Class*. Cambridge, MA: Harvard University Press.

Newman, J., Cardinal. [1852] 1907. *The Idea of the University*. London: Longmans, Green and Company.

Northouse, P. 2004. *Leadership Theory and Practice*. Thousand Oaks, CA: Sage Publications.

Oppenjuru, G., and N. Jaitli (eds). 2015. Knowledge Democracy. *Action Research* (Special Issue) 13(3): 219–314.

Pappe, I. 2010. *Out of the Frame: The Struggle for Academic Freedom in Israel.* London: Pluto Press.

Pateman, C. 1970. *Participation and Democratic Theory.* Cambridge: Cambridge University Press.

—— 2012. Participatory Democracy Revisited. *Perspectives on Politics* 10(1): 7–19.

Peters, S., N. Jordan, M. Adamek, and T. Alter (eds). 2005. *Engaging Campus and Community: The Practice of Public Scholarship in the State and Land-Grant University System.* Dayton, OH: Kettering Foundation Press.

Pfeffer, J. 1981. *Power in Organizations.* Cambridge, MA: Ballinger Publishing Company.

Piketty, T. 2014. *Capital in the Twenty-first Century* (translated by A. Goldhammer). Cambridge, MA: Belknap Press.

Polanyi, K. 1944. *The Great Transformation: The Political and Economic Origins of Our Time.* New York: Farrar and Rinehart.

Price, D. 2004. *Threatening Anthropology: McCarthyism and the FBI's Surveillance of Activist Anthropologists.* Durham, NC: Duke University Press.

Pusser, B. 2003. Beyond Baldridge: Extending the Political Model of Higher Education Organization and Governance. *Educational Policy* 17(1): 121–140.

Reason, P., and H. Bradbury (eds). 2001. *Handbook of Action Research: Participative Inquiry and Practice,* Los Angeles: Sage Publications.

—— (eds). 2008. *Handbook of Action Research,* second edition. London: Sage Publications.

Rhodes, F. 2001. *The Creation of the Future: The Role of the American University.* Ithaca, NY: Cornell University Press.

Robbins, L. [1932] 1937. *Essay on the Nature and Significance of Economic Science,* second edition. New York: Macmillan.

Ross, D. 1992. *The Origins of American Social Science.* Cambridge: Cambridge University Press.

Ruch, R. 2001. *Higher Ed, Inc.: The Rise of the For-profit University.* Baltimore: Johns Hopkins University Press.

Sahlins, M. 1972. *Stone Age Economics.* Chicago: Aldine-Atherton.

Saltmarsh, J., and E. Zlotkowski (eds). 2011. *Higher Education and Democracy: Essays on Service Learning and Community Engagement.* Philadelphia: Temple University Press.

Samuels, R. 2013. *Why Public Higher Education Should Be Free: How to Decrease the Cost and Improve the Quality at American Universities.* New Brunswick, NJ: Rutgers University Press.

Samuelson, P. 1948. *Economics.* New York: McGraw-Hill.

—— 1954. The Pure Theory of Public Expenditure. *Review of Economics and Statistics* 36(4): 387–389.

Scharmer, O. 2008. *Theory U: Learning from the Future as It Emerges.* San Francisco: Berrett-Koehler Publishers.

Schmidt, J. 2001. *Disciplined Minds: A Critical Look at Salaried Professionals and the Soul-battering System that Shapes Their Lives.* London: Rowman and Littlefield.

Schön, D. 1983. *The Reflective Practitioner: How Professionals Think in Action.* New York: Basic Books.

Schrecker, E. 2010. *The Lost Soul of Higher Education: Corporatization, the Assault on Academic Freedom, and the American University.* New York: The New Press.

Schumpeter, J.A. 1943. Capitalism in the Postwar World. In S. Harris (ed.), *Postwar Economic Problems.* New York: McGraw-Hill, pp. 113–126.

Scott, J. 1999. *Seeing Like a State: How Certain Schemes to Improve the Human Condition Have Failed.* New Haven: Yale University Press.

Senge, P. 1990. *The Fifth Discipline: The Art and Practice of the Learning Organization.* London: Century Business.

Shin, J. C., R. Toutkoushian, and U. Teichler. 2011. *University Rankings: Theoretical Basis, Methodology and Impaces on Global Higher Education.* Houton: Springer Netherlands.

Shumar, W. 1997. *College for Sale: A Critique of the Commodification of Higher Education.* New York: Routledge.

Slaughter, S., and L. Leslie. 1997. *Academic Capitalism: Politics, Policies, and the Entrepreneurial University.* Baltimore: Johns Hopkins University Press.

Slaughter, S., and G. Rhoades. 2004. *Academic Capitalism and the New Economy: Markets, State, and Higher Education.* Baltimore: Johns Hopkins University Press.

Soley, L. 1995. *Leasing the Ivory Tower: The Corporate Takeover of Academia.* Boston, MA: South End Press.

Stagic, T.M. 2003. *Transformative Leadership and Synergy Motivation: Transforming Individuals though Group Synergy.* Cabo Bahía, CA: Aventine Press.

Stech, E. 2004. *The Transformed Leader.* Victoria, BC: Trafford.

Stevens, M., and M. Kirst (eds). 2015. *Remaking College: The Changing Ecology of Higher Education.* Stanford: Stanford University Press.

Strathern, M. (ed.). 2000. *Audit Cultures: Anthropological Studies in Accountability, Ethics and the Academy.* Oxford: Routledge.

Taylor, F.W. 1911. *The Principles of Scientific Management.* New York: W.W. Norton and Company.

Thorsrud, E., and F. Emery. 1964. *Industrielt demokrati* [Industrial Democracy]. Oslo: Universitetsforlaget.

——— 1970. *Mot en ny bedriftsorganisasjon* [Toward a New Industrial Organization]. Oslo: Tanum.

Tomusk, V. 2007. *Creating the European Area of Higher Education: Voices from the Periphery.* Dordrecht: Springer.

Trist, E. 1981. *The Evolution of Socio-technical Systems.* Toronto: Ontario Ministry of Labor.

Trist, E., and K. Bamforth. 1951. Some Social and Psychological Consequences of the Longwall Method of Coal Getting. *Human Relations* 4: 3–38.

Tuchman, G. 2009. *Wannabe U: Inside the Corporate University.* Chicago: The University of Chicago Press.

von Bertalanffy, L. 1969. *General Systems Theory: Foundations, Development, Applications,* revised edition. New York: George Brazillier.

Vroom, V., and A. Jago. 1988. *The New Leadership: Managing Participation in Organizations.* Englewood Cliffs: Prentice-Hall.

Washburn, J. 2005. *University, Inc.: The Corporate Corruption of American Higher Education*. New York: Basic Books.

Weber, M. 1947. *The Theory of Social and Economic Organization* (translated by A. Henderson and T. Parsons). New York: Oxford University Press.

Weick, K. 1976. Educational Organizations as Loosely-coupled Systems. *Administrative Science Quarterly* 21(1): 1–19.

Weisbord, M., and S. Janoff. 2010. *Future Search: Getting the Whole System in the Room for Vision, Commitment, and Action*. Oakland, CA: Berrett-Koehler Publishers.

Wellmon, C. 2015. *Organizing Enlightenment: Information Overload and the Invention of the Modern Research University*. Baltimore: Johns Hopkins University Press.

Westbrook, R. 1991. *John Dewey and American Democracy*. Ithaca, NY: Cornell University Press.

Whelan, A., R. Walker, and C. Moore (eds). 2013. *Zombies in the Academy: Living Death in Higher Education*. Chicago: Intellect Ltd. and University of Chicago Press.

Whyte, W. 1948. *Human Relations in the Restaurant Industry*. New York: McGraw-Hill.

———— 1994. *Participant Observer: An Autobiography*. Ithaca, NY: ILR Press.

Whyte, W. (ed.). 1991. *Participatory Action Research*. Newbury Park: Sage Publications.

Wildt, M. 2003. *The Uncompromising Generation: The Nazi Leadership of the Reich Security Main Office*. Madison: The University of Wisconsin Press.

Wright, S. 2003. Enhancing the Quality of Teaching in Universities through Coercive Managerialism or Organizational Democracy? In D. Jary (ed.), *Benchmarking and Quality Management*. Birmingham: CSAP Publications, pp. 115–142.

———— 2005. Processes of Social Transformation: An Anthropology of English Higher Education Policy. In J. Krejsler, N. Kryger and J. Milner (eds), *Pædagogisk Antropologi - et Fag I Tilblivelse*. [Educational Anthropology: A Work in Process] Copenhagen: Danmarks Pædagogiske Universitetsforlag, pp. 185-220.

Wright, S., and J. Ørberg. 2009a. Paradoxes of the Self: Self-owning Universities in a Society of Control. In E. Sørensen and P. Triantafillou (eds), *The Politics of Self-Governance*. Farnham: Ashgate, pp. 117–135.

———— 2009b. Prometheus (on the) Rebound? Freedom and the Danish Steering System. In J. Huisman (ed.), *International Perspectives on the Governance of Higher Education*. London: Routledge, pp. 69–87.

———— 2011. The Double Shuffle of University Reform: The OECD/Denmark Policy Interface. In A. Nyhagen and T. Halvorsen (eds), *Academic Identities – Academic Challenges? American and European Experience of the Transformation of Higher Education and Research*. Newcastle upon Tyne: Cambridge Scholars Press, pp. 269–293.

Wright, S., D. Brenneis, and C. Shore. 2005. Getting the Measure of Academia: Universities and the Politics of Accountability. *Anthropology in Action* 12(1): 1–10.

Wright, S., D. Greenwood, and R. Boden. 2012. Report on a Field Visit to Mondragón University: A Cooperative Experience/Experiment. *Learning and Teaching* 4(3): 38–56.

Zuboff, S. 1984. *In the Age of the Smart Machine: The Future of Work and Power.* New York: Columbia University Press.

Index

◆◆◆

A

Aarhus University, 191
academic freedom, 54, 56, 57–61, 146
  in classes, 95
  teaching methods, 97
academic integrity, 54, 55, 56, 61–62
accountability, 24, 84–87
action research
  behavior and speech codes, 183–84
  budget development, 186–87
  building new public universities,
    155–58
  collaboration, 159–60
  conventional change models
    versus, 155–56
  core organizational processes,
    174–89
  critiques of, 165–66
  curriculum development, 175–77
  defined, 158–61
  developments after 1960, 164–65
  difference Action Research could
    make, 194–97
  employee takeovers, 191–92
  in existing public universities,
    188–89
  history of, 162–66
  intervention, 182
  maintenance, 187
  Mondragón University, 190
  as organizational change strategy,
    153–67
  Ozyegin University, 189–90
  participants, 159
  personal participation, 164
  physical plant development, 187
  pragmatism and, 168–69
  processes, 181–82
  and public goods, 161
  in public universities, 168–93
  redesign, 187
  role of research-based knowledge,
    163
  Sabanci University, 189–90
  as scientific research practice,
    160–61
  search conferences, 169–74 (*See
    also* search conferences)
  service to local communities,
    182–83
  socio-technical system design
    (STSD), 187–88
  strategic planning, 185–86
  trust universities, 191
  university research agendas,
    179–81
action teams, 174
activist democratic workforce, 9
Actor Network Theory (ANT), 111,
  119–22
  actors and actants, 119–20
  decisional power, 120–22
  obligatory passage point, 120
  transformation of interests, 120
actors, democratic, 34–36
adaptation, work organizations, 83–84
administrative subsystems, 103–06
administrators
  authority of, 107–08
  duties of, 105, 106
  networking, 130
  view of students, 100
Afghanistan, 71
alienated labor, work organizations,
  87–88
Alternatives to Hierarchies, 116

altruism, 109
American Association of University
    Professors, 57
American Council on Education, 27
American university model, 39–40
analysis (SWOT), 171, 178, 184
apical leaders, 142
Argyris, Chris, 51, 85
Aristotle, 62
armchair research, 156–57
Arnstein, Sherry, 148, 149
Australia, 170
authoritarianism
    versus *Bildung*, 147
    free market, 144
authority relations, 95, 113

B
Babüroğlu, Oğuz, 189
Baldridge, J.V., 112
Becker, Gary, 30
behavior
    action research, 183–84
    leadership, 142
    Model O-I, 85
Bildung (education as human
    development), 5, 6, 7, 8, 11, 14, 15,
    38, 39, 54–57, 192
    academic freedom, 57–61
    authoritarianism, 147
    corporate organizational models,
        131
    democracy and, 70–72
    linking research and teaching, 50
    Neue-Bildung, 151 (*See also*
        Neue-Bildung)
    premises based on, 147
    social, 155
    for stakeholders, 168 (*See also*
        action research)
    work organizations, 80–81
boards of trustees, 141
Boden, Rebecca, 190
budget development, 186–87

C
Carey, Kevin, 196
casino capitalist, 123
change
    possibility of, 157–58
    in work organizations, 83–84
change strategies
    action research, 153–67
    building new public universities,
        155–58
    definition of action research,
        158–61
    history of action research, 162–66
Clark, Burton, 79, 112
classes
    academic freedom in, 95
    duration of, 94
classrooms, social interaction in, 153,
    154
closed systems, 93
co-generative learning arenas, 170–71,
    172
Cold War, 59
collaboration, 14, 142, 154
    action research, 159–60
    issue identification, 171
    organizational learning processes,
        158
commercialization of research, 30
commissions, 142
commoditization of research and
    teaching, 89–91
community engagement, 182–83
competition, 145
compliance, 27
conferences, search, 169–74. *See also*
    search conferences
conflicts, work organizations, 83
connected networks, 106–07
conventional change models *versus*
    action research, 155–56
cooperation, 146
core organizational processes, 174–89
    action research intervention, 182
    curriculum development, 175–77

university research agendas,
179–81
Cornell University, 162
corporate organizational models,
130–32
corporatization, 9, 14, 122–24
course schedules, 95
curriculum
with action research applied to
development, 177–78
development, 175–77
customers, students as, 24

D
Dahl, Robert A., 65, 66
Danish public universities, 154
debates, 148
debt, 5
Declaration of Human Rights, United
Nations (UN), 63, 64, 66
degrees (university), 11
composition of programs, 95
deliberative democracy, 73–74
democracy, 56, 62–67
action research, 159
and *Bildung* (education as human
development), 70–72
competing meanings of, 64–66
concept of, 62
current state of in higher
education, 72–75
deliberative, 73–74
direct, 68–70
elements in as social institutions,
66–67
participative, 74–75
practicing in universities, 67–72
public goods, 21–36
and public universities, 1–14
representative, 68, 72–73
role of in higher education, 54
Democracy and Education, 65
Democracy and Its Critics, 66
democratic actors, 34–36
Denmark, 137
Dewey, John, 57, 64, 65, 154

direct democracy, 68–70
discourses, 148
distribution of products, 29–30
*Diversity Management: Triple-loop
Learning,* 149

E
economic security, 11
education
liberal, 45–46
professional training, 46–47
technical training, 45
types of, 45–47
vocational, 45
elites, 4, 8, 13
Emery, Fred, 114, 162, 163, 170
Emery, Merrelyn, 170
employee takeovers, 191–192
The Encyclopedia of Action Research,
174
Europe, 14
social mobility in, 33
European public university systems, 42
European Union (EU), 182
Excellent Sheep, 71
existing public universities, action
research in, 188–89
expansion of administrative positions,
104

F
facilitator roles, 171
factor proportions, 29–30
faculty networking, 125–27
fascism, 35
fee-for-service researchers, 8
financial impacts on networks, 122–24
financial structures, 122–23
Flood, Robert, 149
forces for change in higher education,
144
Ford, Henry, 10, 137
for-profit colleges/universities, 43–44
freedom of speech, 184
freedom to teach, 39
free market authoritarianism, 144

free markets, 6, 34
free speech, 55, 58, 59. *See also* academic freedom
full-time professors, avoiding teaching, 97
funding agencies, 60
The Future of Academic Freedom, 57
future in search conferences, 172

G
garbage cans (universities as), 107–09
German Nazi security police, 71
Germany, 38, 39
Geuss, Raymond, 30
global elites, 8, 21
goals
    of higher education, 28–29
    of public higher education goal models, 53
    of universities, 141
grants, 98
Great Britain. *See* United Kingdom (UK)
Greenwood, Davydd J., 75, 76, 95, 98, 153, 159, 161, 166, 168, 171, 176, 190, 191
groups
    research, 98
    semi-autonomous, 116
    work organizations, 81–82

H
Habermas, Jürgen, 65, 70
Handbook of Action Research, 174
Herbst, Phillip, 114, 116
higher education. *See also* public universities
    control over, 144–47
    current state of democracy in, 72–75
    deliberative democracy, 73–74
    forces for change in, 144
    goal models, 28–29
    institutions of, 111 (*See also* universities)
    models, 37–53
    neoliberal construction of, 22–28

participative democracy, 74–75
    public benefits of, 31
    representative democracy in, 72–73
    role of democracy in, 54
    social availability of, 13
    types of education, 45–47
    types of universities, 38–44
Higher Learning, Greater Good, 30
hired gun consultants, 105
history of action research, 162–66
homogenization, 22, 25
How the University Works, 112
human beings, needs of, 23
humanities, 179
Humboldt University model, 38–39
Hyatt, Susan, 112

I
ideal future, search conferences, 172
ideological preferences, 26
individual research projects, 49
industrial democracy, 116
Industrial Revolution, 7
integration of work organizations, 106–07
International Monetary Fund (IMF), 34, 71
interpersonal utilities, 25
Introduction to Action Research, 171
Iraq, 71

J
John Dewey and American Democracy, 65
John Lewis Partnership Trust, 191
just-in-time principles, 104

K
Kerr, Clark, 139
Kirst, Michael, 112
knowledge organizations, 111. *See also* universities
knowledge society, 4

L
Labour Party (Great Britain), 2

land-grant universities, 22, 42, 43
leadership, 147–49, 196
  behavior, 142
  control over higher education,
    144–47
  forces for change in higher
    education, 144
  public universities, 135–49
  skills, 148
  socio-technical systems design
    (STSD), 116–17
  as steering, 136–38
  and steering contrasted, 140–43
  work organizations, 82, 138–40
learning processes, 88–89
Learning Under Neo-liberalism, 112
Levin, Morten, 5, 69, 76, 83, 95, 98,
  135, 147, 153, 161, 166, 168, 171,
  174, 176, 189
Lewin, Kurt, 83, 156, 162, 166, 173
liberal arts
curriculum, 13
liberal education, 45–46
literature, critical 3
loosely coupled systems, 107–09
Lovejoy, Arthur, 57

M
maintenance, action research, 187
management
  fads, 105
  participative, 147
Management Fads in Higher Education,
  139
Manning, Kathleen, 112
market fundamentalism, 30
marketization, 122–24
marketizing, 22
markets, free, 6, 34
Marxism, 87
McCarthy era, academic freedom in, 57
McCarthyism, 58
McMahon, Walter, 30, 31
medieval university model, 38
Menand, Louis, 57
Mendiberri Project, 190

meritocracy, 108, 109, 145
meritocratic individualism, denial of
  work organizations, 84–87
Messer-Davidow, Ellen, 145
Mills, C. Wright, 65
Model O-I, 85, 113, 118, 136
models
  accountability, 84–87
  American university, 39–40
  for change, 133–34
  conventional change *versus* action
    research, 155–56
  corporate organizational, 130–32
  democracy, 73 (*See also*
    democracy)
  dysfunction of current models, 154
  European public university
    systems, 42
  for-profit colleges/universities,
    43–44
  higher education, 28–29, 37–53
  Humboldt University, 38–39
  liberal arts, 40
  Newman university, 39
  policy, 22
  private universities, 40–41
  public higher education goal, 53
  public universities, 42–43, 51–53
  research, 48–51
  steering, 137
  teaching purposes, 47–48
  types of education, 45–47
  vocational colleges, 41–42
modes, meanings of teaching, 44–45
Mondragón University, 190, 196
Morrill Act of 1862, 43
multiple networks, 106–07

N
Nazi security police, 71
Neary, Mike, 190
neoliberals, 1, 4, 6, 7, 11, 14, 15
  construction of higher education,
    22–28
  corporatization, 123
  policies, 122

Reagan, Ronald, 13
    steering, 143
neo-Marxist perspectives, 144
neo-Taylorism, 9, 10, 11, 88–91, 138
neo-Tayloristic authoritarianism, 75
neo-Taylorists
    corporatization and marketization,
        123
    network destruction, 124
    redundancy of parts, 134
    steering, 143
networking for power, 118–24
    Actor Network Theory (ANT),
        119–22
    administrator networking, 130
    faculty networking, 125–27
    financial impacts on networks,
        122–24
    neo-Taylorist network destruction,
        124
    student networking, 128–29
    university subsystems, 124–30
networks, multiple, 106–07
Neue-Bildung, 5, 11, 15, 151, 178, 184,
    195, 196, 197
Newfield, Christopher, 84, 89, 90, 104
Newman university model, 39
new public administration, 140
Norway, 184
    class duration in, 94
    goals of universities, 141
    student networking, 128
Norwegian Arctic University, 5
Norwegian Business School, 58
Norwegian Industrial democracy
    Program, 55
Norwegian University of Science and
    Technology (NTNU), 5, 177

O
one-way knowledge transfers, 96
ongoing disciplinary research, 48–49
open systems, 93
organizational change strategies
    action research, 153–67

building new public universities,
    155–58
definition of action research,
    158–61
history of action research, 162–66
organizational dynamics of universities,
    112–14
organizational learning processes, 158
Organizational Theory in Higher
    Education, 112
organized anarchies, 107–09
Organizing Enlightenment, 90
Ozyegin University, 189–90

P
participants, action research, 159
Participation and Democratic Theory,
    68–69, 74
participative change processes, 115
participative democracy, 74–75
participative management, 147
participatory democracy, 2, 4. See also
    democracy
part-time workforce (students), United
    States, 100
Pateman, Carol, 68, 74
personal participation in action
    research, 164
physical plant development, 187
Places of Inquiry, 79, 112
Plato, 62
Polanyi, Karl, 6
policies
    agendas, 141
    neoliberals, 122
    restrictions, 60
    statements, 3
policing functions, 142
policymakers, 3, 7, 107
policy models, 22
power relations, work organizations, 83
power sharing, 14
private goods, public goods and, 30–33
private university models, 40–41
problems

focus through shared history,
171–72
identification, 169
processes
action research, 181–82
core organizational, 174–89
organizational learning, 158
work organizations, 111–34
product mix, 29–30
professional training, 46–47
profit, 32, 37
"Prometheus (on the) Rebound?
Freedom and the Danish Steering
System," 136
public goods, 21–36
action research and, 161
democratic actors, 34–36
neoliberal construction of higher
education, 22–28
and private goods, 30–33
products, 29–30
public higher education goal
models, 28–29
Public Goods, Private Goods, 30
public higher education goal models,
28–29, 53
public universities, 21–36
action research in, 168–93 (*See
also* action research)
collapse of, 34
core organizational processes,
174–89
Danish, 154
democracy and, 1–14
difference could make, 194–97
focus on, 33–34
as gatekeepers, 12
leadership, 135–149
models, 42–43, 51–53
theories of, 51–53
"The Pure Theory of Public
Expenditure," 30

Q
quadrivium, 38

R
Reagan, Ronald, 1, 13
realpolitik, 106
redesign, action research, 187
redundancy of tasks, 117
Remaking College, 112
representative democracy, 2, 68. *See
also* democracy
in higher education, 72–73
research
action (*See* action research)
agendas, 179–81
armchair, 156–57
commercialization of, 30
commoditization of, 89–91
conflicts in, 99
groups, 98
individual research projects, 49
models, 48–51
ongoing disciplinary, 48–49
restrictions, 60
subsystems, 98–99
Taylorist structure of universities,
88–89
and teaching, 50
teaching linkages and, 49
without teaching, 50
research-based knowledge, role of, 163
researchers, 24
fee-for-service, 8
responsibilities, 158
retention, 154
rights, 158
roles
facilitators, 171
of research-based knowledge, 163
Romm, Norma, 149

S
Sabanci University, 189–90
Salaita, Steven, 58, 59
Samuelson, Paul, 30
Scandinavia, 60, 170
schedules, course, 95
Schön, Donald, 51, 85
scientific research practice, 160–61

search conferences, 169–74
  action teams, 174
  co-generative learning arenas,
    170–71, 172
  ideal future, 172
  probable future, 172
  problem focus through shared
    history, 171–72
  problem identification, 169
  stakeholder inclusion, 170
Second World War, 22, 33, 59
  reconstruction of British industry
    after, 114
  reindustrialization after, 162
  social democratic developments in
    Europe after, 55
self-determination, 195
semi-autonomous groups, 116
service to local communities, 182–83
Shear, Boone, 112
single-loop carrot-and-stick behaviors,
  118
social availability of higher education,
  13
social *Bildung* (education as human
  development), 155
social democracy, 2, 14. *See also*
  democracy
  processes undermining, 3
  reconstructing, 7
social interaction in classrooms, 153,
  154
social sciences, 179
socio-technical systems design (STSD),
  111, 114–118, 162
  action research, 187–88
  applied in university context, 134
  best practices, 124
  comparing to Taylorism, 118
  leadership, 116–17
  participation, 117–18
  participative change processes, 115
  redundancy of tasks, 117, 147
  strategic networking, 127
  technology, 115–16

solidarity, 109, 146
speech codes, 183–84
stakeholders, 142
  action research, 159
  Bildung (education as human
    development) for, 168 (*See also*
    action research)
  competition, 145
  deliberation, 2
  homogenization, 25
  identification process, 170
  search conferences, 170
standardized teaching segments, 94
steering
  leadership as, 136–38
  and leadership contrasted, 140–43
  models, 137
  neoliberalism, 143
  neo-Taylorists, 143
  public universities, 135–49
stereotypes, 25
Stevens, Mitchell, 112
strategic networking, 126. *See also*
  networking for power
strategic planning, action research,
  185–86
strategies
  building new public universities,
    155–58
  definition of action research,
    158–61
  history of action research, 162–66
  organizational change (action
    research), 153–67
strengths, weaknesses, opportunities,
  and threats (SWOT) analysis, 173,
  178, 184
structures
  class durations, 94
  financial, 122–23
  Taylorist structure of universities,
    88–91
  work organizations, 81–82
student networking, 128–29
  Norway, 128
  United States, 128–29

students
    as customers, 24
    social interaction in classrooms, 153, 154
    subsystems, 99–103
systems thinking, work organizations, 93

T
task forces, 142, 170
Tavistock Institute of Human Relations, 114, 162
taxes, 24
Taylor, F.W., 138
Taylorism, 138, 192
    action research, 165
    comparing to socio-technical system design (STSD), 118
    redundancy of tasks, 117
Taylorist structure of universities, 88–91
teaching
    autonomy in, 95
    avoiding, 97
    commoditization of, 89–91
    Taylorism structure of universities, 88–89
teaching purposes, 47–48
    application of new knowledge, 48
    application of prior knowledge, 47
    creation of competence, 47
    critique of prior knowledge, 47
    generation of new knowledge, 48
transmission of prior knowledge, 47
teaching subsystems, work organizations, 93–97
team-based organizations, 35
teams, 116
    coordination, 142
technical training, 45
technology (STSD), 115–16
Thatcher, Margaret, 1, 13
theories of public universities, 51–53
Thorsrud, Einar, 114, 162
tokenism, 149
Toyota, 104, 105
transfers, one-way knowledge, 96

transparency, 24, 195
Trist, Eric, 114, 163
trivium, 38
trust universities, 191
types
    of democracy, 67–72
    of education, 45–47
    of universities, 38–44

U
The Uncompromising Generation, 71
United Kingdom (UK)
    John Lewis Partnership Trust, 191
    Labour Party, 2
    University of Lincoln, 190
United Nations (UN), Declaration of Human Rights, 63, 64, 66
United States, 14, 170, 171
    boards of trustees, 141
    class duration in, 94
    part-time workforce (students), 100
    social mobility in, 33
    student networking, 128–29
universities
    Aarhus University, 191
    boards of trustees, 141
    goals of, 141
    loosely coupled systems, 107–09
    Mondragón University, 190, 196
    networking for power, 118–24
    organizational dynamics of, 112–14
    Ozyegin University, 189–90
    practicing democracy in, 67–72
    public (*See* public universities)
    research agendas, 179–81
    Sabanci University, 189–90
    socio-technical system design (STSD), 114–18
    subsystems, networking for power, 124–30
    Taylorist structure of, 88–91
    transformations, 154
    trust, 191
    types of university, 38–44
    work organizations, 93–110 (*See also* work organizations)

University of Illinois at Urbana-
   Champaign, 58
University of Lincoln, 190
U.S. Department of Education, 141

V
Vietnam, 71
vocational college models, 41–42
vocational education, 45
von Humboldt, Wilhelm, 54, 64

W
Wannabe U, 112, 139, 140
Weick, Karl, 84, 107–09
welfare, 33
Wellmon, Chad, 90
white papers, 8
Who governs?, 65
Winn, Joss, 190
working groups, 142
work organizations. *See also*
   universities
      adaptation, 83–84
      administrative subsystem, 103–06
      alienated labor, 87–88
      Bildung (education as human
         development), 80–81

conflicts, 83
corporate organizational models,
   130–32
groups and structures, 81–82
integration of, 106–107
leadership, 82, 138–40
loosely-coupled systems, 107–09
meritocratic individualism and
   denial of work organization,
   84–87
models for change, 133–34
networking for power, 118–30
organizational dynamics of, 112–14
power relations, 83
processes, 111–34
research subsystems, 98–99
socio-technical system design
   (STSD), 114–18
student subsystem, 99–103
systems thinking, 93
teaching subsystems, 93–97
universities, 79–92, 93–110
World Bank, 34, 71
Wright, Susan, 79, 112, 190, 191

Z
Zionism, 58